GOVERNMENT BEYOND THE CENTRE

General Editors: Gerry Stoker and Steve Leach

The world of sub-central government and administration – including local authorities, quasi-governmental bodies and the agencies of public–private partnerships – has seen massive changes in recent years and is at the heart of the current restructuring of government in the United Kingdom and other western democracies.

The intention of the Government Beyond the Centre series is to bring the study of this often-neglected world into the mainstream of social science research, applying the spotlight of critical analysis to what has traditionally been the preserve of institutional public administration approaches.

Its focus is on the agenda of change currently being faced by sub-central government, the economic, political and ideological forces that underlie it, and the structures of power and influence that are emerging. Its objective is to provide up-to-date and informative accounts of the new forms of government, management and administration that are emerging.

The series will be of interest to students and practitioners of politics, public and social administration, and all those interested in the reshaping of the governmental institutions which have a daily and major impact on our lives.

Government Beyond the Centre

Series Editors: Gerry Stoker and Steve Leach

Series Standing Order

If you would like to receive future titles in this series as they are published, you can make use of our standing order facility. To place a standing order please contact your bookseller or, in case of difficulty, write to us at the address below with your name and address and the name of the series. Please state with which title you wish to begin your standing order. (If you live outside the UK we may not have the rights for your area, in which case we will forward your order to the publisher concerned.)

Standing Order Service, Macmillan Distribution Ltd, Houndmills, Basingstoke, Hampshire, RG21 2XS, England.

Race and Local Politics

Edited by
Wendy Ball
and
John Solomos

MACMILLAN

First published 1990

Published by
MACMILLAN EDUCATION LTD
Houndmills, Basingstoke, Hampshire RG21 2XS
and London
Companies and representatives
throughout the world

Edited and typeset by Povey/Edmondson
Okehampton and Rochdale, England

Printed in Singapore

British Library Cataloguing in Publication Data
Race and local politics. — (Government beyond the centre)
1. Great Britain. Race relations. Role of local
authorities
I. Ball, Wendy   II. Solomos, John
305.800941
ISBN 0–333–51947–7 (hardcover)
ISBN 0–333–51948–5 (paperback)

To our families with love and warm thoughts

Contents

Notes on the Contributors

Wendy Ball is a Research Fellow in the Centre for Research in Ethnic Relations and Lecturer in the Department of Sociology, University of Warwick. She has carried out research on various aspects of equal opportunity policies in education and has published widely in this field. She is currently working on a book based upon her research, and is developing research on community education and anti-racism.

Naomi Connelly is Research and Social Policy Officer at the Greater London Citizens Advice Bureaux Service, and was formerly a Research Fellow at the Policy Studies Institute. She has researched and written widely on aspects of local government and racial equality and the provision of social services in multi-racial settings. She is the co-author of *Policy and Practice in the Multi-racial City* (Policy Studies Institute, 1981) and the author of *Race and Change in Social Services Departments* (Policy Studies Institute, 1989).

Marian Fitzgerald is a researcher in the Research and Planning Unit of the Home Office. She has carried out research on aspects of race and politics, equal opportunities policies and on racial harassment. She is the author of numerous articles on these issues and of *Black People and Party Politics in Britain* (Runnymede Trust, 1987).

Paul Gilroy is a Lecturer in the Department of Sociology, University of Essex. He has researched and written extensively on the politics of racism in Britain and on race and policing issues. He was a contributor to *The Empire Strikes Back* (Hutchinson, 1982) and the author of *There Ain't No Black in the Union Jack* (Hutchinson, 1987).

Paul Gordon is a researcher at the Runnymede Trust. His research has been concerned with issues such as immigration controls, race and policing, and the racial politics of the New Right. He is the author of *White Law* (Pluto, 1983) and co-author of *New Right/New Racism* (Searchlight, 1986).

William Gulam is an Inspector in the City of Manchester Education Department. He has written a number of articles on the role of multi-cultural and anti-racist initiatives in the field of education.

Michael Keith is a Lecturer in the Department of Geography, Queen Mary and Westfield College, University of London. He was formerly a Research Fellow in the Centre for Research in Ethnic Relations, University of Warwick. He has written widely on the issues of race and policing and on the politics of urban unrest.

David Mason is a Lecturer in the Department of Sociology, University of Leicester. He has carried out a number of research projects on the role of equal opportunity policies in the field of employment. He has written widely on this issue and is the author of *Ethnic Minorities and Employment Practice* (Department of Employment), and co-editor of *Theories of Race and Ethnic Relations* (Cambridge University Press, 1986).

Karim Murji is a researcher in the Institute for the Study of Drug Dependence. He has carried out research on the relationship between race and policing and on the politics of urban unrest. He has written widely on aspects of race and policing in contemporary Britain.

Phil Nanton is a Lecturer in the Institute of Local Government Studies, University of Birmingham. He has researched and written widely on issues related to equal opportunity and public policy.

Herman Ouseley is the Chief Executive of the London Borough of Lambeth. He has previously worked for the Inner London Education Authority the Greater London Council. He is the author of *The System* (Runnymede Trust, 1981) and of numerous articles on aspects of equal opportunity policies.

Gurharpal Singh is a Lecturer in the Department of Humanities in Leicester Polytechnic. He has carried out research on Sikh politics in Britain and in India, and on the development of racial equality initiatives in the field of housing.

John Solomos is a Lecturer in the Department of Politics and Sociology, Birkbeck College, University of London. He has researched widely in the fields of the politics of racial inequality, youth unemployment, equal opportunity, urban unrest and local politics. He is the author of *Black Youth,Racism and the State* (Cambridge University Press, 1988), *Race and Racism in Contemporary Britain* (Macmillan, 1989), and co-edited *Racism and Equal Opportunity Policies in the 1980s* (Cambridge University Press, 1987) and *The Roots of Urban Unrest* (Pergamon Press, 1987).

Barry Troyna is a Lecturer in the Department of Education, University of Warwick. He has researched and written extensively on anti-racist education and is the co-author of *Racism, Education and the State* (Croom Helm, 1986) and editor of *Racial Inequality in Education* (Tavistock, 1987).

Ken Young is a Professor in the Department of Political Studies at Queen Mary and Westfield College. He was previously the Director of the Institute of Local Government Studies, University of Birmingham. He has carried out extensive research on the development of equal opportunity policies in local government and on the changing functions of local authorities. He is co-editor of *Ethnic Pluralism and Public Policy* (Heinemann, 1983) and co-author of *Policy and Practice in the Multi-Racial City* (Policy Studies Institute, 1981).

Acknowledgements

Producing an edited volume is usually a long and arduous process. This volume is no exception. Nevertheless we have received various kinds of help and support which have been invaluable in helping us to produce it more or less on time.

Financial support for the conference at which most of the chapters were originally presented was kindly provided by the Nuffield Foundation and the Barrow and Geraldine S. Cadbury Trust. This helped make the idea of the conference a reality, and we thank both organisations for their support.

We would also like to acknowledge the support of Charlotte Wellington, of the Centre for Research in Ethnic Relations, in organising the conference. Without her support we would not have been able to make it the success it was. Rose Goodwin kindly typed most of the individual chapters speedily and efficiently. Gurbakhsh Hundal kindly helped with the conference and with some of the typing.

It must also be said that we have received valuable support from the contributors to this volume. This helped us to make editorial changes speedily and to produce this volume on time. Steven Kennedy, as our publisher, and Gerry Stoker, as an editor of the series in which this book is included, gave us invaluable support and advice. Additionally, we would like to acknowledge the support and encouragement of our colleagues at Warwick and Birkbeck and other institutions. In particular we would like to mention the support of Parminder Bhachu, Adam Crosier, Clive Harris, Syd Jeffers, Richard Jenkins, Errol Lawrence, and Robert Miles.

WENDY BALL
JOHN SOLOMOS

I HISTORY AND BACKGROUND

1 Racial Equality and Local Politics

Wendy Ball and John Solomos

This book explores the central features of local political debates and initiatives about race and racial inequality in contemporary Britain. It provides a timely and authoritative overview of the main trends in this area and of developments in specific policy arenas, discussing the prospects for the 1990s, and suggesting avenues for further analysis.[1]

Although there has been increasing discussion of various aspects of the politics of race and racism in British society the issue of local politics remains relatively neglected. Although it is clear that during the past decade the local state has come to the fore in the public and policy agendas about race and racism in contemporary British society we still know relatively little about the dynamics of this process. This volume is the first to attempt to examine this dimension of contemporary race relations in a detailed and critical manner. It seeks to remedy the general dearth of knowledge about this field by providing a critical analysis of the main processes at work. Some themes are emphasised more in some chapters than in others, but taken together they provide the basis for serious debate about the local politics of race and the options for the 1990s. We hope they will help to stimulate a fundamental rethinking of the role of local race initiatives and link up with current political and policy debates about the future of racial relations and local government in British society.

Before going into the substantive issues that this volume covers we shall attempt in this introductory chapter to provide an overview

of the historical dynamics and broad features of the local politics of
race over the past two decades.

Historical background

One thing that is clear from all the chapters is that along with the
broader racialisation of political debate in British society we have
seen specific types of racialised politics emerge in many urban
localities, leading to intense local and national debate about the
future of 'multi-racialism' in British society. As Paul Gordon makes
clear in his chapter, throughout the 1980s no other race-related
issue has received such a hostile reception from sections of the
media than the actions of those radical local authorities that have
attempted to develop initiatives to promote greater equality of
opportunity for black and other ethnic minority communities. It is
necessary to ask, however, about how we have arrived at the present
situation. Why did the period of the 1980s see such a major
transformation of the local politics of race? What factors helped to
shape policy formulation and practice in this field?

As a first step in locating the concerns of this volume within the
broader historical and political context it may be useful, therefore,
to probe into the origins of the policy initiatives we have seen during
the 1980s. As with many aspects of the local political agenda no
doubt numerous local factors could be adduced to explain the
actions of particular local authorities, but from a number of
research studies it seems clear that two main reasons help explain
this shift.

The first reason seems to have been the belief that, given the
absence of new central government initiatives to tackle racial
inequality during the 1980s, it was important for local authorities to
take more of a leading role in this field. During the early 1980s in
particular, at the height of the move towards 'local socialism' issues
related to race and equal opportunity became a central part of the
local political agenda in many parts of the country.

The second reason that may help to explain the pace of change in
this field during the 1980s is the impact of urban unrest and
increasing black and ethnic minority mobilisation in the local
political system. Major outbreaks of urban unrest during 1981 and
1985 helped to stimulate intense political debate at both national

and local levels about the need for new initiatives to tackle racial inequality. At the same time the role of increasing black and ethnic minority participation within local political institutions helped to encourage a number of local authorities to develop radical programmes to tackle racial inequality in their employment practices and service provision.

There are of course a number of other important factors that need to be taken into account in developing a rounded analysis of the local politics of race. In particular there is the question of changing political, organisational and community agendas within local authorities. A number of the chapters in this volume, particularly those by Ken Young and Herman Ouseley, attempt to look at the interplay between these factors and to test their explanatory power.

At the same time it is clear that recent legislative and political changes have called into question (a) the ability of local authorities to initiate radical policies in this field and (b) their autonomy from the political priorities of central government on race and equal opportunity questions. The 1988 Local Government Act, along with other major pieces of legislation passed over the past few years on issues such as housing and education, has called into question the ability of local authorities to develop radical programmes on issues such as contract compliance and positive action (Stoker, 1988). During the late 1980s it is also clear that hostile media attention has helped to construct a whole mythology around the work of certain local authorities in this field, and to give voice to those who oppose local government's involvement in promoting racial equality. This can be seen particularly in controversies about actions taken by local authorities in relation to issues such as education, housing and employment.

Another dimension which will be looked at throughout this volume is the interplay between the local politics of race and national policies. It is clear that the study of recent developments in the local politics of race also raises important questions about the development and impact of public policies on racial equality more generally. Given the changing terms of political debate on this issue over the past decade two issues have emerged as central in this context. First, the question of the efficacy of public interventions, as compared to private free market initiatives, as mechanisms for tackling racial equality. Second, the relationship between race specific and broader social and economic policy changes (Solomos, 1989). Both of these issues are addressed in this book, and we shall return to them later on in this chapter.

What is the local politics of race?

From the early 1980s onwards much of the public attention and media discussion about the local politics of race has focused on the experiences of a number of local authorities which have introduced radical policy changes in relation to racial inequality. The most notable cases have been the Greater London Council before it was abolished, the Inner London Education Authority and a number of left-wing London boroughs, including Lambeth, Brent, Hackney and Haringey. Nationally, a number of other local authorities, including Manchester, Birmingham and Bradford have attracted attention when they have adopted comprehensive policy statements on racial equality and equal opportunity generally.

In this climate it is easy to lose historical perspective. It is all too easy to forget that as late as the 1970s a common complaint of activists and community groups was that local authorities had failed to develop an adequate policy response to the increasingly multi-racial composition of their populations. Indeed during the 1970s the characteristic form of political intervention at the local level to deal with race issues was still confined in many cases to limited support for Community Relations Councils, financial aid to community groups and the distribution of central government funds made available through Section 11 of the 1966 Local Government Act and the Urban Programme.

Over the past two decades the racialisation of local politics has undergone a number of transformations. The processes which have resulted in the racialisation of local politics are complex, and to some extent they have been determined by the specific histories of particular localities. Broadly speaking, however, they can be divided into three stages. These stages themselves correspond to the transformations in the politics of immigration and race in the period from the 1960s onwards.

It is clear from a number of local community studies that local authorities in areas such as London, Birmingham, Bristol, Wolverhampton and other inner city areas had developed *ad hoc* initiatives about racial issues from the 1960s onwards. In a number of authorities this led to the development of policies about such issues as education, social services and housing. This was often linked to the formation of voluntary committees which consisted of representatives of statutory and voluntary social services, migrant organisations and interested groups and individuals and trade unions. These committees played a particularly important role in areas of the country where race and related issues had already become politicised and aroused the interest of local politicians, the press and voluntary agencies. From the late 1960s such committees begun to receive the support of the Community Relations Commission and became known by the generic term of Community Relations Councils (Hill and Issacharoff, 1971; Gay and Young, 1988).

The main distinguishing feature of the earliest stages of racialised politics at the local level was the use of race as a symbol of the changing nature of local social and economic conditions. The manifest concerns expressed in the local press and in the pronouncements of local politicians were concentrated on such issues as housing, employment and the 'social problems' which were popularly perceived as linked to immigration.

In conjunction with the emergence of race as a local political issue a steady stream of studies looked at various aspects of racial relations and conflicts in particular cities or localities (Rex and Moore, 1967; Richmond, 1973; Lawrence, 1974; Katznelson,1976; Rex and Tomlinson, 1979). The work of John Rex and his associates during the 1960s and 1970s on the position of black minorities in Birmingham represents one of the major trends in this body of work. One of the issues which this research analysed was the role of local and national political processes in structuring the incorporation of black minorities in Birmingham into the institutions of the welfare state and into the employment and housing markets. For example, Rex and Moore analysed the interplay between race and housing in an inner urban area of Birmingham, Sparkbrook, that had a significant black population. Their central concern was to analyse the reasons for the concentration of Asian and West Indian migrants in this declining area. But a central part of their research focused on the role of the policies practised by Birmingham's Housing Department and their impact on the incorporation of migrant communities in the housing market (Rex and Moore, 1967). In a second research project, carried out in the early 1970s, Rex and Tomlinson analysed the position of the 'black underclass' in the Handsworth area of the city (Rex and Tomlinson, 1979). Once again the central concern of this project was to analyse the social position of the black communities in Handsworth, but Rex and Tomlinson did analyse the role of local and national political processes in determining this position. Additionally, they looked in some detail at the political groups that developed within the Asian and West Indian communities in the area. They analysed the history of such groups and their interaction with local political institutions.

Other studies have been concerned with aspects of the incorporation of black and ethnic minorities in the local political system. Important studies from this perspective have looked at the role of racial and ethnic politics in the political life of cities such as Nottingham, Birmingham and Bristol since the 1950s. The work of Nicholas Deakin, David Beetham, Ken Newton, and Ira Katznelson are the best known examples of this type of work (Deakin, 1972; Beetham, 1970; Newton, 1976; Katznelson, 1976). More recently important studies have been carried out by Gideon Ben-Tovim and his associates in Liverpool and Wolverhampton (Ben-Tovim *et al*, 1986) and by Anthony Messina in Ealing (Messina, 1989).

The main themes in this body of work have been the impact of race on both local and national politics, the role of the media, the response of local authorities to the race question and the racialisation of electoral politics. An interesting example of this type of analysis is the study by Susan Smith of the politics of racial segregation in British society (Smith, 1989). Smith's account of the political processes of racialisation and segregation explores the diverse political, social and economic dimensions of racial relations in contemporary Britain. Her account of this process emphasises the need to situate the analysis of the local politics of race within an understanding of how racialisation of residential space within urban localities has come about, and how the local and national political system has responded to this process.

Racial equality and the political climate

The responses of political institutions, groups and individuals to racial issues have, as the various contributions to this volume make clear, by no means been uniform over the past two decades. They have been shaped by both local and national political trends and by changes in the political climate. Changes in both the local and national policy agendas have transformed the kinds of strategies pursued by local authorities in this field.

This is a central theme arising from the research of Ken Young and his associates over the past decade (Young and Connelly, 1981 and 1984; Young, 1985 and 1987), which has emphasised the need to situate the analysis of the local politics of race within a dynamic account of the conditions that have shaped the development and impact of race equality and equal opportunity initiatives. Young has paid particular attention to (a) the context and environment of policy change and (b) the implementation of policy change through particular initiatives and policies. In particular he has looked at what he calls the 'assumptive worlds' of policy makers, meaning the assumptions which are used to develop and implement policy change. According to this framework most of the changes in this field over the past decade have been unplanned and unintended, resulting from the diverse impact of pressures for change both at a local level and from the impact on local authorities of the urban unrest of 1981 and subsequently (Young, 1985: p. 287; and chapter in this volume).

Young and Connelly's by now classic study of policy change in a number of local authorities looked particularly at two aspects (Young and Connelly, 1981). First, the environment of policy change, and the variety of local political actors that make up this environment. Second, the content of the policy changes which local authorities have actually adopted and the processes by which they have sought to implement change. This account has influenced much of the debate about the local politics of race, and has helped to sharpen the interest of researchers in the analysis of the actual processes of policy making and diffusion in local multi-racial settings.

A somewhat different framework of analysis has been offered by Herman Ouseley, who has worked at various levels of local government during the past two decades and who has specialised on equal opportunity issues. In Ouseley's account of policy development in this field the central role is occupied by the actions of black communities, local black politicians and administrators and by the political debates surrounding the 1981 and 1985 riots

(Ouseley, 1981 and 1984). From his own extensive experience of work in a variety of local government contexts he argues that the key to change in the practices of local authorities lies in the combination of pressure from within and without the institutions of local politics and policy making.

From this perspective in order to understand the changing role that local authorities are playing in relation to racial issues it is necessary to look at such factors as the role of black community groups, the voluntary sector, black political leadership, the role of Community Relations Councils as well as the shifts in local and central government politics (Ouseley, 1982; and chapter in this volume).

Whatever theoretical framework one starts from, however, it is possible to identify a number of factors which have shaped policy change in this field. First, there are the issues we have touched upon already, namely the urban unrest that has been much in evidence during the 1980s and increasing black political mobilisation. The second important factor, at least during the early 1980s, was the push by a number of left-wing local authorities to use the issue of equal opportunity as a mechanism for widening their basis of support among ethnic minorities and other constituencies. Third, there is evidence that within a number of local authorities officials and decision makers have become intimately involved in both initiating and implementing policy change in relation to equal opportunity issues.

In terms of policy content local policies on race and equal opportunity have addressed three main issues. The first addressed the central question of who gets what?, and the emphasis has been on establishing equality of treatment and equality of outcome in the distribution of local government services. For example, in relation to housing, local authorities have sought to monitor mobility within the local housing stock and the quality of distribution, and to challenge procedures that contributed to discriminatory outcomes.

The second policy change has addressed the question of the employment of black staff within local authority departments. This has resulted in a number of authorities linking the promotion of racial equality with the representation of black and ethnic minority staff in local government departments. Consequently, in many local authorities targets have been established to increase the employment of black and ethnic minority staff.

Finally, a number of local authorities have introduced promotional measures that are intended to improve communications with black and ethnic minorities, and awareness of racial inequality. These include such measures as publicity about racial discrimination, the translation of policy documents into ethnic languages, and race awareness and equal opportunity training.

The changing role of local government

After the flurry of policy activity and change in this field during the early 1980s the last few years have been a period of conflict, negative media publicity about racial equality policies and in some cases resistance to change by the local white population. The debates during the late 1980s about multi-racial education in areas such as Brent, Bradford, Dewsbury and Manchester, have focused attention on the weaknesses of anti-racist initiatives and the emergence of Islamic fundamentalism as a potentially divisive issue in this context. At the same time the media coverage of the activities of the so-called 'loony left' in a number of local authorities in London and elsewhere, and the changing electoral strategy of the Labour Party has helped to put even previously radical authorities on the defensive (Lansley, *et al*, 1989).

In some cases what is already clear is that the public prominence given in the media to attacks on anti-racism and the emergence of Islamic fundamentalism as a political force has tended to take attention away from the persistence of racial inequality and direct critical attention to these issues. Interestingly enough, those local authorities attempting to allocate resources to minority groups are increasingly under scrutiny because their actions are seen as contributing to the present malaise.

The experience of local authorities thus seems to mirror that of central government initiatives, since there has been a gap between the promise embodied in policy statements and the actual achievements of policies. Most importantly, perhaps, the increasing fiscal constraints imposed by central government and pressure on the resources available to local authorities have left little room for the maintenance of the initiatives already introduced or for new developments.

During the early 1980s, at the height of local authority intervention in the area of racial equality, much hope was placed in the role of local authorities as an agent of change, particularly in the context of the neglect of racial equality by the Thatcher administrations. Indeed one study of the local politics of race argued that the local political scene has 'provided important sites of struggle, particularly for local organisations committed to racial equality' (Ben-Tovim *et al*, 1986: p. 169). Yet in recent years the experience of a number of local authorities seems to indicate that any gains in this area were both fragile and vulnerable to pressure from central government.

By the late 1980s, however, there were already signs that even previously radical local authorities were adopting a lower profile on issues concerned with racial equality. This seems to be partly the result of the increasingly negative public attention given to the policies and programmes pursued by a number of local authorities in London and other authorities such as Manchester and Sheffield. Additionally, the Labour Party has increasingly sought to distance itself from being directly identified with the actions of the urban left in these local authorities and to encourage them to give a lower profile to issues which are seen as either controversial or minority causes.

Perhaps one of the most widely publicised features of this retreat is the increasing attention given by the popular media to the activities of local authorities that have traditionally been seen as at the forefront of race equality initiatives. It is perhaps a sign of the nature of the present political climate that increasingly it is not racism which is presented as the central problem but the work of the 'anti-racists'.

This is why 'anti-racism' has come to occupy such a central position in debates about the local politics of race in British society. It has become a catch-all phrase to which various meanings are attributed. It has also become the target of much critical debate and attack in a number of policy arenas. Indeed over the past few years there has been a noticeable trend to either dismiss the relevance of anti-racism or for the neo-right and the media to articulate an anti-anti-racist position, which sees the anti-racists as a bigger political threat than the racists.

In certain arenas, such as education and social welfare, the issue of anti-racism has become a source of conflict and resistance. This became evident particularly in the late 1980s when public and media debate about 'anti-racism' and 'multi-culturalism' reached a high point.

This was evident in its most extreme form in the context of educational politics. It was during this time that the educational policies of a number of radical Labour LEAs attempting to implement anti-racist programmes came under close scrutiny. The controversy that surrounded the views of Bradford head teacher Ray Honeyford in the mid-1980s attracted both local and national political attention to the debate about the role and function of 'anti-racist' policies in education. The ramifications of the Honeyford affair went far beyond the boundaries of Bradford (Murray, 1986; Honeyford, 1988b; Halstead, 1988). During 1986 another controversy developed around the attempts by Brent Council to sack another headteacher, Maureen McGoldrick, because of her alleged views about the policies it was pursuing in relation to anti-racist initiatives in education. There have been numerous other, perhaps less publicised cases about educational issues over the past few years (see Chapter 10 in this volume).

More recently the controversy about the policies pursued by Manchester Council in the field of anti-racist education, particularly in the case of Burnage High School, has highlighted the problematic nature of policy developments in this field even further (Macdonald *et al*, 1989). This experience is looked at in greater detail in Chapter 5 of this volume.

In 1989 a new dimension to this situation was added by the vociferous public debate about Salman Rushdie's *The Satanic Verses*, and the subsequent public interest in the role of fundamentalism among sections of the Muslim communities in various localities. The full impact of the Rushdie affair on both the local and national politics of race is not as yet clear, but even at this stage it seems likely that it will have an influence on debates about such issues as 'multi-culturalism' and 'anti-racism' in British society.

This is likely to happen at two levels. First, in the context of national debates about the position of black and other ethnic minority communities in British society. There are already signs that the Rushdie affair has given a new impetus to debates about issues such as immigration, integration and public order. The second level at which the Rushdie affair is likely to have a direct impact is in terms of local politics, both in terms of formal and informal political processes. The high profile claimed by various local Muslim political activists in areas such as Bradford, Leicester, Birmingham and elsewhere suggests that the affair will have important reverberations both locally and nationally.

Hostile media coverage of the events surrounding the political mobilisations around the Rushdie affair served to reinforce the view that minorities who do not share the dominant political values of British society pose a threat to social stability and cohesion. Some commentators argued that as a result of the Rushdie affair more attention needed to be given to the divergent political paths seemingly adopted by sections of the Afro-Caribbean and Asian communities (Parekh, 1989; Banton, 1989).

The Rushdie controversy has also given added impetus to debates about the multiple cultural and political identities that have been included in the broad categorisation of 'black and ethnic minority communities'. The *Daily Telegraph*, for example, alleged in an editorial headed 'Races apart' that the events surrounding the publication of *The Satanic Verses* highlighted the 'difficulty of integrating Moslem communities into British life'. It went on:

> In the wake of *The Satanic Verses*, there must be increased pessimism about how far different communities in our nation can ever be integrated, or want to be (*Daily Telegraph*, 17 May 1989).

Arguments such as this show the complex way in which the Rushdie issue has helped to push back on to the agenda questions about the integration of minority communities and help the case of those who question the viability of an ethnically plural society. It has also given an added impetus to the argument that the development of ethnic pluralism raises problems for social and political cohesion in British society. The full impact of developments such as this is likely to be felt both locally and nationally during the 1990s, and in this sense the Rushdie affair can be seen as a sign of things to come.

What is clear already is that such controversies have helped to create a political climate which is much less friendly to the development of anti-racist initiatives than was the case in the early 1980s. But perhaps the most important constraint on the role that local authorities will be able to play in the promotion of racial equality is that within the overall political programme of Thatcherism there seems to be little room for positive initiatives on racial equality or to the political autonomy of local government. On the first point, the language which Thatcher has used to talk about the impact of the black presence on urban localities has tended to lend support to what she sees as the legitimate 'fears' of the majority white community. In the context of the controversies over actions of local authorities on such issues as multi-racial education the interventions of Mrs Thatcher and her ministers have helped to emphasise that Mrs Thatcher's 'swamping' statement of 1978 was by no means an isolated utterance but an affirmation of a more deep seated commitment by large sections of the Conservative Party to the rights of the white majority as against those of minority communities. Mrs Thatcher's role in the controversies about Ray Honeyford in Bradford and the dispute between white parents in Dewsbury and the local education authority emphasise this point (Halstead, 1988; Honeyford, 1988b).

At the same time the massive changes which the Thatcher Governments have introduced in relation to local government emphasise the limits which central government can impose on the autonomy of local authorities. Within this context it seems likely that local authorities will be (a) less willing to experiment with innovation in areas which are controversial, and (b) less responsive to demands for more resources from previously excluded groups. There is increasing evidence that this process of marginalisation has already started, and the consequence of this can be seen in the disputed nature of race equality and anti-racist initiatives.

The increasing incorporation of black politicians and community groups within the local political system may have some impact as to how far black interests will be ignored or put on the back burner. Already there is evidence that black politicians are beginning to exercise a degree of influence in a number of local authorities. The extent and permanence of this influence remain to be seen, and as a number of chapters in this volume argue it is by no means clear that representation on its own can help to challenge the roots of racial inequality.

This does not mean, however, that the racialisation of local politics is completely in retreat. Rather, it seems likely that the politics of race will remain a central feature of the local political scene in many localities over the next decade, but its impact on the policy agenda may be more limited. In making any assessment about the possibilities for bringing about racial equality through local initiatives it is important to bear in mind both the fundamental changes which local politics has undergone over the past decade and the legislative and political actions which the Thatcher Governments have taken to transform the operation of local government finance, housing and education. Such measures have already transformed the face of local government and are likely to have an even bigger impact during the 1990s (Stewart and Stoker, 1989).

Themes and arguments

Before moving on to the substantive chapters in this volume it may be useful to outline briefly the central themes and arguments that run through them. The various chapters in this volume address all the key aspects of the local politics of race over the past decade. The book has been organised into three interrelated but distinct parts. It may be useful at this point to say something about the rationale and content of each part.

Part One looks at the broad contours of the local politics of race in contemporary British society. The key themes of this part, apart from the discussion in this chapter, are explored in Ken Young's contribution which reviews the historical and governmental context of the development of local authority policies on equal opportunity and race. This chapter looks particularly at the main phases of local authority policy changes and the problems faced in implementing local authority initiatives. Young also explores the changing role of equal opportunity policies within the present environment of fundamental reforms in the role of local government.

Part Two analyses in detail the core policy arenas that go to make up the local policy agenda on racial equality. We have chosen to concentrate on the issues of employment, social services, education, housing and policing. David Mason's chapter explores those policies which have aimed to tackle racial discrimination in local government employment. This area has become one of the main priorities on the policy agendas of radical local authorities and has been the source of much conflict and debate over the past decade. Mason looks both at the impact of local authority policies on patterns of discrimination in the labour market and the ways in which policy change has been implemented.

Naomi Connelly's chapter addresses one central question: how far have local authority social services departments moved in the direction of race equality in the past decade? It begins by looking at what has happened in this area over the past decade, the processes of policy change and implementation and the impact on practice thus far. From this follows an account of the changes in social service provision that are currently in process, or are likely to happen in the next few years. Connelly's account concentrates particularly on policy changes in relation to the employment of black social workers, work with black families, children and particular groups with special needs.

Of all the issues on the local race agenda education has been at the forefront of many of the conflicts over the past decade. This issue is explored by Wendy Ball, Bill Gulam and Barry Troyna in a chapter which focuses on the likely impact of the 1988 Education Reform Act on Local Education Authorities committed to promoting anti-racist initiatives. The arguments are illustrated by a case study of Manchester LEA, a pioneer in the development of anti-racist education. This provides evidence that central government's increasingly restrictive funding policies, coupled with other measures, have proved an effective mechanism in enforcing radical LEAs to retreat from their commitment to anti-racist education.

John Solomos and Gurharpal Singh provide an analysis of the development of race equality policies in relation to public sector housing. This chapter starts by locating the national and local political context within which race equality policies in relation to public sector housing emerged, and includes an analysis of policies which attempted to deal with unequal access to public housing. It then looks at the processes of policy development and change within local authorities over the past decade, concentrating particularly on the role of initiatives in relation to allocation, investment and the employment of black staff in housing departments. The chapter concludes by discussing the likely impact of recent legislation on housing and related issues for racial equality in housing.

The chapter by Michael Keith and Karim Murji examines the development of policies about race and policing, particularly in the aftermath of the political debates surrounding the riots of 1981. The issue of policing has been particularly influential in local political debates in London, but it has also been a factor in the politicisation of racial issues in other localities. The chapter looks closely at the experience of those local authorities that have been at the forefront of policy development in this field, and at the role and influence of what are called 'left realist' accounts of race, crime and policing on the policies that they have developed. Within the context of continuing tension between the police and black communities the question of policing is likely to remain part of the political agenda during the 1990s and the chapter concludes by examining prospects for the future.

The final chapter of this part, by Herman Ouseley, provides a unique insight from a practitioner about the resistance to reform that he confronted in attempting to implement effective race equality policies. He addresses the issue of the limits of local authority strategies for racial equality by analysing the local political and internal institutional processes within which such policies were developed. Drawing on experience from Lambeth, the GLC and similar left local authorities it analyses the reasons why the impact of race equality policies has been severely limited in practice, even in the local authorities with a real political commitment to change. It looks in detail at the institutional resistance to new practices aimed at promoting racial equality, both within the local government bureaucracy and among political parties. It also addresses the question of what action needs to be taken to facilitate change and ensure that policies are translated into practice.

The chapters in Part Three explore the question of the future role of local government initiatives on racial equality from a number of angles. In so doing they highlight the intense disagreement that has emerged over the appropriate course of action for local authorities in this field.

Philip Nanton and Marian Fitzgerald develop a controversial critique of the role of local race equality policies by looking critically at the experience of local government in developing and implementing race policies. In particular, they question what they see as the static and discrete conceptualisation of race on which these policies have been based. They illustrate the problems that may arise by specific reference to the approach local authorities have taken to dealing with racial harassment. The chapter concludes by outlining a range of alternative approaches to developing race policies for the future, particularly within the context of the changing role of local government in the 1990s. The core argument of the chapter questions the need for race specific policies, and is thus at variance with the position adopted by ourselves and other contributors to this volume.

Paul Gordon looks in some detail at an issue raised in passing in a number of other chapters; namely, the relationship between the arguments of the New Right, Conservative Government policy and the race policies developed by local authorities. It looks at the policies developed by various New Right think tanks and pressure groups on the reform of local government, in particular the Institute of Economic Affairs, the Centre for Policy Studies, the Social Affairs Unit and the Adam Smith Institute. The chapter explores the question of the influence of these think tanks by looking at the development of Conservative Government policies and the extent to which they were influenced by the New Right. It looks in particular at the controversies around the issue of education, which has been one of the key themes taken up by the New Right, but it also covers related issues such as contract compliance, recruitment, social services and policing. Inevitably, this chapter also takes up the issue of the role that the media has played in political debates about the policies adopted by local authorities on race issues.

The chapter by Paul Gilroy looks at an issue that has attracted much attention over the past decade: namely, the vexed question of anti-racism. It seeks to uncover the ideological and political basis of anti-racism and to analyse the main aspects of debates surrounding this question at the local political level. It begins by analysing the competing meanings attached to the term anti-racism, particularly in the context of the initiatives undertaken by a number of left-wing local authorities. It then looks at the language and politics of New Right discourses on anti-racism, and their impact on recent political debates about this issue. The chapter then concludes by looking forward to the 1990s and the prospects of developing initiatives to challenge racism which go beyond the limits of contemporary anti-racism.

The concluding chapter, by John Solomos and Wendy Ball, takes up the question of the impact of a number of new initiatives within this field which have been specifically aimed at overcoming the gap between policy and practice. These are contract compliance,

programmes of positive action and race awareness training. Such
initiatives have been typically presented as attempts to overcome
resistance to reform and change, but their actual impact on
practices within local authorities remains little understood. By
exploring the role of these initiatives in detail this chapter will link
up with the question raised in Ouseley's chapter about the limits
faced in the implementation of race equality initiatives within
specific institutional contexts. We shall look at the development and
impact of these initiatives and explore the controversies which have
arisen in those local authorities that have sought to implement
them.

Taken together we hope this volume provides a critical analysis
of policy conflict and change in this field during the 1980s, and that
it provides food for thought for those who are interested in
understanding what has happened and what is likely to happen in
the 1990s. The question of how to overcome racial inequality
remains a key issue for those who are interested in seeing a Britain
in which equality and social justice are an everyday reality. Sadly, as
the chapters in this volume show, we have still got a long to go if we
are to achieve this objective. But they also indicate avenues for
future action at the local political level that can help make racial
equality a reality.

Notes and references

1. It was at the height of public debate about this issue that we organised
    the conference at which most of the papers included in this volume were
    presented. The conference brought together some of the academics and
    professionals working in this field in order to encourage serious debate
    and discussion of the substantive issues involved. It attracted an
    audience of academics, researchers and local government professionals,
    community workers and representatives from central government.

    The conference papers and discussion concentrated particularly on a
    number of inter-related themes. First, the historical background and
    context of the policy developments in the general field of the local
    politics of race over the past decade. Second, there was substantial
    discussion about the experience of policy change and conflict in the
    areas of employment, education, social services and housing. Third, the
    role of new initiatives in this field, such as race relations advisers and
    contract compliance, in bringing about institutional change. Finally,
    much of the discussion involved critical exchanges about prospects for
    the future and proposals for more effective reforms.

The conference was jointly organised by the Centre for Research in Ethnic Relations and the Birkbeck Public Policy Centre and held at the University of Warwick, September 24-25, 1988. Financial assistance towards the organisation of the conference was generously provided by the Nuffield Foundation and the Barrow and Geraldine S. Cadbury Trust.

2 Approaches to Policy Development in the Field of Equal Opportunities

Ken Young

Introduction

The 1980s have been a decade of debate as regards the development of equality of opportunity in local government. It is of course too soon to attempt a definitive assessment of the achievements of that decade. The significance of the changes which have occurred, the distinction between rhetoric and reality, can be confidently judged only in a longer perspective. This chapter sets out to clear the ground for such an exercise, providing both a narrative account of the development of policy and an approach to the analysis of its implementation.

The first, descriptive, part of the chapter rehearses the recent history of British race relations policy, setting it in its governmental context and identifying three phases of development. The second, analytical, section explores the factors which underlie the 'implementation gap' or shortfall in achievement, and shows why attempts to secure real change in local authority practice are fraught with difficulty – possibly (and hence paradoxically) with greater difficulty than in most organisations of comparable size. The concluding section takes stock of the present and likely future situation, arguing that the most striking feature of the decade has not been the concrete activities and programmes that have flourished (and perhaps atrophied) but rather the spread of conceptual and linguistic conventions in the context of which they have been conceived.

The development of local authority approaches

The extent to which local authorities now seem to occupy centre stage in the politics of race can distract attention from the recency of that interest. We have seen dramatic and sudden changes in the positions adopted by some authorities, often (but not always) in the wake of a change of political control. However, in taking stock of the local authority situation it is important to have regard to the roles of central government (variable, but with some continuing encouragement and pressure), of the Commission for Racial Equality and of local non-statutory groups and alliances. It is also wise to take a longer view of the many considerations which preoccupy local politicians and officials, a view which suggests that issues and causes may have a life-cycle of their own. Three distinct periods may be readily delineated.

Responding to immigration

The earliest responses of local government to ethnic minorities in Britain were shaped by a desire to incorporate newcomers into British society. Immigration from the West Indies began as early as 1948 and increased throughout the 1950s. It was followed by immigration from the Indian sub-continent, both flows being limited by the introduction of the first controls on entry in 1962, which were followed in turn by further and more stringent controls in 1968, 1972 and subsequently. Central government policy throughout this period was characterised by immigration control on the one hand and encouragement to the newcomers to 'assimilate' on the other. From 1965 this encouragement was reinforced by the first of a series of Acts prohibiting racial discrimination.

If central government was the effective gatekeeper, it fell to local authorities and to voluntary bodies to ease the transition of the settlers at the local level. Initially at least, groups of concerned citizens led the way in organising inter-racial social events and challenging acts of racial discrimination (Hill and Issacharoff, 1971). These groups eventually took on a more formal aspect as Community Relations Councils, under the central tutelage of National Committee for Commonwealth Immigrants, and later the Community Relations Commission, receiving additional financial support from the local authorities. Thus began the curious arrangement whereby the lead role in race relations at the local level was taken by voluntary bodies, sometimes representative of the minority communities, sometimes not, and funded jointly by a national agency and by the local authorities. Local government was however the minor partner in this relationship. Very few local authorities gave more than token support for the administration of what were generally small and powerless organisations, and that often on the tacit understanding that they would refrain from criticising their benefactor (Gay and Young, 1988).

By 1964 it was becoming apparent that anti-immigrant sentiment could be exploited for political ends, and the Labour Government, anxious to stem the potential for racial conflict, introduced a modest funding programme for localities with concentrations of immigrants from the 'New Commonwealth'. This funding became available to local authorities under Section 11 of the Local Government Act 1966. It took the form of grant in aid for the employment of additional local authority staff and was mainly used for the employment of teachers to reinforce English language teaching to Asian children in schools.

The second central government initiative in this period was the launch of what Prime Minister Harold Wilson termed 'a new urban programme'. This similarly provided grant aid to local authorities for a diversity of special projects and was again prompted by the desire to head off a possible mobilisation of anti-immigrant sentiment by channelling funds towards areas of 'special social need', an elliptical reference to areas of immigrant concentration (Batley and Edwards, 1978).

A number of important points need to be made about policy developments in this first phase of local race relations. The first is the inexplicitness of both the Section 11 scheme and the urban programme. Originated by concern for race relations – in the proper sense of inter-community relations – neither source of funding was directly tied to the interests of the ethnic minority communities.

Section 11 was a form of grant aid to local authorities, not to community groups, and was intended to ease the additional 'burden' occasioned by the presence of large numbers of immigrants. In practice, some at least of this assistance came to be seen simply as supplementary funding to schools.

While the Section 11 scheme remained an instrument – indeed, one might almost say the instrument of race relations policy – the urban programme cut loose almost immediately from its origins as a race-related programme. In neither case had it been seen as politically desirable to link the funding too directly to benefiting ethnic minorities; in both cases the ambiguity of intention was advantageous to government. But this inexplicitness sent no clear signals to local authorities, with whom the initiative to bid for funds remained. Nor did this inexplicitness make it any easier to monitor programme performance or even to address the issues raised by the particular circumstances of ethnic minorities in Britain (for a fuller discussion see Young, 1983).

The anodyne nature of race policy in the 1960s has been neatly caught in the titles of just two academic studies of that time: *Doing Good by Doing Little* (Kirp, 1979); and *Promoting Racial Harmony* (Banton, 1985). The assumptions – and the language – of the time constituted what Michael Banton has termed 'Britain's liberal hour'. The common thread was an indirect approach to race issues, tackling them obliquely while maintaining a low political temperature.

The final point concerns the flexibility and longevity of the two schemes developed in that period. Now some 20 years old, they remain the principal sources of funding for schemes targeted on the needs of the ethnic minority communities. Just as it was expedient to downplay these needs from the late 1960s to the late 1970s, so it became expedient to give them more attention in the 1980s, when the ambiguity of the programmes enabled a new drive and a new emphasis to be readily accommodated. It is their very inexplicitness and lack of specificity that enabled Section 11 and the urban programme to act as mirrors of larger political concerns. That these time-worn programmes continue to be significant – indeed, have an enhanced significance – is a measure of the greater political importance commanded by ethnic minority issues in Britain in the 1980s.

Tackling racial disadvantage

The next distinctive phase begins with the Race Relations Act 1976. This was a crucial departure in two senses. First, Section 71 of the Act laid upon local authorities for the first time a statutory duty to take steps to eliminate racial discrimination and disadvantage in the operation of their powers. It read:

> . . . it shall be the duty of every local authority to make appropriate arrangements with a view to securing that their various functions are carried out with due regard to the need
> (a) to eliminate unlawful racial discrimination
> (b) to promote equality of opportunity, and good relations, between persons of different racial groups.

Local authorities henceforth became the local lead agencies in the pursuit of policy goals in respect of race, a status further symbolised by the similarity of the wording of this obligation and that placed upon the new national lead agency, the Commission for Racial Equality.

Second, the Act introduced for the first time a prohibition on indirect discrimination. The existing prohibition on direct discrimination – acting to exclude people on grounds of colour or race – was already well-understood, having been introduced in the 1965 Act and extended in 1968; but it was not clear that it had done much to advance the general well-being of ethnic minorities. There was now added to it a ban on excluding people from access to goods or services by means of requiring irrelevant conditions – for example linguistic skill in an employment setting where it was not required for job performance – which had the effect of discriminating against members of a group. For the first time, then, an 'effects test' could be levelled at local authority decisions. The intention of this new feature of the Act was therefore to tackle not only discriminatory behaviour as such, but the maintenance of practices which perpetuated what was now described as racial disadvantage. Not surprisingly, our review of local authority responses to the 1976 Act undertaken in 1979–81 concluded that the concept of indirect discrimination was shrouded in mystery and ill-understood (Young and Connelly, 1981).

These two legislative provisions – the conferment of a statutory duty and the broadening of the definition of unlawful discrimination – provided the context for local authority policy development over the next twelve years. But the pace of that development was initially slow. By 1981 few local authorities had reconsidered their practices, even though the 'effects test' requirement might be argued both to call for such a review, and to ensure that the voice of people affected by local authority decisions was given a hearing (Young and Connelly, 1984). In a report commissioned by the Home Office in 1979 Naomi Connelly and I commented on the need for a determined promotion effort on the part of local authorities if the intentions of the Race Relations Act were to be realised; a subsequent paper spelled out what might be involved in such an approach (Young, 1982).

In the absence of a strong central lead, diversity of response prevailed. In 1983 we categorised the stance of the hundred or so local authorities within whose areas substantial numbers of ethnic minority citizens lived into four groups:

– those who were testing out the political and legal possibilities and developing approaches which aimed to give a fair deal to black people;

– those who were reviewing their policies and moving cautiously forward in a fairly conventional manner, but with some willingness to accept the need for change;

– those who were aware that a changed social, moral and legal climate presented a challenge to traditional practices but were unsure as to what might be an appropriate response;

– those who as a matter of political preference set their faces against change and were prepared to ignore the requirements of their statutory duties.

It was a reasonable expectation at the time that experience would spread, that good practice would be gradually disseminated, and that local authorities would 'move up the learning curve' towards a greater consistency of practice.

In the event, race policies developed rather differently. The most dramatic impetus came from the urban conflicts of 1981. In the spring of 1981 a senior civil servant explained to us the absence of any policy initiatives on race from his department: race issues 'were on the back burner'. The metaphor was grimly apt; within weeks violence had exploded on the streets of Brixton, to spread rapidly to most large British cities.

Whatever the aetiology of the conflicts, of which those in Brixton and Toxteth were the most severe, they were widely read as a demand on the part of the ethnic minority communities – and young Afro-Caribbeans in particular – for greater equality of treatment. Many local authorities, shocked by the events, began to seriously consider their stance for the first time. Elsewhere, the sense of imminent danger lent urgency to policy review.

But the response came not only from the local authorities. The central departments, and the Department of the Environment and the Home Office in particular, adopted a far more interventionist line, using the flexibility of the urban programme to redirect resources to multi-racial areas, seeking at the same time more immediate and demonstrable benefits to the minority communities. The Commission for Racial Equality and the Department of the Environment intensified their persuasive efforts; the latter gave a junior minister some co-ordinating responsibilities with respect to local authorities and race, and an inter-governmental working party on local authorities and race equality was established.

The Section 11 scheme has been in a state of continuous revision since then, with new guidelines emphasising the need both for consultation with minority groups and more stringent of the deployment of staff. Central funding was providing to establish the Local Authorities Race Relations Information Exchange (LAR-RIE) as clearing house for practice. If 'racial harmony' was the slogan of the earlier period, 'tackling racial disadvantage' might be fairly said to be that of the early 1980s (Young, 1985).

From consensus to conflict

What then of today? While it would be an overstatement to describe the early 1980s as a period of consensus, it was at least one in which a new orthodoxy had emerged, around which Conservative ministers and local politicians of both parties could negotiate. That orthodoxy might be summarised in terms of an acceptance of racial disadvantage – the historic accretion of generations of discrimination – as a problem to be tackled by central and local government in partnership. Being explicit about race was seen as a necessary precondition for measures of 'positive action' – purposive interventions to ensure a fair share of goods and services as well as respect and prestige to the minority communities. And central government at least as active an architect of the new orthodoxy as were the local authorities.

Today the scene is one of confusion and acrimony. Political changes in some localities have produced a picture of even greater diversity in approach than that which prevailed 10 years ago. A concern for equality of opportunity has been eclipsed by a growing commitment to equality of outcome, a preoccupation which, I argue elsewhere, generates a far sharper conflict (Young, 1987). Indeed, the comfortable notion that equal opportunity(or fairness) would in itself lead inexorably to equal outcomes (or justice) is no longer so widely or confidently subscribed to. Similarly comfortable and even pleasurable notions of multi-culturalism characterised local education policies for a period of more than 10 years, only to be eclipsed by harder-edged notions of 'anti-racist' education, which have in turn come under bitter attack as counter-productive. The so-recently-established orthodoxy has already given way to a plurality of antagonistic goals. The 'racialisation' of policy debate has revealed its flaws and shortcomings. Something approaching an intellectual crisis has emerged at the centre for race policy in Britain.

A political crisis too. As local councillors have turned their attention to race issues, the working of their own local authorities – and the roles and relationships that underpin that working – has come under critical scrutiny. Local authority officers, as the continuing or permanent element in local administration, have in some cases become the scapegoats for years of political failure. Political demands are made in a spirit of impatience, demands which can be met in some cases only at some cost to the good government of the locality. The standard of administration and the quality of working relationships in some local authorities has fallen below any tolerable level, bringing deep discredit to local government and putting at risk what is left of central government's willingness to tolerate a measure of local authority discretion. This is not to say that race is the only issue to have had such an impact on local government; rather, it is one of a series of questions on which issues of power and responsibility have in the last five years come to turn.

In other localities recent developments have been in quite the opposite direction. Here the flirtation with race equality issues – or at least with their pursuit through the high-profile route of special committees and administrative units – has proved brief. There is an emerging view, openly put, that such overt gestures to the minority communities may incur heavier electoral costs than benefits. Today, the local politics of race has become polarised around a more intense espousal of race-specific measures on the one hand, and their more dismissive disavowal on the other.

A sober judgement must be that the movement towards adapting local authority practices to better meet the challenges of a multi-racial society has reached a critical point. On the one hand there is a steadily spreading recognition among many of the less urban local authorities that past exclusionary practices must be dropped and steps taken to promote equality of opportunity. On the other hand, there is now markedly less confidence that an acceptable body of knowledge and practice exists which can be drawn upon by the 'learners'. On the one hand, more blatant forms of racism have been tempered. On the other, many local councillors and officials quietly wait for the concern with race equality to burn itself out.

The feasibility analysis of organisational change

The recent history of approaches to equal opportunity in local government teaches some hard lessons. Unrealistic expectations, and a failure to understand the sheer intractability of large bureaucratic organisations have compounded the ever-present difficulties that stem from covert racial hostility or entrenched professional attitudes. This second part of the chapter explores some of the dynamics of organisational change and argues that while local authorities have readily declared themselves in favour of equal opportunities, their own internal processes are to a remarkable degree inimical to its achievement. Indicative rather than conclusive, the approach outlined here provides a set of concepts for exploring the implementation of policy change through the assessment of feasibility.

Any feasibility analysis must deal with two fundamental aspects of the situation that is under scrutiny; put simply, with what the relevant people believe and with the power relations between them.

The two are of course not wholly independent dimensions: beliefs and values encompass issues of power and independence; formal relationships can underpin the way we see the world. Nevertheless, what I shall call the appreciative context of the organisational context of change have independent effects upon outcomes. I shall use the example of efforts to achieve equal opportunities in employment to illustrate the argument, parts of which are set out at greater length in earlier publications (Young, 1987 and 1988).

The appreciative context of equal opportunity policies

By the appreciative context I mean that constellation of images, beliefs, judgements, values and perceptions that are to be found within any organisation. They may be largely held in common, sufficiently shared and consistent enough to enable us to speak of the 'assumptive world' (Young, 1979) or 'culture' of the organisation, or they may not. Professional world views or ideologies can play an important part in constituting the appreciative context of a public service agency, although there may be marked disparities between what is believed and valued by its managers and what is held to be so by those who deliver its services. Equally, different professions may construe common issues in radically divergent ways.

Appreciative gaps of this type are endemic in organisations, but in a local authority presents the extreme case of multi-professional bureaucracy under the control of popularly-elected party politicians, among whom there may or may not be consistent assumptions about means, ends and actions. I want to deal here with the ways in which 'equal opportunity' is understood; with the scope and content accorded to the policy; with instrumentalities, or the processes by which it is thought to be carried forward; and with the implementation difficulties peculiar to the various constructions of equal opportunity.

The appreciative context of a local authority is specific to a particular policy area. Different policies mobilise different forces within the organisation. Universalist policies designed to change behaviour within the organisation as a whole at all levels – of which an equal opportunity policy is an example *par excellence* – are likely to face the most complex of problems in their implementation. This is because the issues which such a policy seeks to address – in this case recruitment to the organisation - will be differently construed by people at different points in the organisation.

Understandings of equal opportunity

There is a wide range of understandings of what an equal opportunity policy might entail, and different constructions of the purpose of a particular policy can co-exist within a particular authority. Equal opportunity policies may be broad or narrow in their scope, and can espouse goals that range from marginal adjustment of the procedures of the authority to far-reaching changes in its patterns of recruitment. Given that such goals represent a range from the immediately achievable to the intrinsically difficult, it is a matter of some importance that a given policy commitment can be understood very differently by different people within the same authority. The appreciative context of equal opportunity policies is typically one of ambiguity, inexplicitness and confusion.

The first emphasises procedures, and takes at least the initial aspiration of policy to be the reform of procedures and routines so as to (i) preclude the exercise of directly discriminatory judgements by recruiters, and (ii) to remove indirectly discriminatory barriers. Here the emphasis is on tackling practices and procedures that may have intended or unintended exclusionary consequences. Such an approach recognises that managers exercise discretion and discrimination in the recruitment process; the aim is to ensure that such judgements are fair and lawful – that they are made on the basis of what the Institute of Personnel Management has called 'fair discrimination'. Insofar as such a policy is concerned with equality, it seeks to ensure that candidates for employment are accorded equal treatment.

The aims of such a policy are regulatory rather than redistributive. They give prominence to those who will play a role in achieving greater systematisation of procedures: personnel managers and race relations staff. In progressing such a policy of procedural change they may be involved at all stages in the recruitment process, from drawing up job descriptions and person specifications, through advertising and short-listing to selection and monitoring of the selection processes. Associated training programmes may cover any of these areas and include interviewing training for selectors. The criteria for the success of such a policy are generally implicit and the activity seen as self-justifying. This understanding of equal opportunity is principally concerned with fairness.

Different in its implications, although often proceeding in the same manner, is the understanding of equal opportunity as a redistribution of employment in favour of previously excluded groups. Such a policy goal is more explicit in its egalitarianism: it seeks what might be termed equal shares or equal outcomes. In practice, the achievement of equality is usually posited on some notion of ethnic representativeness, in which the ethnic composition of the local authority is seen as properly reflecting that of the community which it serves.

The programme inherent in such a policy position usually subsumes and transcends the concern to eliminate discrimination. It poses as the test of policy its success in changing the pattern of recruitment and, in the longer term, the composition of the authority's workforce. To that end it may support more positive measures to reach out and encourage recruitment from the minority communities. This position may be more common among councillors than among officers, although many officers also support it, some believing it to follow naturally as the consequence of the very procedural changes which they are attempting to effect. This second understanding of the nature of equal opportunity is principally concerned with justice.

Either understanding, if explicit and shared, can provide a coherent basis for policy. But such explicitness is rare, and the co-existence of contrasting understandings within the same organisa-tion more common. Inexplicitness about outcomes probably smooths the path for the adoption of an equal opportunities policy in some at least of these authorities. However, the effect of such ambiguity is to postpone conflict from the policy formulation stage to the point where concrete proposals are put forward for implementation.

The scope and content of equal opportunity policies

Not only do understandings of the meaning of equal opportunity vary between and within local authorities, the actual substance of policy is itself highly variable. The principal issue here might be posed in terms of 'equal opportunities for whom?'

The precise form which an equal opportunity policy takes may be shaped by the ethnic composition of the locality, the recruitment issues and efforts taking different forms according to the linguistic or other characteristics of the local communities. An equal opportunities policy might be explicitly geared to opening up blue collar employment; or it might concentrate (perhaps for reasons of internal political or administrative opportunism) on the white-collar grades; or it might cover both.

But local authorities also place quite different emphases on equal opportunities for ethnic minorities, for women, for disabled people or for gays and lesbians. The coverage of 'equal opportunity' is then a major facet of policy variation, and one which has direct implications for implementation. For example, measures to achieve greater consistency and fairness in recruitment procedures (through for example the redesigning of application forms) might be of benefit to black people and women in equal measure. The development of a training strategy might be seen as a vehicle for reducing the significance of race, sex or sexual orientation as a barrier to recruitment or advancement. Some changes in personnel policy aimed at achieving greater flexibility might particularly advantage women who are currently in the labour force. The establishment of equal opportunity units within the authority might have the inadvertent consequence of strengthening the competitive advantage of white women vis-à-vis black men.

There are few safe generalisations to be made. Local authorities equal opportunity policies are often additive in nature, the initial agreement that some characteristic – for example race – should not be a basis for adverse discrimination being readily followed by the specification of a (possibly extensive) list of characteristics the possession of which might similarly be or have been a basis of exclusion. It seems likely that in some authorities (but not in others) the linking of sex and race in an equal opportunities strategy can add impetus and aid agreement. Extending the coverage of equal opportunities to disability may have a similar effect. Extending it further to cover sexual orientation or spent criminal convictions may lead to resistance. That resistance may or may not then spillover to effect the prospects for implementation of earlier-agreed measures. These are dynamic relationships with unpredictable outcomes.

The instruments of policy

The third major source of variation in the appreciative context of equal opportunity relates to the processes by which it is expected change will come about. Some of the people concerned with progressing equal opportunity policies choose to emphasise procedures and the need for compliance with them. On such a view, equal opportunities are achieved by changing the rules and standard operating procedures of the organisation and enforcing and policing their observance. Others emphasise the need to change appreciations through essentially declarative policies, through interventions to change the culture of a department, or through training strategies to enhance awareness – reflects perceptions of power relations within the authority as well as perceptions of the change process itself.

Whatever the approach and the assumptions underlying it, it can only be carried into effect through the identification within the authority of those who are to act as the principal instruments of policy. Such a change in the organisational context of the authority in turn reflects notions of instrumentality; an equal opportunities policy may be seen as 'everyone's concern' or as the province of specialists. It may be seen as a management issue or as a matter of all staff. It may be led and monitored through the political structures – thus becoming a 'member's issue' – or it may be seen as something to be built into the mainstream of management practice. Finally, its achievement may be seen as something to be sought through the absorption of a generalised moral concern into the normal run of decision-making or as something to be handled programmatically, through specified targets and action plans.

The nature of policy and implementation difficulties

Each of these three sets of issues – understandings of equal opportunity, the scope and coverage of the aspiration to equalise, the means by which such ends can be sought – bear in different ways upon the relative difficulty of implementation. Over time, the experience of attempting to implement a change policy may itself feed back into the appreciative context of the authority, with failures and shortfalls fostering a sense of this type of change as 'too difficult', and with successes extending the sense of the possible.

The achievement of the limited aspiration to fairness or equal treatment lies more readily within reach than the more ambitious programme of achieving justice or equal outcomes. This is not to underestimate the practical and political difficulties of achieving such procedural changes. But in this case the goal is specified in terms of the arrangements of the authority itself and is not predicated on uncertain responses from the labour market. It enjoys a greater inherent feasibility.

Similarly, the achievement of the limited aspiration to equality (of whatever kind) for distinct and specified groups in the population lies more readily within reach than does the broader ambition of equality for everyone. Indeed, given the financial resource and internal labour market conditions of local authorities, the more broadly based equal opportunity policies run the risk of having no visible results to display to any one of the would-be beneficiary groups. Ultimately, all members of otherwise excluded social groups are in competition with one another for that scarce resource, employment.

Finally, the pursuit of equality (of whatever kind, for whomsoever) by means of purposive action, carefully delineated programmes and a clear designation of responsibilities maximises the possibilities of achievement against the purely declarative policy which is not followed through. But while this is now increasingly conceded, any such approach must still be assessed in the light of, and tailored to the realities of, the organisational context within which policy is first proposed and then pursued.

The organisational context of equal opportunity policies

The organisational context comprises the formal and informal structures of power, authority and influence, and the procedures, controls, incentives and sanctions through which they are expressed. In the case of change strategies which are led from the top, the organisational context of a particular institution may be favourable or unfavourable to a successful outcome, supportive or subversive of the desires of management. To some extent this is a matter of the formal characteristics of centralisation and decentralisation and the mechanisms of communication that sustain them, and to some extent a matter of traditions built up in the authority over a long period, perhaps since reorganisation in 1965 or 1974. However, even where the formal authority of management may appear to sustain powerful interventions, the informal authority of lower participants, the operational discretion of middle management ('managers must manage'), or custom and practice in labour relations may effectively undercut and nullify it.

I want now to indicate some of the key sources of variation in the organisational context of the authorities, as they impinge upon the implementation of equal opportunity policies. These are, respectively, the problem of organisational scale; the range of local authority functions and the degree of differentiation stemming from it; the strength of 'central' integrating mechanisms; and the significance of informal power relations.

Points of entry: the problem of scale

The potential for exclusionary racial discrimination is inherent in the large organisation. Every public service bureaucracy has a multitude of points of entry. Few of any size take all or even most of the decisions over appointment at a central point, although there is evidence that the personnel function is more dispersed in local authorities than elsewhere in the public sector. So the problem of the implementation of any change policy immediately arises. The greater the autonomy of lower level management to appoint, the greater the problem of securing consistency in practice.

The implications of this vertical division of power are most evident where the organisation has a territorial locus, for the larger the territory the greater still the necessary decentralisation. A large shire county may employ 30–50 000 people over a large territory, operating through area offices with substantial delegated authority. In terms of the difficulties facing those who seek to introduce an authority-wide employment policy, the difference between such an authority and a shire district employing perhaps a tenth of that number in a compact urban area is crucial.

The smallest and most compact local authorities have a sufficiently limited number of points of entry for the achievement of consistency in recruitment to be a feasible aim. In the medium

sized but non-education authorities the number of points of entry
might be around 3–400. In the shire counties it may be in excess of
3000. In practical terms, this precludes any possibility of the
effective monitoring of recruitment processes, as distinct from
recruitment outcomes.

Functional range and horizontal differentiation

Some public service agencies provide a single function or service.
Local authorities however provide a range of services, leading to a
departmental form of organisation and the further lateral division
of management responsibility. Indeed, local authorities are so
sharply differentiated in this regard – having grown as semi-
autonomous departments around separate statutory functions
through the medium of distinct professions – that they might be
fairly regarded as multi-organisations.

   The degree of departmental differentiation is least in the shire
districts. The London boroughs and metropolitan districts are more
complex, with social services being an important department in
both. The shire counties are more differentiated still, with education
departments enjoying more apparent autonomy than in the
metropolitan districts. The organisational context of pronounced
vertical and lateral differentiation tends to militate against the
implementation of any universalist policy, the more so where the
central integrating functions – chief executive, personnel, management services – are weak or limited in their scope.

Integrating mechanisms

One popular route to non-exclusionary or anti-racist practice is
through the tightening of procedures to limit the discretion from
which discrimination can flow. In the local authority case this often
takes the form of some kind of reinforcement of central services.
That may call for an expanded and more active personnel
department. But there are few local authorities where the remit of
personnel runs wide enough to act as a vehicle for such a policy.
Education departments in particular may be effectively off-limits
for central services.

   Race relations units – or their equivalent – are a further form of
integrating mechanism which may share or contest 'ownership' of

an equal opportunities policy with the personnel department. In most instances, however, the central race function suffers even more severely than personnel from the absence of an effective organisational resource for challenging and intervening in the decisions of service-providing departments. Low status, and the inability to meet departmental chief officers 'eye to eye' hampers the performance of the integrating role. In the early stages of an equal opportunities policy personnel and race relations staff may each be preoccupied with the need to gain organisational advantage over the other. The growing tendency to accord the heads of equal opportunity units chief officer status can be read as a deliberate attempt to overcome this difficulty.

The power and influence of personnel departments (or central personnel sections in chief executives' departments) varies widely. To some extent this reflects the type and size of the authority, the larger authorities tending to have a more developed departmental personnel function. However, in these cases the links between the centre and the departments are typically weak, personnel providing a support role to departmental staff and operating in an essentially reactive mode. Moreover, the scope of central personnel varies considerably even between authorities of similar size and type, largely for local and historical reasons. Where race units are established, their role is highly variable and in some cases is undergoing rapid change, as they seek to establish a strategic position within the authority, while their competitors seek to counter their power.

Informal organisation

Informal power relations in practice pervade the formal organisation. This is most particularly true for local authorities, where a pattern of political direction by elected members of the council is superimposed upon the conventional departmentalised bureaucracy. The responsiveness of the politicians to community, party or labour union groups who may have little contact with or visibility to managers can vastly complicate – or in some circumstances simplify – the implementation of an agreed policy line.

A nationally 'tight' organisational structure with apparently strong channels of central influence may be undercut by trade union power and networks of influence linking elected members and union officials. Such networks may cut across the authority not on a departmental basis but according to grade, where (for example) white-collar unions may be weak and blue collar powerful. The formal structures which underpin the personnel function - organisation as a separate department rather than as a central services section, reporting lines to a full committee rather than to a sub-committee – seem to provide only approximate indicators of power. More important is the *derived power* that flows from the engagement in personnel issues of the authority's most senior politicians.

It is through informality also that the impediments posed by the organisational context so far described may be subverted. An authority which normally operates in a highly departmentalised manner in the delivery of services with weak central resources may be open to powerful issue-specific integrating leadership from political leaders whose influence runs throughout the authority. A race relations adviser occupying a relatively junior position in the formal hierarchy may have private and political channels of influence that count for more than grade when issues are in dispute. The formal aspects of the organisational context may be visible and stable; the informal aspects are not immediately apparent and are likely to change over time with shifts in the patterns of political influence and interest.

Towards an assessment

Notwithstanding my initial disclaimers, it is appropriate at this point to attempt some provisional assessment of the significance of this past decade of policy development and to seek pointers to the next. The account given in the first part of this paper lends little credence to the gradualist assumptions of epidemiological models of policy change. The analysis set out in the second part emphasises that the outcomes of such change are indeterminate, contingent as they are upon a complex interplay of thought and language, process and power.

The predominant characteristic of that interplay is ambiguity – the ambiguities of language, and the ambiguities of power. Such ambiguity is the very stuff of taken-for-granted ideas undergoing transformation. These shifting ides of rights and relationships that are encompassed in the term 'equal opportunity' are on a par (allegorically speaking) with the construction of such apparently diverse social phenomena as scientific orthodoxy, fashion, or popular rumour, for each is concerned with shifts in taken-for-granted assumptions. Each is a way of talking about and giving stability to uncertain realities, of fixing temporarily the flux of experience, of making sense of situations, vesting them with order and hope, replacing one plausible story with another.

Equal opportunity issues are highly charged, addressing as they do the boundaries of identity in the contained and constrained social order of the workplace. The burden of fear and uncertainty is eased by the collective adoption of safe ways of talking about them. To bring off that adoption is the essence of the political challenge, for politics is at root a linguistically constituted activity. Changes in modes of thought – even modish thoughts – should not be considered trivial or insubstantial. Rather, they provide the means of framing the issue, the better to address it. Thus the history of equal opportunity in this past decade may best be read as a history of what people have learned to say, rather than as a history of concrete accomplishment.

This is comforting, for at first sight the prospects of any further concrete accomplishment during the 1990s appear to be diminished. The current transformation in local authority powers, responsibilities and management practices actually removes from political control much of the scope for the decisions which those who represent or hope to advance ethnic minority interests might have hoped to influence, while the restriction of co-option and twin-tracking will take a significant number of them out of the political arena. Changes in housing (choice of landlord, House Action Trusts) and education (opting out, core curriculum, devolved management) together with the extension of compulsory competitive tendering to a wider range of services, are intended to diminish the role of local authorities as providers of services in favour of an as-yet vaguely-defined role as 'enablers' (Ridley, 1988; Stewart and Stoker, 1989). To the existing ambiguity of language will be added a new degree of ambiguity of power.

But these changes do not spell the end of the politics of equal opportunity. Rather, the coming decade promises to be every bit as fertile a period of political argument as was the last. For example, the simple concept of an identity of interest among all ethnic minority citizens, attributing to them a shared black experience regardless of their actual communal, religious or political affiliations is likely to continue to break down. The glib implications of the term 'racial disadvantage' may be increasingly challenged. The organisational practice of ethnic labelling will evoke continuing unease as to its meaningfulness, while prevailing notions of multiculturalism will be seen as failing to capture the dynamic and interactive processes by which human identity is managed over time. What will be at issue in the 1990s is the way in which we construe ethnicity itself. The more important manifestations of the politics of race in the 1990s are then likely to be less concerned with programmes than with language and concepts, as we struggle to find a mode of discourse that can do justice to the subtlety and variety of the influx of social experience.

II POLICY ARENAS

3 Competing Conceptions of 'Fairness' and the Formulation and Implementation of Equal Opportunities Policies[1]

David Mason

Introduction

The disadvantaged position of black people in the British labour market is well established and does not need to be spelt out in detail here (Bhat, 1988; Brown, 1984; *Employment Gazette*, 1988; Wrench, 1989). Our concern in this chapter is to examine the attempts by local authorities to tackle racial disadvantage in employment and their role and impact. However, there are some features of the position of black workers in employment and of recent changes in the labour market which are particularly relevant to the discussion in this chapter.

Brown (1984: pp. 160–164) has shown that much of the limited improvement in the occupational placement of black people which occurred between the 1960s and 1980s is to be accounted for by the relatively greater success of black people in penetrating the public sector and especially local authorities. This is of considerable importance because of the way in which both levels of local authority spending and the scope of their services and competences have been increasingly constrained in the 1980s.

Against this background, the challenge facing local authorities committed to the promotion of greater racial equality, is to develop policies which can address this new context. It is by no means clear, however, that all authorities have yet met this challenge by developing such policies in the context of their existing relatively centralised operations. There is evidence (Ben-Tovim *et al.* 1986; Young, 1987) that confusion, uncertainty and reluctance to act are almost as prevalent here as in the private sector (Jenkins, 1986). One difficulty is a continuing lack of agreement not only about the details of equal opportunities policies but also about the underlying principles on which policy is, or should be, founded.

This chapter is addressed to the consequences of this second kind of uncertainty. It sets out to explore certain persistent confusions, about the character and purposes of equal opportunities policies in the field of employment, which are related to competing concep- tions of 'fairness' or justice. It seeks to identify the possible sources of such confusions and to suggest some of the mechanisms by which they are reproduced in everyday interactions in an employment context. It will suggest that there are some features of the local authority situation which are particularly conducive to the reproduction, and manipulation, of such confusions.

This chapter does not seek to adjudicate between the policies associated with the competing conceptions on offer. This is partly because to do so invokes moral and political questions which, in principle, are matters for collective consultation, discussion and determination within the framework of a democratic polity. In this connection, it may be argued that a central requirement of policy development in this area is consultation with those whom policy is designed to assist. In addition we should note that recent trends in the labour market have highlighted a differentiation in the experiences of members of different groups (Field, 1987; Hamnett and Randolph, 1988). Put another way, not all those who experience racism do so in the same way; not all experiences of racial inequality are the same. It follows that the policies which might be most effective in tackling one pattern of inequality might well be ineffective, or even downright deleterious, with respect to another. For example, it is sometimes argued that the establishment of quotas (which are, of course, illegal in Britain) might be effective in increasing the representation of disadvantaged or excluded groups, particularly in occupations with relatively low skill requirements. Equally, however, a quota system could, in principle, serve to exclude well-qualified members of such groups from some jobs requiring particular skills or qualifications. This would be likely to occur if the proportions of members of such groups possessing high levels of relevant skill or qualification exceeded their representation in the population as a whole. In this context we should note that evidence points to an increasing diversity of educational achievement among members of different ethnic categories in Britain. It follows that the policies which most directly meet the needs of one group are not necessarily those that are most appropriate for others.[2]

The operation of differing conceptions of fairness is associated with competing conceptions of equal opportunities policies. The confusions which arise in practice as these conceptions overlap and interact give rise to debates and unclarity about a range of policy principles and objectives. The most striking, and that most frequently giving rise to misunderstanding and dispute, concerns the relative appropriateness of positive action and positive discrimination. I shall return to this in due course. For the moment it is appropriate to identify three main sources of confusion.

The first is a straightforward intellectual unclarity. Here confusion results from a failure to think through the implications of one's position, to disentangle incompatible principles and to identify points of contact and divergence between competing policy proposals. It will be suggested below that this source of confusion is associated with the coexistence of individualist and collectivist principles in both conceptions of policy identified below. The second source is deliberate manipulation and obfuscation as politicians and others seek to find ways of promoting or resisting particular policy developments. In addition, it will be argued that not only struggles over equal opportunities policy but also unrelated power struggles within organisations may contribute to unclarity and confusion. Thus a third source of confusion arises out of the process by which policy makers, and those charged with implementation, seek to reconcile competing objectives, satisfy diverse demands for results and mediate between competing interests within and outside the organisational structure of the authority. It will be argued that these second and third sources of confusion are particularly prevalent in a local authority context.

Conceptions of fairness

It is a commonplace to argue that all acts of employment selection
are acts of discrimination. They entail making a selection between
candidates on the basis of some standard of judgement or
preference (Jewson and Mason, 1986a: p. 44). Thus a discrimination based on the possession of measurable skills which are
demonstrably relevant to a given task will typically, in Western
industrial societies, be regarded as a model of fairness.

Note that there are several components which contribute to this
judgement of fairness. First, it is assumed that jobs can be specified
in terms of a number of particular tasks requiring given skills or
aptitudes. Second, it is assumed that people are invested with skills
or aptitudes which match up with the elements of the job
specification. Third, it is assumed that such skills or aptitudes are
measurable in ways which permit judgements of what Richard
Jenkins (1982; 1986) has called 'suitability'. Finally, it is assumed
that such skills or aptitudes are properties of *individuals*. Thus fair
selection processes are typically said to be those which select the
best person for the job (IPM, 1978). This interpretation of fairness
is in line with the ideology of Western capitalist societies and is the
standard against which unfairness is judged. Unfairness is typically
seen to inhere in any system of selection in which *collectivist* rather
than *individualist* principles are invoked. Thus the usual conception
of discrimination is one in which people are judged, and treated, not
as individuals but as members of categories and as carriers of the
putative characteristics of those categories. Thus, in everyday
parlance, 'discrimination' typically refers to the negative treatment
of all members of a particular group, often justified by the
mobilisation of collective stereotypes.

This contrast between fair (individualist) and unfair (collectivist)
principles is not without its problems. First, it is clear that not all
decisions of an individualist kind will necessarily be seen as fair.
Thus forms of favouritism, earmarking and patronage will typically
be labelled unfair. Second, even those most strongly committed to
individualist principles are able to recognise (for example, in the
total exclusion of particular groups from a given occupation) the
existence of a collective injustice, even if they explain this in terms of
an absence of fair, individualist, decision making. In both cases the

judgements of fairness being invoked involve the rooting of the contrast between individualism and collectivism in a particular image of social action, including the recruitment process, in Western capitalist societies.

As will be clear from what has been said above, the image of the recruitment process underlying this interpretation of fairness is one which draws heavily on the experience of middle class, professional and academic occupations where functional criteria, and means of validation and certification, are readily available. It is of course by no means clear that such certification is a *necessary* condition of functional performance and there is a large literature which demonstrates its importance as a mechanism of control and closure (Johnson, 1972; Larkin, 1983). What is, however, clear is that for a very large number of manual and routine non-manual occupations, it is very difficult if not impossible to specify functionally or technically relevant selection criteria. As Richard Jenkins (1982; 1986) and others have pointed out, for many, if not most, such jobs, acceptability criteria (whether or not a person will 'fit in') are of much greater significance. What this means is that for many such occupations almost anyone would do. The object is to provide the required number of labour units. In such circumstances there may well be a kind of negative selectivity at work. There are certain kinds of people who are not acceptable. This almost by necessity invokes a collectivist standard of acceptability, if only because the judgements of moral and personal worth entailed in acceptability are difficult either to pin down or establish in the case of any given individual who is unknown to the selector in advance. In these circumstances, employers may well resort to what Michael Banton (1983) has called statistical discrimination – the probability that any given person will display the alleged characteristics of the category of which she is a member and which are thought to be known on the basis of past experience.

Given the prevalence of negative stereotypes about many different categories of people in the labour market – the young, black people, women, people with disabilities, the old, those with stigmatised sexual orientations – such a system generates myriad opportunities for unfair discrimination. It should not be thought, however, that judgements of acceptability are entirely absent from even the most technically specific occupations. Moreover, even here, the notion of selecting *the* best person for the job may be more a matter of ideology than of everyday practice. In reality, criteria of *adequate* performance, or the ability to meet *minimum* technical standards, may be the prelude to final decisions based on acceptability. We should also note that it would not be correct to say that acceptability criteria are always and inevitably unjustifiable or irrelevant.[3]

To summarise, then, the conventionally mobilised conception of fairness in Western capitalist societies is one which emphasises individual talent. It invokes an image of the recruitment process which is at odds with the realities of much, if not all, day to day recruitment practice. Given this clash between rhetoric and reality, it is perhaps not surprising that there is scope for confusion about both the character of racial disadvantage in the labour market and the means by which it is to be countered. It is to these means that I turn in the next section. Before this issue is addressed,however, a final comment on conceptions of fairness is in order.

The problem of competing conceptions of fairness, and their implications for policy, is much more acute in the public sector that in private industry and commerce. This is because the conceptualisation of fairness in individualistic terms is rarely challenged in the private sector (Jenkins, 1986; Jewson and Mason, forthcoming). Managers typically conceive fairness to consist in the provision of opportunities for individuals to compete with one another for positions and rewards. Attempts – for example, by the CRE – to argue for attention to collective benefits or wrongs are typically met with a mixture of incomprehensions and suspicion or with the claim that they amount to pleading for special treatment.

The local authority context is very different. Here policy is ultimately the responsibility, not of managers, but of elected politicians. Politicians derive policy from a number of sources including: their own ideological commitments; pressure from constituents; the demands of central government; the advice of full time professional officers. The complex interrelationships of these various influences creates much greater scope for, and a greater likelihood of, conflict or confusion about the underlying principles upon which employment policy should be built. Each of these sources is dealt with in more detail below.

Liberal and radical conceptions of equal opportunities policy

In an earlier paper (1986b) Nick Jewson and I sought to identify and explicate two contrasting approaches to the development and operation of equal opportunities policies. These we called the 'liberal' and the 'radical' approaches. There is not space here to reiterate our argument or to present the research evidence on which it was based. It will, however, be helpful to sketch the main features of the two approaches as we conceived them.

The liberal approach is one which draws heavily on the theories of classical liberalism. It defines the task of equal opportunities policy as securing free competition between individuals and the elimination of barriers to that competition in the form of unfair discrimination. It typically takes the form of devising fair, bureaucratic procedures and rules for recruitment and selection decision making. This is often combined with training in the correct application of procedures. The only interventions contemplated in the pattern of free competition between individual candidates is a recognition that programmes of positive action may sometimes be necessary to permit members of disadvantaged groups to enter the competition on equal terms. For liberals the aim of policy is to ensure that justice, in terms of the individualistic conception of fairness outlined above, is done and seen to be done.

By contrast, those committed to a radical policy approach reject the individualistic conception of fairness and the view of talent as an individual attribute on which it is based. Though they concede that discrimination affects individuals, its operation can only be identified at the level of the group. Fairness, from this perspective, is identified with equality of outcome. The absence of fair distribution is, *ipso facto*, evidence of unfair discrimination. Thus neither fair procedures nor the operation of the market are of inherent interest to radicals. What matters is whether these, or any other mechanisms, deliver the goods. The disinterested, professional operation of fair procedures has no value in itself. Thus radicals typically seek the politicisation of decision making. Similarly they are willing to set aside the judgements of the market in the search for fair outcomes. Positive discrimination poses no problem from a radical perspective since radicals both embrace the collectivity as the object of policy and reject the individualistic conceptions of talent on which the liberal approach is founded. Radicals set great store by the need to raise the consciousness of both the oppressed and oppressors and training programmes are frequently directed to securing this end.

This outline of the two approaches does not do justice to the two conceptions of policy which it seeks to describe. It does, however, draw attention to some critical contrasts of principle which are relevant to the discussion that follows. It hardly needs to be stressed that this somewhat crude characterisation does not reflect in a simple way the positions of respondents in our research who typically were rarely theoretically or logically consistent. Indeed uncertainty and confusion were both contingent and, we believe, at times necessary features of the organisational contexts in which policy was developed and put into operation. Confusion and the manipulation of competing conceptions were both conditions for, and the outcome of, those struggles for power in the workplace which centred on equal opportunities policies. Some aspects of this confusion are discussed below.

Some intellectual and cultural sources of confusion

(i) Individualism and collectivism

It was suggested above that conceptions of fairness in Western capitalist societies are heavily laden with individualist values. Nevertheless, it was argued, even the most individualist of approaches can recognise the existence of collective unfairness – even if this consists of no more than an aggregation of individual injustices in the form of acts of discrimination. It is this conception of fairness which is enshrined in the liberal conception of equal opportunities policy as outlined above. The recognition of collective unfairness (as an aggregation of individual discriminations) manifests itself in the emphasis on the need to develop procedures which are fair to individuals and in the willingness to secure effectiveness by admitting limited measures of positive action. Note that what positive action does is to address individual disadvantage (an inability to compete equally) by designing policy measures aimed at collectivities. Both individualistic and collectivistic principles, then, are involved in the *practice* of liberal policy measures.

By contrast the radical conception of policy outlined above focuses from the outset on collectivities. The notion of equality of outcome necessarily involves concepts of collective fairness or justice. Measures of effectiveness invoke the relative success rates of collectivities. Notions of meritocracy, individual merit or equality of individual opportunity are held to be smokescreens behind which powerful collectivities pursue their interests. Effective policy demands, therefore, a focus on group interest and procedures for securing equality of outcomes judged in terms of collective benefits. Paradoxically, the means for securing this is positive discrimination; that is, discrimination between individuals at the point of selection. Thus, although radical policy is collectivist in conception, it is individualist at the point of operation.

The implication of this is that both liberal and radical conceptions of policy invoke individualist *and* collectivist principles. Positive action is individualist in conception but collectivist in policy action. Positive discrimination is collectivist in conception and individualist at the point of policy action. The fact that both collectivist and individualist principles are involved in both conceptions of policy is of considerable importance. It helps to explain why positive action and positive discrimination are persistently confused (Jewson and Mason, 1984–5 and 1987). At one level there is a straightforward potential for misunderstanding. More crucially, however, there is scope for considerable manipulation of people's understanding. Thus opponents of all attempts to secure greater equal opportunities will frequently seek to portray all such measures (and particularly positive action programmes) as special treatment of individuals; in other words as positive discrimination. The interplay of collectivist and individualist principles in both conceptions of policy outlined above help to make this manipulation of perceptions possible. To the extent that advocates of radical policy measures may seek to play on the same confusion by passing off policies of positive discrimination as positive action they both help to reinforce the confusion and lend weight to the charges levelled by the opponents of all anti-discrimination measures that they amount to nothing more than attempts at special (and hence necessarily unfair) treatment for collectivities.

(ii) US–British contrasts

Although differing from it in a number of important respects, British anti-discrimination law has drawn on some aspects of the United States legislation and experience. More importantly the American experience, and the relatively greater effectiveness of American law and practice, has led many in Britain to seek to draw lessons from across the Atlantic. This is not the place to explore systematically the contrasts between the British and US experience. However there is one matter relevant to the theme of this chapter which merits comment. This concerns the relative legitimacy of individualist and collectivist principles in the two societies.

Many writers have noted the relatively early development in England of individualist forms of consciousness. Whether or not these can be traced back as far as Macfarlane (1978) would argue, it is relatively commonplace to argue that individualism as a principle of social and political organisation developed earlier in Britain than in most other European societies. This entrenched individualism has been used to account for phenomena as diverse as the relative weakness of socialism among the British working-class and the recent electoral dominance of Thatcherite Conservatism.

The United States is also frequently seen as a haven of individualism: the ultimate societal expression of meritocracy and rags to riches individual achievement. However the history of the United States, and its present political structure, belies this simple image. In fact, the United States is a society of collectivities; particularly ethnic collectivities. US politicians are only too well aware of this and election campaigns revolve around securing this or that ethnic allegiance. Moreover, the structure of government, and particularly of local government, reflects the significance of the ethnic collectivity. Not only does the accepted structure of US politics provide channels of upward mobility for members of collectivities (as it did for successive waves of European migrants and as it has, to a much more limited extent, for a burgeoning black middle class) it also creates an environment in which the conceptualisation of policy in terms of the needs, demands and rights of collectivities is readily understood and accepted. Notwithstanding recent neo-conservative assaults on such measures as affirmative action and quota setting, this difference in the legitimacy attaching to notions of ethnic collectivity is a crucial one. It may well help to explain why measures which are taken for granted in a US context meet with greater resistance in Britain. It may also be that attempts to invoke or draw on the US experience serve only to reinforce the confusions attending the relationship between individual and collectivist principles as seen from a British point of view.

This is not to say that the 'city boss', and local politics rooted in community, are unknown phenomena in mainland Britain. They have, however, much more commonly been expressed in class terms. With the emergence of a situation in which political fortunes in particular local areas depends on being able to secure the allegiance of members of particular ethnic groups, both the major political parties, have in appropriate circumstances, become much more responsive to their needs. The dominant tendency, however, has been to continue to present policy initiatives in either class or area terms (see below). Where reference has been made explicitly to the needs of groups defined in ethnic or racial terms, proposals have tended to be regarded with much less legitimacy. The treatment, in the press, of redressive initiatives by some London boroughs is a case in point. Similarly, reactions to demands for services which meet specifically ethnic requirements (and leaving aside the question of their merits on other grounds) – such as the attempt to secure funding for single sex Muslim schools – suggest that ethnic collectivities are not so easily seen as legitimate participants in the political process as they are in the United States.

(iii) Local authorities: service provision versus employment

A third source of confusion which may be specific to local authorities concerns contrasts between what is possible in the field of employment and what is possible in the area of service provision. In the area of employment, positive discrimination is unequivocally illegal and is readily definable in terms which clearly breach the individualistic assumptions outlined above. By contrast, positive discrimination in favour of geographical areas has become a well-established feature of inner city policy (Edwards and Batley, 1978). It is possible, as Young and Connelly note (1981: pp. 165–6), that the use of the term positive discrimination to refer to policies in both these areas is itself a source of confusion within local government.

Edwards (1987: pp. 28–31) has noted that as area based policies became increasingly identified with the needs of particular (ethnic and gender) groups, so the old consensus that had surrounded area-based positive discrimination began to evaporate. It is probable that much of this opposition (emanating from the political right) was based on a straightforward hostility to the groups involved. However, a likely further source of difficulty was that the identification of area with particular groups raised the issue of the appropriateness of collectivities as recipients of services or as loci of need. Taken together with the simultaneous use of the term positive discrimination to refer to illegitimate discrimination between individuals at the point of selection for employment, the scope for confusion and mischievous manipulation is difficult to miss.

That confusion, moreover, may be enhanced to the extent that the operation of area-based service delivery policies requires or permits the employment of specially designated staff (as Section 11 of the 1966 Local Government Act). In these circumstances the question arises of whether post holders require special knowledge of, or empathy with, specific population groups resident in the geographical areas concerned. It is often argued that such qualities represent 'genuine occupational qualifications' (GOQ) for the posts in question and hence justify the preferential selection of members of particular groups or categories. At this point, of course, geographically-based service delivery and employment policy recombine and new terrain is opened for struggle over whether and to what extent such GOQs exist and whether membership of a particular collectivity is the *sine qua non* of their possession. At this point such consensus as exists over area-based positive discrimination is likely to break down and charges of illegitimate 'positive discrimination' as between individuals to re-emerge. Here again, those opposed to all attempts to redress disadvantage are likely to exploit the confusion to bolster their resistance while those whose aim is to pursue radical policy may well seek to use the measures to pursue their own policy objectives.

Institutional sources of confusion and resistance

(i) Struggles over policy

The nature and extent of a local authority's equal opportunities policy will depend on a number of factors. Like any other employer,

a local authority is subject to the requirements of the 1976 Race
Relations Act. In addition, however, a number of measures, such as
Section 11 of the 1966 Local Government Act or Section 71 of the
1976 Race Relations Act, either place duties on, or offer
opportunities for, local authorities to act in the promotion of
greater racial equality. The existence of such provisions places
pressures on local authorities to develop policies in this area. It also
gives those who are, for reasons of ideological commitment or
political survival, keen to do so the necessary means and
opportunity.

Perceived pressure from constituents is another powerful source
of policy. Where councillors consider that their political futures
depend on their being able to demonstrate a responsiveness to the
needs of particular ethnic communities, the pressure to develop
equal opportunities policies will be greater. In addition, it is in the
nature of the political cycle that the time very rapidly approaches
when the need arises to produce and demonstrate results. This is
likely to produce a greater emphasis on the outcomes of policy than
merely on a commitment to procedural rectitude. In turn, this may
make it desirable or attractive to develop policy which is, or can be
presented as, radical in the sense defined above.

Differing ideological commitments are obviously central to both
policy development and the day to day operation of much local
government. In particular, it hardly needs to be said that Labour
councillors are, in general, more likely than their Conservative
opponents to embrace collectivist principles in policy development.
This does not, of course, mean that Labour controlled councils have
always been quick to develop equal employment opportunities
policies (partly because their collectivism has often been deeply
rooted in a class politics which has been slow to come to terms with
the realities of a multi-ethnic society (Ben-Tovim *et al.* 1986:
pp. 76–7). Nor does it mean that no Conservative-led councils have
taken initiatives in this area. Nevertheless, the cleavage between a
Labour Party generally more sympathetic to collectivist conceptions
of social action and a Conservative Party increasingly committed to
radical individualism is an important source of dispute, in many
local authorities, about the principles of fairness which should
underlie policy.

In the paper referred to above (1986b), Nick Jewson and I
explore some of the ways in which confusions between competing

conceptions of equal opportunities policy can be exploited and manipulated by those who wish to promote a particular policy or oppose another. Proponents of the liberal version may seek to argue or imply that such policies are capable of delivering radical policy outcomes. Proponents of radical policy may seek to legitimate their proposals in terms of the rhetoric of the liberal view in order to gain acceptance or minimise opposition. Opponents of all policies aimed at redressing inequality and disadvantage may seek to tar all proposals with the brush of those thought to be illegal or most unpopular. In other words the confusions between conceptions of fairness, and principles of policy, referred to above are not simply fortuitous nor are they merely a product of intellectual error or unclarity. Rather they are systematically promoted and manipulated as part of a struggle for power in the process of policy formation.

(ii) Organisational struggles

Disputes over policy are not the only struggles for power in local authorities and other large organisations. As Richard Jenkins (1982; 1986) has noted there are also typically organisational struggles in progress which may have little or no direct relevance to issues of equal opportunities but which have significant bearing on policy development and outcomes. In private industrial and commercial organisations, one of the most critical of these concerns struggles for power between personnel and line managers. Such struggles for power will typically be concerned either with the promotion of a particular set of objectives (getting the job done versus 'good employment practice'; or equal opportunities versus management discretion) or with the relative placement of the groups concerned within the organisational hierarchy. In the latter case the successful promotion of an equal opportunities policy may well be seen as a means of increasing the role of personnel at the expense of line management. Resistance to the policy on the part of line management may then be a manifestation of a disagreement over policy but it may equally be motivated by considerations of power unrelated to the policy in question. In either case competing conceptions of fairness of the kind described above will typically be mobilised and attempts made to question the legitimacy of the opposing position. Once again the generation of confusion may be an integral part of the struggle (see also Jenkins and Parker, 1987; Jewson and Mason, 1984–5; 1986a; 1986b).

In a local authority context, there may well be similar intra-organisational struggles at management level (Young, 1987: p. 100). In addition, however, the cleavage between elected members and officers is likely to be of significance. Officers are charged with advising on policy matters and with implementing policy once it is determined. In practice they make, *de facto*, much day to day policy either through the process of implementation or because their 'professional' expertise is not challenged by elected members in many areas. This has two implications for the development of equal opportunities policy. Firstly, it is possible that officers will opt for a quiet life and see their main occupational tasks in terms of organisational efficiency and getting the job done. Policy innovation is by definition a nuisance and equal opportunities policy is likely to be seen as secondary to the main service delivery function of the authority (Ouseley, 1981: p. 179). When it comes to advising or commenting on policy, moreover, they are likely to conceive of fairness in individualistic terms which are congruent with the structures of their own career hierarchies (Young, 1987: p. 100).

Secondly, officers are likely to be suspicious of attempts to 'interfere' politically in their 'professional' advice-giving functions. The development of equal opportunities or race equality policies always involves challenging the way things are presently done. It not infrequently involves a relatively high degree of politicisation of matters which had previously been seen subject to 'professional' judgement and procedure, and hence 'non-political'. As a result, policy development is not only likely to be marked by disputes over policy itself but to also become the site of struggles over powers, competences and degrees of autonomy within the organisation (on these matters, see Ouseley, 1981). These processes will be even more marked in authorities (typically, though not necessarily, Labour controlled) where elected members take a strongly politicised view of all policy formulation and implementation. Once again such terrain is ripe for the manipulation and reproduction of confusion invoking competing conceptions of fairness and contrasting principles of policy (Jewson and Mason, 1986b).

Conclusion

The prospects for effective initiatives by local authorities to promote equal opportunity in employment are not good. Recent changes, such as the growth of competitive tendering and the increasing development of specialised agencies (like inner city task forces), places limits on the range of employment opportunities over which local authorities have direct control. By its very nature, competitive tendering involves increasing devolution of control over employment matters to independent and localised units. This is likely to be true even if contracts are won by in-house units. Moreover, Young (1987: p. 103) has noted that, especially in large authorities, there is already a considerable degree of devolution of control over recruitment matters. There will be impetus to use trends in the labour market, such as increased part-time working and casualisation (Wrench, 1989), to reduce costs in order to win contracts. All of these developments reduce employment opportunities in a context where black people are already over-represented among the unemployed. Moreover, cost pressures can be expected to ensure that matters such as equal opportunities are a low priority among managers. Finally, the increasing devolution and decentralisation implied by competitive tendering is likely to reduce progressively the need for extensive central organisation and control of services. This, in turn, would place further constraints on precisely that sector of the economy where black people have made the most progress – notably in non-manual occupations.

This chapter has sought to identify the ways in which contrasting conceptions of fairness, reflecting individualistic and collectivist assumptions, interact in the struggle over the formulation and implementation of equal opportunities policies in the field of employment. It has traced a number of intellectual, cultural and institutional sources of confusion and obfuscation. It is important to note that the argument being advanced is that such confusion is not simply fortuitous. It is the outcome of struggles within and outside the workplace in which the participants are not equally matched in terms of power. Moreover, space has not permitted an exploration of the ways in which the terms of the debate may be subject to agenda setting from outside. However, it is impossible to conclude without mentioning two possible sources of such agenda setting. One concerns the way in which equal opportunities matters are portrayed in the media. In our recent research conducted in private commercial organisations, press characterisations of the alleged activities of local authorities have frequently been cited as evidence for the illegitimacy of all but the most minimal commitment to equal opportunities. Secondly, it is difficult to escape the conclusion that the electoral dominance of new right conservatism in the 1980s has succeeded in transforming the political agenda in ways which prioritise individualism and deny legitimacy to collectivist conceptions of all kinds. We are, after all, even told there is no such thing as society.

Notes and references

1. The ideas which form the basis of this chapter have been developed in collaboration with Nick Jewson. The same is true of the research which underlies and informs them. Nick, therefore, shares the credit for whatever merits this chapter may have. I alone, however, am responsible for its errors and deficiencies.

2. Another good example of how such conflicts in policy may occur concerns the operation of seniority as a criterion of promotion. Dennis Brooks (1975) has shown how seniority worked to the advantage of ethnic minority workers in the underground railway operations of London Transport allowing a good deal of upward occupational mobility, at least within the manual grades. However, it is usually recognised that seniority systems work to the disadvantage of women workers given their typical experience of discontinuous careers. In Brooks's example, moreover, the advantageous effects of seniority depended on a relatively low rate of labour turnover among ethnic minority workers within the overall context of labour shortage.

3. A case in point is provided by the notion of a genuine occupational qualification. Very often, the idea that particular services can only be provided effectively by members of the group for which they are destined is founded on the application of acceptability criteria. Members of any group might possess the right technical qualifications but it is thought that only co-members are able to empathise with the special problems of the group or are likely to be acceptable, for cultural or religious reasons, as service providers, advisers or confidants. Such arguments have often been invoked to explain or justify particular appointments under Section 11. Whether or not such arguments are justified can, of course, only be decided in the light of the circumstances of each case. The point at issue here, however, is that acceptability criteria are not everywhere unjustified nor do they always, inevitably, work against the cause of greater racial equality.

4 Social Services Departments: The Process and Progress of Change

Naomi Connelly

Introduction

In 1978 the Association of Directors of Social Services (ADSS) and the Commission for Racial Equality (CRE) produced their joint report on *Multi-Racial Britain: The Social Services Response*. If that document did not itself prove to be the catalyst for change which the directors involved perhaps had hoped, it provides us now, at least, with some picture of the social services world just over a decade ago. Together with other information we can use it as a baseline from which to consider the progress which has been made.[1]

There are important reasons for taking stock now at the beginning of the 1990s. These are critical times for social services departments, with many uncertainties about what their roles and responsibilities will be over the coming years. Among the changes underway are shifting boundaries between social services departments and the health service, the voluntary sector and the commercial care sector; closure of long-stay institutions and developments in community care; moves to ensure greater choice and greater voice for service users; a decreasing role for social services departments as providers of support and care, and an increasing role as case managers or managing agencies for services provided by others.

Amidst all these changes, what are the prospects for moves towards race equality? Can we assume that awareness has increased, that policies and practices are well enough understood and that implementation of change is far enough advanced so that possible race dimensions will routinely be taken into account in the new and challenging situations which social services departments will be facing? Or is there a danger that some years from now we will look back on the 1980s and see them as having been a fairly self-contained period of development, built on subsequently here and there in the social care world, but by and large coming to an end as the new challenge arose for departments?

Although there have been some significant changes over the past decade, it would be unwise (to say the least) to be at all complacent about the inevitability of further progress. Four steps are therefore required as we move into the 1990s:

1. Take stock of what has been achieved thus far, and what can be learned from the experience of the past years about the most effective methods and the most essential elements in the move towards race equality in social services.
2. Take a hard and realistic look at what is happening now and what is likely to happen in social services and in the wider health and social care worlds over the next few years.
3. Consider how to ensure that relevant race dimensions are not lost or overlooked, but rather are included appropriately at the early stages of planning (at national, regional and local levels) for all new developments affecting social services provision, whether in the statutory, voluntary or private sectors.
4. Aim to go beyond this and maximise the opportunities presented by a period of such general change, devising ways of short-cutting the painfully slow process of change towards race equality.

We shall look at each of these issues in turn, and will conclude by examining the prospects for the 1990s.

Looking back

After examining what was happening in social services departments across the country, the 1978 ADSS/CRE report said:

Our conclusion is that the response of social services departments
to the existence of multi-racial communities has been patchy,
piecemeal and lacking in strategy . . . few departments have
specifically and explicitly worked through the implications to
social services of a multi-racial clientele (ADSS and CRE, 1978:
pp. 14-15).

Over the next few years, other observers of the social services
scene came to much the same conclusions. In my own research in
1980–81 in social services departments, carried out as part of a
larger study of local authority race equality policies and practices
(Young and Connelly, 1981: Chapter vi), most changes were found
to have come about because of initiatives by individual practitioners
and managers. It was rare to find that any issues relating to local
black populations had been discussed at senior management levels,
and the role of councillors was hardly mentioned; social services
staff interviewed disclaimed any knowledge of departmental or local
authority policies on race equality.

It is perhaps too easy to look back to that period and judge that
nothing of value was happening in social services departments, or
nothing worth our continuing consideration. That is not only
untrue, it is also unjust to all those people, who were implementing
change as far as they could within their own work, or struggling to
get race issues taken on board at a policy level. Certainly there was
a widespread and determined adherence to colour blindness in
social services departments at that time. But there were many other
positions on the spectrum of awareness, and a variety of approaches
to practical change, from the multitude of reasons given for
continuing to provide a standard service through a range of
adjustments and additions aimed at meeting needs of local black
populations.

The variation within and between departments was so great that
generalisations about lack of response at that time require
immediate qualification. By the beginning of 1981, for example,
Leicestershire Social Services Department had set up its carefully-
designed interpreting service, Coventry Social Services had
appointed a Training Officer (Ethnic Minorities), and Race
Relations Advisers were in post in Lambeth and Lewisham Social
Services.

It can be argued that a period of predominantly practitioner-driven change is a necessary stage in the development of new ideas and new methods. Although there is some validity in this, clearly the approach has severe limitations and drawbacks in social services, where the issues are those of support and care for frail or vulnerable people. Because the response was (as the ADSS/CRE report said) 'patchy' and 'piecemeal' it was inequitable. Whether a black person in need of support and care was able to obtain these was very much a matter of luck; and in all departments whole areas of work were untouched by change. Besides being inequitable, the situation was a very wasteful one. There were few opportunities for committed staff to improve their practice by learning from each other; or to pool their experience and draw on that of local black groups in order to go beyond case by case consideration and find general ways of easing access and increasing the sensitivity and appropriateness of services.

Perhaps most important of all was that the system allowed ample scope both for individual acts of discrimination and racism, and for the continuance of indirectly discriminatory policies and practice.

None of this could change while the prevailing ethos was one of colour blindness. There are still many people at all levels of social services departments who have found it difficult or impossible to give up this frame of reference. However, sufficient change has now taken place to provide the potential for policy consideration and the more strategic approach which the ADSS/CRE found lacking. There are many reasons why this change has occurred, with some variation from area to area, but certainly the disorders in the inner cities in 1980 and 1981, and the increasing participation of people from black communities in local politics, have been important.

Writing at the end of 1981, Juliet Cheetham noted that:

Whereas in 1979 senior administrators (in social services departments) said frequently that it would be political dynamite and counter-productive to raise ethnic questions at policy level, by 1981 race relations and related policy questions had been moved firmly on to local authority agendas (Cheetham, 1981: p. v).

Unfortunately, in many cases such questions moved off agendas fairly rapidly. But in those authorities and those departments where they remained matters of policy-level concern, substantial time and energy had been devoted throughout the decade to coming to grips with the issues and their resolution. This has been a complex and difficult process.

Even when there is acceptance that there are issues to be discussed there has to be some agreement about what those issues are, both at a general level and in relation to particular aspects of social services provision. There has to be a willingness to discuss the issues, opportunities to do so critically and constructively, and ways of carrying out decisions about changes in policies, procedures and practices. Ideally, there would be initial review of the functioning of a department, then careful consideration of the necessary scope and content of change, then allocation of resources and implementation of change directed towards particular objectives over particular time-periods. Although some departments have attempted this, so systematic and strategic an approach has rarely been possible. What there has often been instead is a continuation of an *ad hoc* and piecemeal approach - although this time within at least a minimal policy framework, initiated or encouraged at senior management or social services committee levels, and thus likely to have a wider significance and impact than the earlier practitioner-initiated changes.

As with all local authority and social services department activity, many disparate pressures influence what steps are taken. Included among these are, for example, concerns voiced by local black communities, implementation of local authority equal opportunity employment policies, current professional interest in a subject, apparent political benefits to be derived, and the availability of resources in the form of Section 11 funding[2] (together with the Home Office's requirements relating to consultation, evaluation and strategy). At least equally important are constraints: racism on the part of key councillors or officers, lack of awareness or lack of commitment, officers' views of how far councillors are prepared to go and vice versa, other resource priorities, obstruction by some groups of staff and the cumbersome working of bureaucratic procedures.

Notably absent as a possible influence on change has been any statement from the Department of Health and Social Security about the responsibilities of social services departments, such as that from the Home Office in a 1988 'Policy statement on Race Issues and the Probation Service':

> The Home Office is wholly committed to the elimination of racial discrimination from all aspects of the work of the Probation Service, and to a policy of racial equality. There must be no racial discrimination of any kind, conscious or inadvertent, whether by Home Office staff, by the Probation Committee as an employer, by the managers of the Service or by the staff of the Probation Service itself in their working environment or in their provision of services. (Home Office, 1988)

In contrast, in relation to social services the subject has generally been kept at arm's length, with the central department supporting development activities rather than giving guidance either on the responsibilities of social services departments or on details of policy and practice. However, the Department's Social Services Inspectorate in late 1988 issued a paper which discussed the issues and set out the Inspectorate's 'Policy on Race Equality' (Pearson, 1988).

Taking stock

Looking back over the 1980s, there has been considerable change in the way a great many social services departments approach issues of race equality. But the journey has proved to be a long and difficult one; from acceptance that policy level consideration is possible and necessary, to some understanding of the implications and complexities of this, to the implementation of appropriate change.

In considering how far we have come and what is different now, here are a few suggestions:
1. Race equality is widely accepted as an appropriate subject for social services discussion. Indeed, race equality issues now have a high profile. Week in and week out the social services press includes relevant news items, descriptions of projects, articles about training or other issues, reports of conference discussions, advertisements for specialist posts.
2. There is a wider geographical spread of change. This is probably due mainly to awareness of the presence of hitherto

'invisible' (to departments) black populations, either because of
pressure from local black communities or for other reasons. In
some cases it is due to political or professional recognition that
provision of social services in a multi-racial society goes beyond
questions of provision of services to individuals within sizeable
local black communities; there are other important issues such
as how white staff deal with racism among white service users.

3. The relevance and scope of change are defined differently.
Although many people in social services departments still see
multi-racial populations as 'a problem' for service-providers,
there has been increased acceptance that 'the problem' lies with
departments, and that their responsibilities include informing
themselves about need and ways of meeting this, easing access
and ensuring more equal treatment. The subject is increasingly
seen as relevant to all staff (receptionists and senior managers
as well as social workers and nursery nurses), and to all aspects
of social services. Recently, for example, there has been an
encouraging if belated recognition that there are issues to be
addressed about appropriate assessment, support and care for
black people with physical or mental disabilities.

4. Contacts between social services departments and local black
communities have multiplied, and in many departments now go
well beyond the old pattern of white service provider and black
service user, or department funding of a few black voluntary
projects. There are increasing numbers of black staff and black
councillors, experimentation with a variety of advisory and
consultative arrangements, and joint working in relation to
action-research and other projects.

5. There are some signs of a greater understanding of the
complexity of change. The simplistic reliance on one step –
such as issuing a policy statement, or training, or ethnic record
keeping, or appointment of a race adviser or liaison officer –
has diminished, although unfortunately by no means disappeared. Diversity is accepted somewhat more readily, although
the amount of diversity which it is appropriate and feasible for
departments to meet is a matter of continuing debate. The role
of policy and its inter-relationship with practical change is
beginning to be better understood. In general, the constraints
and the opportunities are clearer, as are the dangers of
marginalisation and compartmentalisation of change.

These are the kinds of points which come to mind when trying to answer the question of how far social services departments have moved in the direction of race equality. What is striking, however, is that they are all about the *process* of change. They relate to shifts in ways of thinking about race equality and social services provision, and about establishing the conditions in which something further can happen. As such, they are to be welcomed. But they need to be differentiated from 'real' change: change in outcomes. The struggle over these past years to widen social services departments' view of their responsibility for change has involved many people in tremendous efforts. How much of that energy has found its way through, in the end, to create change apparent to individual black people with needs for support or care?

The amount of information available is limited and fragmentary. Perhaps the only answer we can hazard is: 'not enough'. But the experience acquired, often so painfully, does at least provide a good basis on which to build with some confidence. Or, rather, it might have done so, if so many changes were not imminent in social services.

The changing social services world

The social services world is never a static one. Departments almost always seem to be in the throes of change, either because of their latest restructuring or in response to the latest focus of professional or media concern. However, the changes which are now underway or under discussion are exceptionally far-reaching, raising questions about all roles and responsibilities of social services departments. For example:

1. Care in the community/community care. The running down and closure of long-stay institutions for frail elderly people, people with learning difficulties (mental handicap), mentally ill and physically disabled people require major adjustments from social services departments. The return of people from such institutions to local areas (the 'care in the community' initiative), and establishing alternative provision for them and for others, are providing significant resource and professional challenges to all departments. As well as issues about appropriate and feasible forms of support and care there are issues about changing boundaries with the health service and

social security, joint working with housing associations and voluntary organisations, responses to the needs of carers as well as people with disabilities, and others. Central government delay in clarifying its intentions following Sir Roy Griffiths' 1988 report on community care (Griffiths, 1988) and the 1989 White Paper on the National Health Service (Department of Health, 1988) have exacerbated uncertainty and the difficulties for departmental planning.

2. 'Consumerism' and 'user empowerment'. Coming from a variety of viewpoints ranging from confidence in a market-oriented approach to concern with social justice and human rights, ideas about 'consumerism' and about 'user empowerment', about 'choice' and 'voice', present departments with critical questions about professional ethos and responsibilities as well as the practicalities involved in readjusting the balance of decision-making between departments and their users.

3. Private sector support and care. The growth of the private sector has mainly affected residential care (particularly for frail elderly people), but private day and domiciliary services are expanding. Compulsory competitive tendering for some aspects of local authority work will be increasing over the next few years: commercial firms may soon be providing catering, cleaning and perhaps other services to many more social services departments (although doubtless some contracts will be won by in-house groups and others by voluntary organisations). A new development is a not-for-profit private sector, taking on responsibility for specific aspects of departments' work such as residential provision for people with learning difficulties.

4. Social services departments as managing agencies. All these and other pressures mean that the social services department role as direct provider of services is being eroded: increasingly departments will be managing agencies for services provided by others. This development, requiring a new approach and new skills, raises many issues about standards, assessment, evaluation and accountability. It is not clear how far the shift will go, nor indeed is there agreement about how far it ought to go. The possibilities include the contracting-out of care for individuals on a much greater scale than hitherto; or contracting-out services in part of a local authority area, or

services for a whole group of vulnerable people; or individual establishments of a variety of kinds may he hived off. Providers may include self-help organisations and user groups as well as traditional voluntary organisations and private sector agencies; current local authority employees may be involved in new relationships with social services departments through direct service organisations or in other ways.

5. The changing political/professional balance. Across a range of fields ideas have shifted as to what are appropriate 'professional' concerns and what are matters which should be subject to political decision. At the local authority level, politician–chief officer relationships have sometimes altered as a result; and central government has, through legislation and subsequent regulations, increasingly changed the parameters within which these and other relationships operate. Such developments have affected social services as much as other local authority departments. There have, of course, always been differences of view within social services about priorities and methods, for example in the exercise of their control functions; about the relative roles of casework, group work, community work and community development; about the amount of diversity which can be met and the amount of flexibility a bureaucracy can sustain. But the increasing politicisation of social services (whether from the right or the left) has made substantial inroads into whatever degree of professional consensus previously existed.

In addition to these changes affecting social services departments directly, they are already or soon will be affected by changes taking place in local authority housing, education and leisure services departments; by the introduction of the Social Fund and other of the 1988 and 1989 social security changes; and by the substitution of the poll tax for rates.

Crucial elements in change towards race equality

Given these major changes to the social services world, what is likely to happen to race equality policies and practices? Will we be able, after all, to build constructively on the experience of the 1980s or is there a danger that momentum will be lost? If that danger is to be avoided, we need to be as clear as possible about what the lessons of the past years have been. We need to distinguish the crucial elements which make change in the direction of race equality more likely – and not just process change, but changes in outcomes.

There are likely to be many views about what these crucial elements are. What is important is that the question should now be specifically addressed, so that the great variety and wealth of experience – inside and outside of departments – can be drawn on quickly and applied effectively. The most obvious candidate for such a list is political and senior managerial commitment; among others might be administrative and organisational competence, mainstream change as the priority, and – closely associated with this – building on existing skills and existing methods.

1. Political and senior managerial commitment. Experience in social services departments has shown that much can be achieved by dedicated and energetic staff who take their courage in their hands and press on with change, even when there is little interest and enthusiasm at higher levels of the department. But the strains on such staff are great, necessary resources are likely to be hard to come by, and the lack of explicit policy makes it difficult for black groups and individuals outside the department to contribute to development. Political and senior managerial commitment really needs to go beyond 'letting things happen' for real progress to be made.

2. Administrative and organisational competence. Many race relations and equal opportunities advisers in local government and in voluntary organisations have found that a basic impediment to achieving change is that the organisation seems to function in too haphazard a way for change of any kind to be systematically introduced, let alone change relating to so emotive an area as race equality. (This lack of effective organisation is well recognised by many personnel staff, who have taken up the cause of equal opportunities with enthusiasm as a vehicle for introducing the kind of training and uniformity of procedures in recruitment and selection which they have long wanted). Social services departments are perhaps particularly liable to find themselves in a state of organisational disarray, whether as a result of their never-ending search for better structures to deal with their complex responsibilities; or because

support services are cut back drastically in order to keep desperately-needed frontline services in place, so that the administrative infrastructure for translating policy into action effectively disappears. In this situation, even the most basic changes directed towards lessening racial discrimination or disadvantage have little hope of effective implementation, let alone positive action to improve the quality of provision for local black populations. Politicians and managers need to recognise the importance of administrative and organisational competence if activity directed to increasing race equality is not to be dissipated or wasted, and if those with advisory or development responsibilities are not to be overwhelmed by the immensity of the task.

3. Mainstream change as priority. It is difficult to judge how much of the attempted change over the past decade has been in the form of 'special' arrangements or services added on to existing provision, and how much has been in the form of mainstream change: the former tend to be much more visible than the latter. The dangers in 'special' provision are well known: marginalisation, compartmentalisation, inadequate resources, overlooking common needs in the concentration on 'extra' needs; and many others. As awareness and experience have increased, departments have begun to find ways of planning for the mainstream in ways which take fuller account of diversity – and often in ways clearly beneficial to a wide range of staff and service users, not only those from black communities.

For example, flexitime for employees can overcome some of the issues relating to religious observance; flexible budgets for practitioners can help them meet a variety of needs in a more appropriate way. Where substantial numbers of service users have little command of English, interpreting services can be built into the 'ordinary' resources available rather than being 'special', and hence difficult and perhaps stressful for practitioners or users to obtain. There are probably as yet few departments which routinely build race equality dimensions into the mainstream, but the knowledge and experience now available make it increasingly possible to find creative ways of doing so.

4. Building on existing skills and existing methods. One of the most difficult tasks for those trying to progress race equality in

social services has been to find the right balance between using 'ordinary' skills and methods and developing new ones. Building on what already exists in a social services department (although not overlooking the point made above about organisational competence) has many advantages – lessening possible resentment, avoiding the deskilling of staff which has inhibited constructive change, producing quicker and more durable results. As with mainstreaming service change, specific attention to race equality aspects continues to be necessary. However, the stage has now been reached in many departments where these aspects can then be drawn on positively: emphasising and developing the skills professionals and others already have, taking fuller account within race-related training of what is known about how adults learn about other topics, involving black groups in the department's usual consultative or advisory bodies, ensuring that race equality issues are taken account of within the preparation of plans for particular groups of users rather than as separate exercises, and so on.

Looking forward

Experience over the past decade suggests the importance of these four factors: political and senior managerial commitment, administrative and organisational competence, mainstream change as a priority and building on existing skills and existing methods. The task then is to consider how these and other crucial elements can be translated into the new situation of social services departments. There are problems in doing so – but also opportunities. Being alert to the problems, but identifying and taking advantage of the opportunities, is the challenge which has to be met if there is to be any hope of maintaining progress and increasing the speed of change.

In some ways, political and senior managerial commitment are now even more important than they have been in the past. Over the next few years social services departments will be engaging in many new or expanded activities, in each of which there ought to be a race equality dimension: devising contract specifications, liaising with other agencies about joint provision, choosing among possible providers, systematising assessment procedures, and building quality assurance measures into performance monitoring. Such general concepts as 'meeting needs of local ethnic minority communities' will hardly be sufficient. The content of services and how they are to be delivered will have to be much more clearly specified, and it is difficult to see how this can be done in a way which takes adequate account of race equality aspects unless senior backing is given to it.

On the other hand, if political and senior managerial commitment are insufficient, individual staff will still have the opportunity they have always had, of making what adjustments they can in their own work. But in addition, individual black managers, or local black groups, or voluntary groups with a strong ethos of multiracial work, have a new opportunity: to ensure that they are equipped to bid for sites or services hived-off by the department, or to enter the competitive tendering process.

As noted above, a reasonable level of organisational and administrative competence is likely to be a necessary – although by no means sufficient – condition for implementation of change towards race equality. It is difficult in mid-1989 to envisage how social services departments will respond to the many pressures on them over the next few years, and what the implications will be for such competence. Some of the ideas being canvassed envisage social services departments as filling a residual role, with the bulk of provision under other (especially private) auspices. Others envisage a substantial role for social services departments in planning, assessment and monitoring of support and care services, but with little actual involvement in direct provision. Yet others expect social services departments to exercise central responsibility for ensuring that local populations have access to appropriate support and care, with this necessarily requiring a continuing service delivery role as well as new managing agency functions.

If there is fragmentation of departments and provision under many different auspices, it is hard to see how we can avoid returning to the position which the 1978 ADSS/CRE report characterised as 'patchy, piecemeal and lacking in strategy'. On the other hand, some of the organisational and administrative changes currently under discussion could contribute to implementation of more systematic approaches towards race equality – if opportunities are grasped. Examples include the stress being laid on performance measurement, and on outcomes rather than inputs; consideration of training needs of front-line staff; examination of decision making points in departments; concern to find ways of hearing the voice of the 'customer', 'consumer', 'user', 'citizen'. The general shaking-up of departments and the enforced examination of their responsibilities, the questioning of what they are doing and why, ought to provide scope for clarifying their role in a multi-racial society and then building on this.

Ideally, that role would include routinely taking on issues of race equality: adopting a strategic approach which treats as priorities mainstream change and building on existing skills and methods. But many things about the new position of social services departments may make that less likely, and may force even committed departments back to 'patchy' and 'piecemeal' provision, and the *ad hoc* funding of small black voluntary groups. Equal opportunity recruitment and selection procedures, working parties dealing with race equality issues, support arrangements for people in specialist posts: all these and other aspects of the infrastructure of departmental and local authority-wide change have costs. When resources are severely constrained, or when groups of department staff are competing with private sector firms for contracts to provide services, such arrangements may come to be seen as dispensable frills.

The arguments for moving towards mainstreaming and routinisation are those of social justice, reinforced now by recognition of the amount of learning which has taken place over the last decade. But they are pragmatic, too: if anything is to be saved, it may have to become part of the 'ordinary' work of the department. Individual employees may have more autonomy within the department; or they may move outside the department to consultancy firms, or to commercial, not-for-profit or voluntary sector service-providing agencies. Departments concerned with race equality need to ensure that such staff are equipped to apply their learning in very different settings.

In addition, in departments' new relationships with a wide range of agencies (through contracts, assessment, monitoring, joint working) they may be able or even expected to give guidance on issues which relate to support and care for local multi-racial populations. They need the capacity for seeing what is crucial in moving towards race equality, whatever the setting. In this, special posts and special arrangements clearly still have a place – but only after mainstreaming and its implications have been carefully considered.

In looking back over the 1980s we can see that social services departments have at least made a start on the process and progress of change towards race quality. However tentative and uncertain this has sometimes been, it now provides a basis on which to build constructively. The many new challenges facing the social care world cannot be allowed to inhibit further – and more rapid – development.

Notes and references

1. This chapter draws on research funded by the Department of Health and Social Security and by the Economic and Social Research Council (Grant GOO 232237): I am very grateful for their support. For a fuller discussion of the issues see *Care in the Multi-racial Community*, Policy Studies Institute, 1988, and *Race and Change in Social Services Departments*, Policy Studies Institute, 1989.

2. Under Section 11 of the Local Government Act 1966 the Home Office is empowered to pay part of the salary costs of local authority staff employed 'in consequence of the presence within their areas of substantial numbers of immigrants from the Commonwealth whose language or customs differ from those of the community'. The history of Section 11 and the issues which have arisen in its use are discussed in Cross, Johnson and Cox (1988) and Johnson, Cox and Cross (1989).

5   Pragmatism or Retreat? Funding Policy, Local Government and the Marginalisation of Anti-Racist Education[1]

Wendy Ball, William Gulam, Barry Troyna

Introduction

The structural decentralisation of the education system in England and Wales has, until recently, permitted a degree of autonomy at the local level and it is within this 'space' that campaigns for racial equality in education have been waged in the last 10 years, albeit with different degrees of commitment and vigour (Troyna and Ball, 1986; Troyna and Williams, 1986). The 1988 Education Reform Act (ERA) will almost certainly deny this 'space', a prospect which has deleterious implications for the promotion of anti-racism. The Tories' educational (and social) policy package will denude local authorities of their powers, a project which, of course, was already well underway before the enactment of the ERA. As we have witnessed over the last decade or so, the Conservative policy imperative eschews any semblance of respect or deference to the other members of the partnership in education which since 1944 have, to a greater or lesser degree, taken responsibility for decision-making. Roger Dale has summed up the far-reaching consequences of this shift in responsibility like this: 'LEAs and teachers become the agents of central government on terms laid down by central government rather than being consulted by it' (1988: p. 53).

On the whole, the debate on the implications of the 1988 Education Reform Act for anti-racist education and related egalitarian measures has centred, primarily, on the national curriculum and the associated targets of attainment with assessment at ages 7, 11, 14 and 16. Interestingly, this narrow construction of the problem mirrors that of earlier debates in the area of multi-racial education. In 1982, Andrew Dorn and Barry Troyna commented on the failure by most commentators to engage with the broader issue of the politics of decision making on 'race':

> The bulk of the literature (both academic and practical) in this field has been classroom, teacher and child-centred, and discussions have been dominated by the issues of language, curriculum development, pupil-teacher interaction and compara- tive academic performance (Dorn and Troyna, 1982: p. 175).

Without wishing to underestimate the negative effects of age- related testing and the so-called 'entitlement curriculum' on racial equality in education it is our view that the radical changes in funding of state education constitute the principal cause for concern for those wishing to promote egalitarian initiatives in education. In this chapter, then, we want to try and redress this imbalance by concentrating on the ways in which changes in the funding of state education inhibit the potential for the development and implementation of anti-racist and related egalitarian initiatives. We begin by specifying the changes before considering their implications.

Changing the rules: from permissive to prescriptive modes of funding

Spurred on by a determination to undermine the role of local authorities in policy-making processes, successive Thatcher admin- istrations have radically changed the rules by which funding is allocated. Traditionally two thirds of local authority funding derived from central government through the rate support grant with the remainder raised through local taxes – the rates. By changing the criteria for the allocation of grants with a move towards categorical funding (Harland, 1987) and imposing stringent limits on how much can be raised through the rates, central government has been able to assume a determinant role in how, when and where money is spent at the local level. Additionally during the period since the mid-1970s overall levels of central government support for local authorities have been reduced. More recently the 1988 Local Government Finance Act introduced the community charge to replace rates, and has thus instituted further changes in the funding of local government which will have a major impact during the 1990s (Stewart and Stoker, 1989).

As education is the largest spender in the local authorities, accounting for around 50 percent of the annual budget, it is especially vulnerable to the demands for accountability which this process implies. Put another way, the move from permissive to prescriptive modes of funding under Thatcher has ensured that particular views of education are pre-eminent and diffused throughout LEAs up and down the country. However, despite the fundamental impact of this move on the educational landscape the critical role of funding arrangements in the trend towards the aggrandisement of central power has been ignored in a number of recent analyses of the antecedents of the ERA (see for example Johnson, 1989; Whitty and Menter, 1989). We want to rectify this imbalance here.

The move towards categorical funding in education has been addressed elsewhere (for example Fulton, 1987; Harland, 1987; David, 1988). What we want to do is provide sufficient insight into this trend to sustain our general argument. That is, by increasing the tendency to allocate funds to local authorities on the understanding that certain criteria are met, the centre assumes progressively tighter control over the financial management of education. In consequence, the centre has unprecedented power to define and confine priorities and emphases at the local level. As Brian Knight observes, this style of management constitutes 'a very powerful device . . . to effect change in education' (1987: p. 212). And, of course, this 'change' is determined by the centre. This move from permissive funding, where grants without strings has been the conventional mode, towards prescriptive funding, where strings are attached, naturally alters the relationship between central and local government. Whilst it permits local authorities the opportunity to shape its bid in accordance with perceived local needs and concerns, it rests on the principle that the criteria established for the location of funds are sacrosanct. Harland conceives of the relationship in terms of a contractual agreement between central and local spheres of government. In her view, categorical funding:

> acts as an effective, even if temporary, substitute for legislation; in so far as it relates to funding agencies to do something which the principal to the agreement either cannot or does not wish to do for itself, categorical funding comes very close to the kind of sub-contracting arrangements common in industry (1987: pp. 238–9).

From this perspective then, it is possible to appreciate how far the LEA has been subordinated to the centre by this new funding arrangement. What is more, it allows us to perceive the differences between, say, TRIST (TVEI-related in-service training), GRIST (grant-related in-service training) LAPP (Lower Attaining Pupils Programme) and Education Support Grants (established under the 1984 Education Act) and their accompanying rhetoric as more apparent than real. The imperative for each is the same; to rigidify and reinforce particular conceptions of education.

This move towards categorical funding and the trend towards centralisation in general draws its rationale from the neo-conservative group within the New Right and its commitment to strong government as a pre-requisite for securing the unity of the nation, amongst other things. But with the introduction of Local Financial Management (LMS) through the 1988 Education Reform Act we see a move towards the devolution of power. This is in line with the concerns of the neo-liberal group within the New Right to 'roll back the state', give priority to the freedom of the market and individualism and to champion consumer participation (Troyna, 1990). Other proposals in the ERA also reflect this neo-liberal perspective: that is, open enrolment, opting out into grant maintained status, financial delegation, increasing powers of governing bodies and the creation of City Technology Colleges are, ostensibly in opposition to state control. On the other hand the introduction of the national curriculum, with targets of attainment at 7, 11, 14 and 16 is geared towards centralisation. However, this does not imply that the proposals introduced through the ERA are contradictory. What unifies these proposals is their role in denuding LEAs of their powers (Ball and Troyna, 1989).

So, more specifically, what are the consequences of Local Financial Management (LMS) for the balance of power, control and accountability in education? The key issues here concern the implications for the structure and power base of LEAs. As Dinah Tuck (1988) points out LEAs will be faced with a substantially reduced role in planning and hence the difficulties of maintaining an equitable spread of resources:

> The role of the LEA to look after the needs of all children it serves seems to me endangered if we perceive of each school as a private company competing rather than collaborating with its neighbours, not least when resources are limited (1988: p. 148).

In other words, LMS is likely to exacerbate the potential for conflict and confrontation between schools.

So how will these shifts impact on the status and future prospects of the promotion of anti-racist education? As Ball and Troyna (1989) have pointed out elsewhere, during the 1980s a substantial number of LEAs has produced policies and provision concerned with the promotion of cultural diversity and/or combating racial inequality in education. It must be acknowledged that the heightened visibility of 'race' as a matter to be addressed by LEAs is not the 'result of a centrally inspired or directed attempt to establish a national policy on multicultural education' (Dorn, 1983: p. 2). Despite the moves we have identified by central government to centralise control over educational policy making and intervene more directly in matters concerning the content of education, it has failed to introduce an explicit national educational policy on the issue of 'race' (Dorn and Troyna, 1982; Troyna and Williams, 1986). The generally dismissive view of Sir Keith Joseph, then Secretary of State, to the recommendations of the Swann Committee of Inquiry into the Education of Children from Ethnic Minority Groups (DES, 1985) exemplifies this stance. Appointments to the National Curriculum Council provide another, more recent example: whilst there is a part-time post for equal opportunities (gender) there is no-one with responsibility for race-related matters. Simply put, race-related initiatives in education remain marginal in terms of the allocation of resources.

The main source of LEA funding for multi-cultural/anti-racist education initiatives is through Section 11 introduced in the 1966 Local Government Act. This empowers the Home Secretary to make payments to local authorities 'who in his opinion are required to make special provision in the exercise of any of their functions in consequence of the presence within their areas of substantial numbers of immigrants from the commonwealth whose language or customs differs from those of the community' (quoted in Dorn and Hibbert, 1987: p. 59). Whilst this is not specifically an educational initiative the bulk of Section 11 funding has been claimed by LEAs (Cross, 1982). The underlying rationale for the introduction of this source of funding was that the presence of black people *per se* constituted a burden on local authority services. Provision is based on the problematic concept of 'special needs' with which a pathological view of the black communities has been associated (Solomos, 1983). As we and others have argued before (Dorn and Hibbert, 1987; Troyna and Ball, 1986) research on LEA usage of S11 suggests this form of funding has served to demarcate rigidly initiatives in multi-cultural/anti-racist education. As Dorn and Hibbert argue it is still

> firmly rooted in a policy tradition that prefers voluntarism to compulsion, inexplicitness to explicitness, assimilation to anti-racism, marginal rather than mainstream, disadvantage rather than racial discrimination (1987: p. 60)

In this context, those LEAs which wish to promote policies and practices which prioritise multi-cultural education as a notion of relevance to all schools or have moved towards the more politicised notion of anti-racist education are constrained by the tight controls operated by the Home Office.

In the next section we will illustrate through a case study how the trend towards the greater use of categorical funding and a reduction in the Rate Support Grant has magnified this problem.

Manchester LEA and the new realism

Historically, Manchester LEA under the leadership of a left of centre Labour Group has been a pioneer in the development of multi-cultural education, introducing its first policy statement in

1980. This is not the place to present a detailed history of the development and implementation of the policy on multicultural education (but see Troyna, 1984; Troyna and Ball, 1983 and 1985). However, a number of points are worth mentioning to contextualise the present discussion.

First, Manchester has experienced a long history of both white and non-white immigration. The largest of the black communities originated from the Caribbean, particularly Jamaica, and from South Asia. The LEA's response to the inflow and growth of its black pupil population in the 1960s and early 1970s was largely typical of LEAs up and down the country; its philosophy and practical arrangements were geared towards the principle of assimilation. There was certainly no recognition of the principle of multi-culturalism as a notion of relevance to all schools. Nor was the question of racism within education on the political agenda. Instead the authority tackled race-related issues within a compensatory educational framework which focused on the 'special needs' of black pupils, an approach exemplified by the Education Committee's decision in 1976 to appoint an Inspector for Special Education who was allocated additional responsibility for Multi-cultural Education. Practical support included provision for English as a Second Language teaching, deployment of staff funded under Section 11 of the 1966 Local Government Act and some extra financial support to schools with a large proportion of black pupils. It was not until 1980 in response to various national and local developments that a policy on multi-cultural education was introduced (see Troyna, 1984 for further details).

The policy statement foreshadowed the recommendations of the Swann Committee (DES, 1985) in its insistence that multi-cultural education as an organising principle should suffuse the administration, pedagogy and curriculum of all schools.

Our subsequent research on school responses to the 1980 policy is reported elsewhere (Troyna and Ball, 1983, 1985). There are, however, two aspects of our findings which are relevant to the present discussion. Our research indicated that the LEA's policy and related initiatives had made a limited impact on the routine practices and procedures of local schools. In seeking to explain this discrepancy between policy and practice we considered the strategies introduced by the LEA to implement its policy. As in many other authorities the main practical support for the policy included the appointment of a specialist inspector for multi-cultural education, the establishment of a multi-cultural unit (with four staff), the expansion of mother tongue provision and in-service training in this area. In other words, specialist administrative initiatives were introduced in preference to a reappraisal of mainstream LEA services. In this way the LEA's stated commitment to the principle of multi-culturalism for all was undermined and the notion of 'special needs' perpetuated in terms of the authority's own internal organisation. This was largely because most of these initiatives were funded through Section 11 of the 1966 Local Government Act underlining the point made earlier that this mode of funding has served to demarcate (and marginalise) initiatives on multi-cultural education. One might argue that if the LEA had been genuinely committed to multi-cultural education it would have introduced initiatives involving a substantial reallocation of mainstream resources. The point we wish to emphasise is that the establishment of specialist services was largely ineffective and inappropriate as a means of intervention in local institutions, and as a strategy designed to embrace *all* schools and colleges. Moreover, the setting up of specialist services made them particularly vulnerable at a time of increased financial contraction as we shall show.

A second point arising from our earlier research concerns the permissive approach taken by LEA policy makers, whereby they appeared willing to devolve ultimate responsibility for the development of multi-cultural education in schools to headteachers and their staff. We argued that notwithstanding the relative autonomy enjoyed by schools in the UK's education system this LEA and others needed to assume a far more prescriptive and directive approach in policy implementation. Styles of LEA intervention no longer constitute the main cause for concern, however. With the enactment of the ERA the key question is whether LEAs will be in a position to take an active lead any longer.

From multi-cultural to anti-racist education

In the mid-1980s a number of factors, including the election of a more radical group of councillors in the May 1984 municipal elections, encouraged Manchester Education Committee to depart from its commitment to multi-culturalism and adopt a more politicised approach focusing on issues of power and the existence of institutionalised racism. A policy statement on anti-racist education was adopted in early 1985 (see Appendix). This was a period in which the implementation of Manchester City Council's policy on equal opportunities was also the focus of development and MEC set up a working party to draft a policy for the Education Service within the context of the City Council's equal opportunities policy. This considered questions of recruitment, staff development, curriculum and working conditions with respect to inequalities of 'race' as well as those relating to women, the disabled, gay men and women and the working class.[2] To summarise, by the mid-1980s Manchester LEA had introduced a series of initiatives to underpin a high profile commitment to promoting a policy on anti-racism in education.

As we have indicated, over the last five years Manchester has been led by a left of centre and radical Labour Group with a substantial majority on the council. It is a city, therefore, without a viable Conservative presence. This has had implications not only for the LEA's policies but also for its relationship with the Central State; that is, the Department of Education and Science, the Training Agency (MSC) and the Home Office. Importantly, in the context of this discussion, the shift from a centralist position by the Manchester Labour Group had abated by mid-1988, but the *image* of a far left Manchester remains. The popular press has played a leading role in reflecting and reinforcing this impression. A *Guardian* interview in 1986 with Graham Stringer, Labour leader of Manchester City Council, for example, reported the arrival in the city of a *Daily Mail* team briefed to expose 'loony left' council policies, of which its commitment to equal opportunities was a major concern (Benfield, 1986: p. 23). It is also seen as a city that consistently overshoots its centrally determined grant-related expenditure assessment. Recent evidence of this is reported in *The Guardian*'s coverage of the response in the House of Commons to the statement on the community charge issued by the Secretary of State for the Environment in 1989. According to the report Sir Fergus Montgomery, Conservative MP for Altrincham and Sale asked: 'If the purpose of the community charge is to make councils more accountable to the electors, could he explain why in my constituency those who are going to have to pay the community charge will have to pay an extra £49 a year in order to bail out socialist extravagant councils like Manchester?' (*The Guardian*, 5 July 1989).

As we now turn to consider the impact of changes in funding on Manchester LEA and its race-related work, it is vital to acknowledge this tense relationship between the central and local state. Along with other urban authorities it has become a city to be penalised via rate-capping and other measures.

Pragmatism or retreat?

We referred earlier to the different ways that central government has been able to weaken the powers of LEAs by its control over resource allocation: on the one hand, the reduction in the rate support grant combined with rate-capping, the introduction of Education Support Grants, the Local Education Authority Grant Training Scheme (LEAGTS) (formerly GRIST) and other forms of categorical funding; and, on the other, the proposals relating to Local Management of Schools in the 1988 Education Reform Act. Taken as a whole LEAs committed to the promotion of equal opportunities are now facing a crisis situation. Simply put, there is little room for manoeuvre. We can illustrate this by looking at the experiences in Manchester during the late 1980s.

Manchester's educational services take up 46 per cent of the city's gross expenditure: indicative, in itself, of the strains it has to bear. This crisis came to a head following the 1987 Conservative General Election victory. When the 1987–88 budget was agreed, under central government's Rate Support Grant process the proposed level of expenditure would have meant little or no grant being paid to the city. Hence, like many other urban local authorities, Manchester had to rely on creative accountancy measures coupled with a total freeze on jobs which has operated since July 1987 to artificially reduce expenditure to central government's assessment.

In order to avoid rate capping it has become a political imperative to operate at a reduced budget.[3] The attempt by MEC to meet a reduced budget has involved substantial job losses of both teaching and non-teaching staff through restructuring as well as reduction in running costs. Whilst this has had effects on all users of

MEC's provision it is felt that certain areas will be disproportionately affected by the cuts imposed to reach the central
government's financial targets. This concern has been most forcibly
expressed in the debate around the impact cuts tend to have on
'developmental work with minority or disadvantaged groups. This
work is seen to be at risk, indefinitely discontinued or even
regressing'. [4] In this context let us consider the evidence of the cuts
on race-related work.

The attempt by MEC to meet a reduced budget has
disproportionately hit provision most used by black students.
There are numerous examples: the freeze on posts which hits
replacements of Section 11 funded teaching staff in schools and
colleges; the freeze on part-time contracts which affect a
disproportionately high number of female and black staff; and the
expedient of feeding English as a Second Language (ESL) students
into fee-generating English as a Foreign Language (EFL) classes.
Now let us discuss two specific cases in detail to illustrate how
financial control has affected race-related work.

Educational provision in the inner city areas was already
pressurised as long term trends involving parental choice of
schools, the movement out to the suburbs and the declining birth
rate produced smaller intakes and hence smaller establishments in
the schools sector. The closure of Birley High School (July 1989), a
pioneer in anti-racist education, has left parts of the inner city
without a co-educational 11–16 school. This sector has also
traditionally met some of the adult/community needs in this area.
The recent cuts have meant a rigourous imposition of correct pupil–
teacher ratios that has in turn usually resulted in reduced staffing in
the statutory sector and the pressure is compounded. The head of
one institution in Moss Side, an inner city area in Manchester
produced a litany of issues that included: frozen teaching posts;
administration and technician posts unfilled; the closure of the
creche in the three months prior to exams; S11 posts and hours not
filled; the run down of the youth club as part-time contracts were
cut. It was, in his estimation, a cuts strategy that disproportionately
hit inner cities and black people which: 'made us suffer to save the
authority peanuts'.

A second example is the MEC attempt to meet the need for more
black teaching staff. Three projects were established within the
LEA. One, the black Access course with guaranteed degree places at

Manchester Polytechnic, has laboured under the handicap of unfilled vacancies that include the critical post of student counsellor. The second is the prototype Qualified Teacher Status (QTS) Course run in conjunction with Manchester University. This QTS course involved the MEC employing black adults, with degree qualifications that the DES would not recognise for qualified teacher status, as instructors in schools. These instructors were then seconded on full pay for two and a half days a week to the University to undertake a course that had negotiated with the DES for qualified teacher status on completion. The cuts and job freeze meant that MEC could not employ, and hence could not in 1987–88 pass a cohort through the scheme. The third project is the prototype course intended for Afro-Caribbean students wishing to train to teach Adult Basic Literacy. Initiated in 1986, with the first passage of graduates in 1987, it found the cuts hitting the course budget, course staffing and job opportunities for its throughput. In the perspective of the course tutors it would have been unethical to repeat the process unless: 'there is some prospect of viable teaching posts for those who graduate'. All in all, then, it is clear that reductions in the general budget have impeded race-related work by Manchester LEA. As the leader of the city's Labour Group has put it:'. . . of course . . . equal opportunities will suffer'.[5]

As the local financial situation worsens, Manchester along with many other urban authorities, is forced to compete for categorical funding in areas prioritised by Central Government. At present, the LEA's race-related work has benefited from Education Support Grants (ESG) introduced in 1984 through the Education (Grants and Awards) Act. Whilst on the face of it this source of finance would seem to be welcome, the terms imposed and the directions for development suggested by the DES are at variance with local political priorities in this area. Despite these contradictions, bids are made as the 'new realism' begins to bite. Hence, it is clear that a reduction in the general grant and the introduction of categorical funding has forced the LEA to play by certain rules. After all, a bid reflecting a high profile commitment to anti-racist work simply will not succeed. Indeed, even Section 11 funding cannot be used to develop anti-racist work. In other words, the LEA is forced to acede in order to secure funds. A similar process is at work in relation to grant -related in-service training (GRIST) now the local education authority grant training scheme (LEAGTS). Under LEAGTS, the formula for funding has changed from payment per pound per teacher to per pound per student. This payment per head on each student naturally hits LEAs with good pupil-teacher ratios as there is less money available to train teachers. The less teachers the higher the allocation to each staff member under this scheme. This has effectively meant that Manchester has had less money available to pursue local in-service education priorities.

As an LEA, the set allocation for race related work from the DES, under the auspices of GRIST, was some £20 000 per financial year. Moreover, this allocation was only for the post-16 education sector. The issue was not deemed a priority for schools. This sum is a pittance and, pragmatically, recourse has been made to the competitive tendering process so beloved of this present government. However successful in terms of bidding the LEA is, the returns are meagre in comparison with the millions lost to this same central state.

It is clear then that central government's funding policies have had a restrictive effect on race-related work in Manchester. With categorical funding there is less room for LEAs to establish independent priorities. They must be compatible with those identified by the DES and this does not include anti-racist education. In the face of the onslaught by central government it is evident that MEC's high profile commitment to anti-racism is in retreat. We have illustrated some of the immediate practical effects of cost cutting on race related work. This is coupled with a shift at a political level with the deracialisation of policy: that is, blurring of the race issue into a concern with equal opportunities as a package. Just to provide a couple of examples: in 1988 the Specialist Inspector for Multi-cultural Education was replaced by a new Senior Inspector for Equal Opportunities. And there are rumours that the race unit in Manchester is likely to be disbanded. It appears that the retreat has been accelerated by the repercussions of the killing of Ahmed Iqbal Ullah at Burnage High School in Manchester in September 1986. The report of the Macdonald Inquiry into the incident criticised the headteacher and senior members of staff for their endorsement of an anti-racist education policy, which privileged the perceived needs of black pupils and ignored those of white parents and students (Macdonald *et al.* 1989). In the face of negative press coverage Manchester is now a local authority on the defensive and there is an increased concern among councillors to cater for their white working class constituents. Moreover, race related issues are now more tightly controlled by a minority of officers: with less public debate, anti-racism has gone underground.

It is in this context that Manchester LEA is seeking to respond to the 1988 Education Reform Act. As we have shown, the marginalisation of race-related work was already well under way. In what ways will the Act exacerbate this process? First of all, as we argued earlier, the Act undermines the powers of LEAs by its proposals to increase the autonomy of individual institutions. Undoubtedly this will make it even more difficult, if not impossible for the LEA to actively pursue city wide policies. As we noted earlier, our research on the implementation of the LEA's policy on multi-cultural education highlighted the refusal of a significant number of schools to engage with the issue. Notwithstanding our criticisms of the LEA's *laissez-faire* approach to policy implementation it could be argued that the LEA will now have no choice but to adopt a more cautious style of operation and to devote its declining budget to working in partnership with those schools or colleges which seek support. A second thrust concerns the introduction of local financial management for schools. This will reduce the LEA's general budget *even further* making the support of extra-institutional specialised units a 'luxury' the LEA may no longer be in a position to afford. With a further £5 million to be cut by MEC the emphasis is to preserve face to face staff and not detached units. We expressed our reservations about the introduction of specialist units for race-related work earlier on the grounds that they remain vulnerable to marginalisation and this is a case in point.

The experiences of Manchester local authority are illustrative rather than unique. What we are witnessing there is more or less common to other authorities which in the past decade or so have been committed to equal opportunity measures. This retreat is exemplified in the views of the adviser for multi-cultural education in 'Cottontown', a local authority in the North West of England:

> To openly describe itself as anti-racist the Authority might suffer the consequences of being branded 'left-wing' or 'extremist' and experience the same negative treatment from central government and the media similar to that experienced by the ILEA and Brent Education Authority (quoted in Sikora, 1988: p. 52)

Table 5.1 Inner London Borough plans for anti-racist/multi-ethnic education

	Camden	Greenwich	Hackney	Hammersmith	Islington	Kensington & Chelsea	Lambeth	Lewisham	Southwark	Tower Hamlets	Wandsworth	Westminster
Acknowledges obligations under 1976 Race Relations Act	yes	yes	yes	no	no	yes	yes	yes	yes	yes	yes	yes
Acknowledges Swann or Eggleston reports	no	yes	no	no	no	yes	yes	no	no	yes	yes	no
Backs anti-racist teaching	no	yes	no	no	no	yes	yes	no	no	no	no	no
Will provide 2nd language support	yes	yes	yes	no	yes	yes	yes	yes	yes	yes	yes	yes
Will provide INSET on race and ethnicity	no	yes	no	no	no	no	no	no	no	no	no	no
Proposes a multi-ethnic Inspectorate	yes	yes	yes	no	yes	yes	yes	no	yes	no	no	yes
Outlines Section 11 plans	yes	yes	yes	no	yes	yes	yes	no	yes	yes	yes	no
Acknowledges work of supplementary schools	yes	yes	yes	no	yes	no	yes	yes	yes	yes	yes	no
Recognises imbalance of black children suspended and expelled	yes	no	no	yes	yes	no	yes	no	yes	no	no	no
policy on the appointment of black teaching staff	yes	yes	yes	no	no	no	yes	no	yes	no	no	no
Offers statistics on black school population	no	yes	yes	yes	yes	no	no	no	yes	yes	yes	no
Proposes ethnic monitoring	no	no	yes	yes	yes	no	no	yes	yes	yes	no	no

Source: London Voluntary Service Unit/Afro-Caribbean Community Development Unit (1989): *The 1988 Education Reform Act and Its Impact on London's Black Communities*, p. 5.

And in Inner London the impact of the 'new realism' is particularly pronounced, as illustrated in Table 5.1.

This shows the role of racial issues in the education development plans published by the 12 London boroughs which assumed responsibility for local services in April 1990. These reflect a patchy and circumscribed commitment to promoting racial equality in education which crosses party political lines. And, as our study of Manchester demonstrates, this retreat can be explained in terms of financial and political expedience.

Conclusion

Our analysis has sought to demonstrate how the Conservative onslaught on local government has served to marginalise policies and practices on anti-racist education. In particular, we have focused on changes in funding policy as a device to control political and social priorities at the local level. Of course, the policies of the Thatcher administration in relation to local government have ramifications beyond the education service and issues of racial inequality. As Hatcher (1987) stresses it is important to locate discussions on anti-racist education in a political framework whereby links can be made with other spheres and in relation to other manifestations of inequality.

The centralising trend has, as we have seen, severely curtailed the potential for equal opportunity initiatives in education and elsewhere. Against this background it is important for educationalists to establish alliances with others committed to social change. As Geoff Whitty observes:

> For Left sociologists of the curriculum, as for other socialist teachers, this suggests that they need to make their project part of a broader programme of political reconstruction on the Left. This will involve abandoning old conceptions of professionalism and developing new ways of working with what are sometimes called the popular constituencies – the labour movement, the women's movement and black movements (1985: 179).

Organised and unified political and professional action is needed to defend anti-racist education along with other radical initiatives.

Appendix

'Manchester Education Committee employ over 17000 people within the city. As an employer committed to confronting and eradicating racism and its damaging effects on all Mancunians the Committee expect their employees to uphold this commitment. All employees, both non-teaching and teaching and of every grade, are expected to contribute fully to an education service founded on equal rights, equal opportunities and mutual respect and social justice.

The Committee expect their employees to behave in a non-racist way towards the public, other employees, students and pupils. More than this, employees are encouraged and given support to be critical of and to help change institutional practices and procedures that work against equal rights, equal opportunities, mutual respect and social justice.

Racist abuse, harassment and discrimination are not acceptable. Employees must know that such behaviour will be subject to disciplinary action possibly leading to dismissal.'

Notes and references

1. We are grateful to Jenny Williams for making available some materials collected during her research into Manchester LEA's move towards anti-racist education policies. Parts of the chapter originally appeared in an article by Wendy Ball and Barry Troyna in *Educational Management and Administration*, vol. 17, no.1, 1989. We'd like to thank the British Education Management and Administration Society for permission to reproduce some of that article.
2. For further details see Gulam (1986).
3. At the time of writing (July 1989) the authority has been told of a further cut of £5 million from its education budget over 18 months.
4. Grimshaw, B. in 'City Wide', MEC publication, Spring 1988: p. 144.
5. Stringer, G. quoted in the *New Statesman*, 5 February 1988: p. 13.

6   Racial Equality, Housing and the Local State

John Solomos and Gurharpal Singh

Introduction

Few aspects of racial inequality have over the years attracted as much attention as housing. From the earliest stages of the arrival of black migrants in post-war Britain the disadvantages they suffered in the housing market were a major issue of concern in some localities. Additionally, during this time anti-immigrant groups found that housing was an emotive issue around which they could attempt to organise political support. One way or another, therefore, it can be said that it is on the question of housing that many local political debates about racial issues have focused.

Systematic research which proved the extent of racial discrimination in public sector housing began to emerge in the mid-1970s (Smith and Whalley, 1975). In London the seminal work of the Runnymede Trust (1975) provided a stimulus for further detailed local studies. Parker and Dugmore (1976) found widespread discrimination in the allocation process of the GLC. Research in Islington drew similar conclusions (Islington, 1977). Other authorities, such as Wandsworth (1979) and Lewisham (1980), also began an examination of their procedures and practices in the light of these findings.

95

During the 1980s the housing question has become inextricably tied up with wider concerns: those of urban decay, unrest and related 'social problems'. There has been an increased awareness that housing conditions are an integral element of urban disadvantage and inequality, and that black communities have been particularly hard hit by the deteriorating social conditions in many inner city localities. In this context the changing role of public housing has been at the centre of much political debate during the 1980s. Additionally, housing issues have attracted much popular attention from the media and other opinion forming agencies.

The development of race equality policies in relation to public housing by a sizeable number of local authorities has been a particular focus in recent political debates. These policies have developed over the past decade, by and large, and there is much dispute about their role and impact on patterns of discrimination in public sector housing. They have also been the subject of regular discussion in local political institutions and in the local and national media

In this chapter[1] we shall examine the history of the formulation, implementation and impact of race equality policies with reference to public sector housing. The key period we shall focus upon is the 1980s, although inevitably we shall also look backwards and forwards in order to contextualise the developments with which we are concerned.

To help to illustrate the main processes we are concerned with we shall use as case studies the experience over the past decade of the London boroughs of Hackney and Haringey. In many ways these boroughs provide useful models of policy change in this field. Both have large black and ethnic minority populations in housing need and public sector housing. Both have a recognised political commitment to establishing race equality within the local government system. And during the last decade both have seen increased mobilisation and political participation by the black and ethnic minorities.

The chapter is divided into three sections: (i) a general outline of the policy initiatives which have become identified with a number of local authorities in the field of race and housing; (ii) an examination of the background to policy change and conflict in the two case study authorities; and (iii) an assessment of some of the problems of policy implementation in this field.

Background and context

Since 1960 housing has become an important area of concern in the study of the racialisation of politics and policy in British society (Ward, 1984; Ratcliffe, 1986; Henderson and Karn, 1987). This growing interest has been influenced by the increasing recognition that equal access to housing (and other local services) is central to determining the overall life chances of black and ethnic minority groups. Indeed, in his report on the urban unrest of 1981 Lord Scarman pointed out that housing represented one of the most enduring sources of conflict in racial relations in many areas (Scarman, 1981; Benyon and Solomos, 1987).

Research into racial disadvantage and housing has been available for some time and there is no need to go through the evidence produced by such studies here. The earliest studies into racial disadvantage in housing were ethnographically based. Concentrating on the tendency of the newly arrived migrants to cluster in inner city areas, these works emphasised the naturalness of the process. This pattern, it was argued, was voluntaristic, conditioned by migrants' expectations of the host community, and was largely unrelated to racial disadvantage (Phillips, 1987).

Coinciding with the growing national importance of race issues during the 1960s and 1970s new studies attempted to unravel processes of discrimination and exclusion in the housing market. This can be seen in Rex and Moore's study of the politics of race and housing in Birmingham. This highlighted the mechanisms which regulated the allocation of housing between racial groups within the private and public sectors. Differential access to scarce housing resources, Rex and Moore argued, was related to the existence of differentiated housing classes, which circumscribed the relative position of black and ethnic minorities and the host community within the public and private sector housing markets. This analysis was also supported by other empirical studies of the housing situation (Daniel, 1968).

Detailed research into processes which perpetuated racial disadvantage began with an increasing demand by black and ethnic minority groups for a fairer allocation of public sector housing in the mid-1970s and early 1980s. The seminal study in this area was undertaken by the Runnymede Trust into council housing in London. This study stimulated further research. Parker and

Dugmore (1976) examined the allocation process of the GLC; and Islington (1977) conducted its own investigation. All these studies provided considerable evidence that the allocation procedures of local councils were discriminatory in their operation towards black applicants. Further evidence that discrimination was systemic was provided by the works of Skellington (1980), Simpson (1981), Phillips (1986) and Henderson and Karn (1987).

The Commission for Racial Equality's own investigation into the Hackney Housing Department (CRE, 1984) also confirmed these findings. In public sector housing the Hackney investigation became a *cause célèbre*, and the recommendations of the CRE on policy changes required of the local authority became a model for good practice in other authorities.

It also seems clear, however, that despite a number of changes over the past four decades the housing situation of black and ethnic minority groups has not improved in any substantial sense. Recent research by Deborah Phillips and Susan Smith on the experience of black and ethnic minority communities in public sector housing over the past four decades points to a pessimistic conclusion (Phillips 1987; Smith, 1989). Phillips, while noting that black and ethnic minority communities have benefited from the general improvement in housing conditions, observes that this change continues to co-exist with a 'pattern of entrenched inequalities' (Phillips, 1987). She argues:

> Looking back over the post-war period, there is no doubt that there have been significant changes in the housing conditions of the ethnic minorities, progress in terms of legislation and advances in the formulation of housing policies sensitive to ethnic minority needs . . . Such advances are significant, but they are not in themselves indicative of fundamental structural change. There is also no doubt that the ethnic minorities have been and still are in a disadvantaged position within the British housing market. Racial discrimination as manifest through persistent inequalities, pervades the housing market. The ethnic minorities know it from their everyday experience (Phillips, 1987: p. 114).

From a broader historical perspective Smith has argued that the politics of race and housing has been a central factor in the construction of racialised politics in post-1945 Britian (Smith, 1989). She draws attention to the diverse political, social and economic dimensions of racial relations in contemporary Britain. Smith's analysis highlights the racialisation of residential space within urban localities, and the political and social responses of agencies, groups and individuals to this process.

What research such as this seems to show is that despite successive changes in policy and legislation, and some improvements in relation to the allocation of public housing, there are deeply entrenched racial inequalities in housing which continue to be reproduced. It is within this context that we can begin to analyse the development and impact of local authority initiatives on racial inequality in housing.

The politics of race and housing

It was during the early 1980s that the adoption of racial equality policies in relation to housing became part of the local political agenda. Against the backdrop of political mobilisation by black and ethnic minority groups, urban unrest, and accumulated frustration, a number of local authorities, most notably in London, adopted policies and procedures to promote and effect racial equality in public sector housing.

Such policy initiatives were based on ethnic monitoring of all applicants for public sector housing, ethnic monitoring of all new property allocations, targeting to obtain ethnic proportionality in housing stock, redefinition of council housing access channels on the basis of need, recognition of the special household requirements of black and ethnic minorities, race awareness training for staff of housing departments, and new race structures.

Collectively these changes were introduced as part of equal opportunity and race equality programmes designed to have a systematic impact within the structure of local government. Such policies were based on two important considerations:
1. That there was, and would continue to be, a political commitment to race equality;
2. the collective provision for housing would remain within the control of local government.

As applied in many radical Labour authorities, including Hackney and Haringey, race equality policies in housing since the early 1980s have had three main objectives:
1. To establish the conditions for allocative equality;
2. To increase the recruitment of black and ethnic minority staff in the relevant departments;
3. To undertake promotional initiatives designed to increase black and ethnic minority participation in, and awareness of, public sector housing.

While we cannot go into all the details of the policy models and philosophies that underlie these objectives it may helpful to clarify briefly the basic issues that they addressed.

Allocative equality

Under the rubric of allocative equality the central question addressed has been: who gets what? Do black and other ethnic minority communities receive equal treatment in the allocation of public housing? The emphasis has been on establishing an equality of treatment and equality of outcome in the allocation process. Ethnic records have been introduced to monitor access channels (waiting lists, decants, homeless, and others), mobility within the local housing stock (transfers), and the quality of distribution (property quality indexes).

A central target has been the elimination of procedures that facilitated discretion and contributed to discriminatory outcomes. In many authorities such procedures have been seen as the main channel through which racial discrimination has been reproduced over time, and much effort has been put into examining and revising discretionary procedures.

Additionally, targeting has been adopted to correct imbalances in black and ethnic minority access and representation. It is around this question that much of the controversy has been concentrated, particularly in the context of a political climate that has in general been unfavourable to positive action measures. We shall return to this issue later on in the chapter.

Employment of black and ethnic minority staff

A parallel feature of initiatives in this field has been the linking of allocative equality with measures aimed at increasing the representation of black and ethnic minority staff in housing departments. Racially discriminatory outcomes, it was argued, were not solely the function of organisational procedures but also related to the under-representation or exclusion of black and ethnic minority staff. Consequently, targets have been established to increase the employment of black and ethnic minority staff in housing departments.

Promotional initiatives

These are measures intended to improve communications with, and awareness of, the difficulties faced by black and ethnic minorities. They include such measures as the translation of housing policies into ethnic languages, race awareness training for housing department staff, and more effective controls against racial harassment. Compared with allocative equality or employment development, however, promotional initiatives generally have low operational costs.

Overall these three dimensions are neither exclusive nor exhaustive: at best they have represented the general parameters within which race equality initiatives have developed. We now turn to how these elements were identified and the success and difficulties encountered in their implementation.

Racial inequality and housing policy

Broadly the process of policy formulation and implementation in relation to racial inequality in public sector housing can be seen as going through three stages. *First*, the issue was identified and became the subject of concern for the local authority. *Second*, local authorities began to formulate policy agendas and alternatives in dealing with the issue. *Third*, there has been a critical evaluation of local authorities responses, including suggestions for alternative courses of action.

This process can be illustrated in greater detail if we look at the experience of such initiatives in those authorities at the forefront of policy change in this field. For the purposes of this chapter we have chosen to draw on research we have carried out in the London boroughs of Hackney and Haringey. These authorities provide an illustration of the processes that have shaped racial equality policies in relation to housing and the gap that often exists between policy and practice. Where appropriate we shall also refer to the experience of other local authorities and broader national trends.

The local political context

As we mentioned above systematic evidence about the extent of racial discrimination and inequality in public sector housing in London began to emerge in the 1970s. The willingness of some London authorities to undertake research was the first recognition that existing policies were perhaps discriminatory. It is perhaps not surprising, in this climate, that Hackney and Haringey, with their large black and ethnic minority populations, could not remain insulated from pressures to change their practices in the housing field.

If we look at the origins of policy formulation in the two authorities we can see more clearly the forces that shaped the political debate in these and other local authorities. Hackney first responded to the issue of race equality in council housing in late 1975 when the Community Relations Commission (CRC) approached the authority with a view to discussing the findings of the Runnymede study of race and housing in London (1975). This report, which was based on 1971 census data, argued that a greater number of families of New Commonwealth origin were living in older property in Hackney than any other borough in London. The CRC's proposal for a new research project to evaluate the post-1971 situation was withdrawn when the Race Relations Board (RRB) expressed an interest in undertaking an investigation of housing allocations in Hackney under Section 17 of the 1968 Race Relations Act.

During its discussions with Hackney councillors and officials in May 1976 the RRB expressed a need for access to tenants' files and a survey of their ethnic origins. The Council's response was emphatic:

It was made clear to the Race Relations Board that the Council was not prepared to allow the Board to inspect tenants' files and, moreover, that this was the ruling generally applied to all tenants' files which debars access by members or other third parties. In addition it was made clear that in the view of the Council a survey of tenants to ascertain ethnic origin and related matters would not be appropriate at that time (Hackney, 1983).

Although we are not aware of the RRB's reply to Hackney's position, it is possible that the enactment of the Race Relations Act (1976) with its powers of subpoena might have led the RRB to postpone its proposal. In 1977 the newly established Commission for Racial Equality (CRE) approached Hackney to undertake a similar investigation as to that proposed by the former RRB. Perhaps recognising the legal difficulty in sustaining further opposition to the CRE's demand, Hackney changed its previous strategy. In response to the CRE request the Council now proposed self-regulation in the form of an internal unit that would liaise with the CRE. The unit, it was suggested, would consist of two officers who would monitor all aspects of the housing service to ensure that it provided fair and equal treatment to the ethnic minorities. The unit would report regularly to the Council and the CRE and the latter was free to monitor its progress and raise matters of concern with the Council. Such a structure, Hackney insisted, would meet the Council's guidelines regarding tenant confidentiality, overcome staff suspicion, and ensure the latter's co-operation and positive motivation in the project as it progressed. Turning misfortune into triumph Hackney now boldly proclaimed that such a scheme would act as a pilot for other authorities with similar problems (Hackney, 1983).

But the CRE was not convinced by this new found radicalism. Despite last minute delaying tactics by the authority the Commission decided upon a formal investigation in May 1978. We shall return to this investigation and its consequences later.

In Haringey similar factors seemed to have influenced the initial stages of policy change, though the initial impetus seems to have been pressure from officials. In October 1976 the Borough Housing Officer wrote a detailed report on the increasing concentration of black and ethnic minorities in unpopular estates such as Broadwater Farm. His suggestion for arresting this development, which was held to be the result of a high allocation to homeless and single parent families to such estates, was a recommendation for a greater social mix (Gifford, 1986). Though it is likely that this concern stemmed as much from popular paranoia at the time about black ghettos as professional concern about racial discrimination, the issue soon became established and could not be ignored.

Policy agendas and alternatives

After the initial stage of response Hackney continued its stance of opposition to the CRE investigation but now combined it with apparent concern. On the one hand the Council resisted CRE calls for access to tenants' files; on the other it projected an image of concern by creating its own Housing and Race Relations Monitoring Review Unit (HRRMU) and adopting a formal equal opportunities policy. The HRRMU was established in 1978 and headed by a researcher previously employed by the CRE itself.

That Hackney foresaw no evaluative or monitoring role for the HRRMU seems to be borne out by its relative inactivity during the first five years of its existence. Moreover, the intellectually combative Director of Housing lent weight to the authority's unofficial policy of race blindness by drawing on the idea of bargaining power. Some black and ethnic minorities, he argued, were in poor quality accommodation not because of racial discrimination, but because bargaining power between those already in public sector housing and those seeking access was unevenly distributed. Since new and recent tenants tended to be allocated low quality accommodation, it followed that the black and ethnic minorities who were heavily represented among them would get a disproportionate share of this stock. There was nothing racial about quality differentials, the Director insisted: they would be overcome in time as black and ethnic minorities moved up the quality ladder and their bargaining power increased *vis-à-vis* the excluded and new entrants (CRE, 1984).

While the Housing Department continued its opposition to the CRE investigation – permission for access to tenants' files was eventually conceded in September 1979 under the threat of subpoena from the Secretary of State for the Environment – the Council leadership seemed more interested in criticising voluntary groups campaigning for a more explicit race equality policy by the authority. The occasion was a review of the Hackney Council for Racial Equality (HCRE) and the undeclared objective seems to have been to undermine the various groups operating under the umbrella of HCRE (*Interview*, 1988).

Unfortunately for the Council leadership HCRE co-operation in the review was only secured after the review team broadened its terms of reference to include the authority's own race relations policies in the context of local and national developments (Hackney, 1981). Though this concession led to detailed consideration of parallel developments in other London boroughs – and a recommendation for the creation of a Race Relations Sub-Committee – the review team dismissed the HCRE's demands on housing (such as ethnic monitoring of allocations and an effective racial harassment policy). Indeed, it spoke warmly of the HRRMU, as 'an excellent example of a unit working exclusively on race issues' (Hackney, 1981).

An indication of the standpoint of the Hackney leadership at the time can be found in an interview given by Sam Springer, a leading black councillor. The interview is worth quoting at length because its illustrative of the contemporary political climate. 'The mere fact the CRE has decided to investigate', commented Springer, 'does not mean Hackney is guilty'. He continued:

Hackney has a progressive and fair policy for allocating council homes. We have a firm commitment to equal opportunities and good race relations. If the CRE wish to investigate we have nothing to hide . . . So far they have come up with nothing. Quite frankly we are getting a little fed up. The CRE has a right to investigate but we are entitled to ask whether it is misusing its powers by a prolonged investigation with apparently no end in sight. One wonders whether those directing such investigations are simply going on a fishing expedition without knowing what they are looking for (*Caribbean Times*, 11 June, 1982).

Yet despite such protestations from within the council within a year the outcome of the CRE's formal investigation forced the council to reverse this stance.

Haringey's response to issue identification was only sightly less contradictory. Following the 1978 elections, which led to the success of Bernie Grant and a small group of left-wing councillors, the authority responded to increasing demands for more action on race equality issues by appointing a Principal Race Equality Officer

(1979) and creating an Ethnic Minorities Joint Consultative
Committee (EMJCC) (1979). This was a consultative forum for
the black and ethnic minorities in the borough. Initially the EMJCC
was successful in raising policy and service issues such as housing
but it seems to have soon become embroiled in conflicts between the
various community representatives. In the context of these
developments steps were taken to promote racial equality in
housing, though at the time little seems to have been done to
make them effective. Thus ethnic minority housing needs were
recognised but only two officers were appointed to process them.
Although ethnic monitoring of housing applicants was introduced,
it was voluntary and was of little value in monitoring changes
(*Interview*, 1988).

As in Hackney the role of officers in Haringey in the promotion
of policy change was limited. Although they seemed to accept the
inevitability of change they were unwilling to lead or encourage it.
As a former critic has noted, at the time the leadership 'was saying
things that sounded okay, but what was said was like jelly: you
couldn't get hold of it. To put it bluntly, they were smart bastards
who were always so charming and liberal' (*Interview*, 1988).

Policy evaluation and critique

The final stage of policy formation which has culminated in the
present policies resulted from critiques of existing policies, the
linking of these critiques with wider notions of race equality, and
iterative modifications arising from implementation.

By formally committing themselves to race equality soon after
the Race Relations Act and taking limited measures to effect it,
both Hackney and Haringey created a policy gap. The discrepancy
between formal commitments and reality, between radical rhetoric
and the space between the words, was seized upon by those Ken
Young defines as policy entrepreneurs and by political activists of
the urban left, and voluntary groups with an interest in housing in
their attempts to define and redefine policies. The development of a
radical critique of existing policies was further enhanced by the
growth of the unofficial information network – an exchange system
where latest initiatives in housing and among local authorities were

discussed and analysed (*Interview*, 1988). Hence when the results of the Hackney investigation were made public earlier critiques of existing housing department policies had extended beyond the prescriptions the CRE was willing to make.

The CRE non-discrimination notice in Hackney required the authority to fulfil four conditions: to introduce ethnic monitoring for all persons applying for housing and being rehoused (identifiable by quality of accommodation); to re-evaluate its procedures and practices in matching applicants and tenants with relevant housing needs; to undertake race training of staff; and to establish a senior post within the housing department who would monitor the implementation of the non-discrimination notice (CRE, 1984).

That the CRE's recommendations were seen as too little too late was apparent in the way radical critics of existing policies used the investigation as a resource. These critics, some of who had been successful in elections to the two authorities in 1982 as followers of the urban left, had always seen housing as an integral part of a holistic conception of race equality. In constructing the two authorities' response to the new requirements, they were successful in establishing the linkage between the service deprivation encountered by black and ethnic minorities and their under-representation within the authorities staff. The central race relations units in Hackney and Haringey, therefore, became the principal agencies for overseeing black and ethnic minority recruitment into housing departments. Occasionally, as for example in the employment of specialist fieldworkers, the imperative of generic recruitment merged with the requirement to cater for the specialist needs of black and ethnic minorities.

Lastly, what distinguished this stage in policy formation from previous ones was that it set in motion a dynamic process of review and reformulation. The increase in the recruitment of black and ethnic minority staff within the Housing Departments, for example, created a constituency of interest – *à la* Black Workers' Housing Groups – that began to question the exclusion or non-representation of black and ethnic minority people in some grades. Similarly, ethnic monitoring of allocations produced some controversial findings that only could be analysed by further detailed research. In short, potentially the limits of policy could be continuously called into question.

Implementation strategies

A number of factors need to be taken into account in looking at the implementation of the policy changes that authorities such as Hackney and Haringey have introduced in relation to housing. As noted above, the recent origin of race equality policies in housing has meant that they have had a limited life span. Further, the complex process of formulation, with its critiques of previous policies, was likely to generate its own complexities in the new cycle of implementation. These difficulties have also been compounded by the simultaneous crisis of local government that has powerfully affected the working of left-leaning authorities such as Haringey and Hackney. Consequently, a detailed assessment of implementation is beyond the scope of this chapter. What follows is a brief summary of the three dimensions identified at the beginning and some reflection on the factors and processes that may have impeded the fulfilment of radical policy objectives.

The official position regarding allocative equality within the Departments of Housing in Hackney and Haringey today is that though they have not achieved perfect equality they are more likely to attain this goal than with previous policies. Both departments have introduced ethnic monitoring and methods of reviewing the results. Both have developed property indexes to identify qualitative differences in allocations. And both have undertaken reviews of allocations procedures. Officer discretion, the main factor in producing discriminatory outcomes has, it is argued, been restricted and minimised. In Hackney even the principle of targeting was applied to allocations for a while to increase quality and quantity of property allocated to black and ethnic minorities. Furthermore, the general change in allocation practices from date-order (waiting list) and bargaining power (transfer and homeless) queues to those based on need has enhanced the race equality strategy in so far as black and ethnic minorities tended disproportionately to be represented in the latter queues.

Yet this official position exists uncomfortably with a reluctant acceptance that racial discrepancies and disparities remain in the allocation process – despite the elusive pursuit of perfect equality (*Interview*, 1988). For example, a recent monitoring report in Hackney produced, incidently, on the termination of the CRE non-discrimination notice, found significant variations in the offers and acceptance of property between white and black groups to the latter's disadvantage. Not unexpectedly it provoked a lively debate among black and ethnic minority councillors, some of whom questioned the integrity and commitment of officers and the Labour Group to race equality (Hackney, London Borough of, 1988a and b).

More importantly it is possible that monitoring evidence for increasing equality on which the official positions are based is related to the homeless initiatives rather than the race equality policies. Since about 1986 almost all the new tenancies in Hackney and Haringey have gone to those in the homeless queue in an effort to reduce the bed-and-breakfast charges in the face of financial crisis. Because black and ethnic minorities have traditionally been more concentrated in this access channel, it is likely that their inclusion has increased the overall representation of the minorities. Certainly the Chair of Housing Committee in Hackney has drawn this conclusion. 'As a direct result', he has observed of the homeless initiative, 'and for the first time in Hackney, black people are getting a fair share of housing' (*Hackney Herald*, May and June, 1988).

If implementation of allocative equality has been a mixed success the emphasis on increasing black and ethnic minority staff within the departments of housing presents a different picture. Housing, in line with other service departments, has attempted to achieve proportionality targets of black and ethnic minority employees that are in keeping with their local population figures. The main direction of this element of race equality policy has been undertaken by the central race relations units, for whom the ability to influence recruitment has been an important source of power.

One source of concern is that the overall distribution of black and ethnic minority staff within the two housing departments is unevenly spread among middle and lower officer grades. Relatively few black and ethnic minority staff in both authorities are represented at either senior officer level or among manual workers. Of course these deficiencies may be due to historical inequalities in the labour market or low staff turnover (Young, 1987). However, there is increasing evidence that black and ethnic minority employees are resorting to authority-switching at the lack of upward mobility within the two housing departments.

Finally, promotional initiatives have occupied an important position in the race equality strategies of Hackney and Haringey.

Sometimes they have been the logical extension of attempts to change awareness of the needs of racial minorities. Sometimes, as in the case of the CRE requirement to train housing staff, necessary legal impositions. Nevertheless all promotional initiatives have had one thing in common: they are essentially educative and aimed at changing behaviour through influencing attitudes rather than the use of sanctions.

Hackney and Haringey, along with other radical authorities, have made a regular use of promotional initiatives. These have included conferences, seminars, race training for staff, audio-visual publicity, and the translation of housing policy material into ethnic languages. Specialist agencies working in housing, such as the Association of Metropolitan Authorities, the CRE, the London Housing Unit, and the London Race and Housing Research Unit, have provided valuable contributions to developing this area of policy.

However, like allocative equality and employment development, promotional initiatives have endured mixed fortunes. Occasionally they have given the appearance of being substitutes for policy. Often when they have threatened to incur substantial cost or change in overall policy, as in the case of racial harassment, they have been quietly de-emphasised. In the mid-1980s both boroughs gave racial harassment a high profile, and promised to punish perpetrators of harassment. More recently, however, this policy has mellowed. Indeed, it has been argued that racial harassment is no longer perceived as a major problem in need of urgent attention, but instead has become another onerous obligation of complex management (*Interview*, 1988).

Indecision and prevarication on the course of policy change have become more apparent in the last few years. Perhaps the most interesting is the training programme required by the CRE non-discrimination notice in Hackney. There seems doubt about the effectiveness of this programme. Not only did it take two years to design but many senior officers were reluctant to participate. To date the manual workers, who comprise an important element within the housing staff, have remained an excluded category in terms of training.

Limits to change

Yet what also seems clear is that we need to go beyond pointing out the gap between policy and practice, and explain why policy change has proved to be so difficult to implement. Are there any common variables that may have influenced the dissonance between radical formulation and radical implementation? In this context there seem to have been four main processes which have shaped policy change and conflict in the field of housing.

First, it seems necessary to evaluate the relevance of political commitment. This may appear paradoxical given the fact that much policy change in this field is associated with the urban left. However, the urban left is not a monolithic bloc. In both Hackney and Haringey after 1982 political power was located in various combinations of left-wing Labour Groups. Not all elements within these groups either accepted or were prepared to privilege the eradication of race inequality above class inequality. Housing was not immune to these tendencies. After 1982, which is usually seen as a watershed in the success of the urban left, the Chair of Housing in both authorities was occupied by councillors who were not totally convinced by the need to prioritise race equality strategies.

Second, and equally significant – if not more interesting – is the need to evaluate the contribution of black and ethnic minority politicians and activists involved in housing. If it is accepted that their mobilisation was central to the development of a radical critique, it is necessary to understand why this mobilisation has not been sustained during the period of political power. There seems to be common agreement that one reason for the recent quiescence in the promotion of racial equality is the fact that former activists have now become less radical in their demands or have lost confidence in the possibility of achieving change (*Interview*, 1988).

The change may partially be explained by the regularisation of conflict within the system and institutions of local government. Whatever the cause, it is evident that existing institutions and procedures for effective monitoring of all race equality strategies are not being adequately utilised. The Housing and Race Relations Sub-Committee (HRRSC) in Hackney provides a relevant illustration. Created to review and monitor race equality policies in the Department of Housing in Hackney, it generated considerable interest among voluntary groups and experienced high participation from among black and ethnic minority councillors. Today the HRRSC is still in operation, but apart from providing an occasional platform for the Housing Black Workers' Group, it does not seem to play an important role.

Third, there is a clear need to demarcate and specify the measure of organisational resistance that has impeded policy implementation. We need to identify the objectives and the resources underpinning it. Organisational inertia, a reluctance to accept radical change, may be an important consideration. Similarly the sublimation of racial opposition in the guise of technical competence requires to be identified. Certainly the systemic nature of race equality policies instituted new technocratic controls within the departments of housing and these may have provided a useful resource for recalcitrant and obstructionist officers. The development of ethnic monitoring, for example, and the parallel computerisation of housing departments, has concentrated considerable knowledge power in the hands of few senior officers (Mullins, 1986). Not unexpectedly one of the arguments put in defence of the HRRSC was the vast amount of complex, elaborate and technical data that its lay membership (councillors) were expected to comprehend.

Fourth, resource constraint seems to be a relevant indicator for further examination. Most new policy initiatives are contingent on adequate funding for their success; race equality strategies are no exception. As these strategies were not primarily distributive but growth-linked, they have suffered disproportionately from central government limitations on local government expenditure and investment, particularly in public sector housing. For example, the decrease in the rate of addition to existing public sector stock (coupled with rising demand) has necessitated a switch to needs-based policies which, though they have been in favour of black and ethnic minorities, are too insignificant to radically alter the historical disadvantage suffered by these communities.

Recent housing legislation and equal opportunity

Finally, an important issue that needs to be taken into account in assessing future prospects in this area is the impact of the 1988 Housing Act, the 1989 Local Government and Housing Act, and other related local government legislation over the past few years, on the ability of local authorities to remain a key actor in the promotion of racial equality in public sector housing.

The housing legislation of the past few years has not been directly influenced by issues related to race. The most important objectives of housing legislation during the 1980s have been (a) the reduction of the role of local authorities as landlords, and (b) encouragement for greater home ownership (Spencer, 1989). These objectives have formed a core theme in the attempts by the Thatcher Governments during the 1980s to change the shape of local authority housing. But whatever the origins of the legislation it is still important to ask about the extent to which it will have an impact on issues related to racial inequality.

The 1988 Housing Act and the 1989 Local Government and Housing Act are the most comprehensive attempt to implement the objectives of the Thatcher administrations in relation to housing. They are only now beginning to have any significant impact and their full implementation will be a feature of Government policy during the early 1990s. But there have already been complaints that if there is a significant reduction in the role of local authorities in the provision of public housing some of the worst hit will be those black and ethnic minority households in greatest housing need (Mullins, 1989).

A number of black and ethnic minority groups involved in the housing field have already begun to mobilise on this issue and to argue that whatever the future of local authority public housing there is a need to take the issue of equal opportunity fully into account, and to develop race equality strategies that will help to meet the new challenges to be faced in the 1990s. Particular areas of concern are the issues of homelessness and racial harassment. These are already areas of concern among many community groups involved in the housing field, and there are fears that the recent legislation will actually make the situation worse.

Under the provisions of the 1988 Housing Act and the 1989 Local Government and Housing Act the Government envisages that local authorities will no longer be major landlords, and will take on the role of being enablers, facilitating the efforts of other agencies to deal with housing problems. The future of equal opportunity initiatives under this system remains unclear, and the Government has done little to clarify the situation or to assuage the fears of black and ethnic minority groups. Whatever happens, however, it seems clear that the role of public housing will be subject to major changes during the 1990s, and that successful race equality initiatives will have to take account of these changes if they are to be successful.

Conclusion

The story of race equality strategies in housing offers some sobering reflections for policy development in this area. The process by which these strategies were formulated into policy entailed a long conflictual discourse and raised hopes of radical changes in practice. Their implementation, however, has failed to realise the original stated objectives. True some processes such as the pursuit of allocative equality and the recruitment of black and ethnic minority staff have been set in motion, but their general contribution to race equality has been limited and they have yet to address historical disadvantage or the housing needs of these groups.

The 'implementation gap' is a common feature of public policy at both central and local government levels. But the failure of the urban left to implement racial equality policies in practice raises important issues for the future efficacy of race equality policies and practices. Central to identifying the cause of the failure to bring about radical change is a fuller understanding of the relevance and the interdependence of political commitment, persistence of organisational opposition, and imposed resource constraint. It is only through such an analysis that we can approach the question of how effective strategies of racial equality in housing can be developed in the 1990s.

Notes and references

1. The chapter derives from research on Race Equality Policies and Public Sector Housing funded by the London Race and Housing Research Unit during 1987–89. Where reference is made to interviews carried out in the course of the research the references are included in the text, and interviews are not listed individually in the bibliography.

7 Reifying Crime, Legitimising Racism: Policing, Local Authorities and Left Realism

Michael Keith and Karim Murji

Introduction

The influence of the politics of 'race' on local authorities has, in London at least, gone hand in hand with the politics of policing. This was particularly evident in the early 1980s, closely following the disturbances of 1981, when a number of Labour local authorities initiated policies both on race equality and police accountability. 'Race' and policing at that time served to both unite and later divide the London local authorities, as evidenced in the political debates about the actions of the Greater London Council in this field, which attracted the attention of a hostile media and critical Conservative politicians (Lansley, *et al.* 1989: pp. 52–3).

This chapter looks at the issue of the local politics of policing and race from a number of angles. First, through a critical review of the key debates about what is perhaps the most important theoretical influence in this field, namely the ideas of what is often called 'left realist criminology' and its role in influencing policy change in this field. We begin by pointing to the centrality of 'crime' as the explanatory variable in left realist theory and argue that in the context of race this leads into a reliance on 'culture' in explaining the conflicts between the police and black people. We then explore the impact of this framework on policy developments in Islington and other left Labour authorities. This part of the chapter also attempts to develop a critique of these policies and of their impact on black people. Finally, the chapter looks at the inter-relationship between local political developments in this field and national politics, particularly in relation to the Labour Party.

'Black youth' and crime

The works of John Lea, Jock Young and others associated with them are perhaps the best known examples of what is commonly called 'left realist criminology' (Lea and Young, 1982a and 1984; Kinsey, Lea and Young, 1986). Their ideas have played a major role in both academic and in local and national political debates about race and policing during the period since the uprisings of 1981.

The arguments developed by Lea and Young have stirred up a welter of criticism and debate from a number of angles, but much of the attention has focused on their analysis of 'race and crime' (Gilroy, 1982a and b; Gilroy and Bridges, 1982; Bridges, 1983; Gutzmore, 1983; Ryan and Ward, 1987; Sim *et al.* 1987). We do not propose to repeat the details of this complex debate here. Rather we seek to highlight some major aspects of the debate of relevance to the focus of this chapter.

Perhaps the most controversial aspect of the writings of Lea and Young has been their suggested explanation of the causes of the urban disturbances in 1981 (Lea and Young, 1982a and 1984; Kinsey, Lea and Young, 1986). The model they propose takes as a central premise the idea that crime is a function of deprivation. While accepting that racism in society leads to a disproportionate element of racial deprivation Lea and Young argue that it is only to be expected that young black people are involved in disproportionate levels of street 'crime'. The failure of the police to combat rising crime levels everywhere prompts a drift towards military policing and a collapse of consensus policing. The strained relations between police and the community deteriorate, thus resulting in cumulatively reduced flows of information to the police and a mobilisation of bystanders against them.

This 'vicious circle', the left realists argue, is seen at its worst within the black communities who are at the sharp end of the 'inner city' economic collapse and who find their own young children stereotyped as universally criminal suspects as a result of the failure of uninformed police to grasp a true picture of the nature of crime. This imagery of black involvement in crime is for left realist criminology an exaggeration of a reality where:

> To take the example of black youth in British Inner Cities – all the evidence points to widespread police illegalities directed towards them. Economic injustice is exacerbated by police injustice and, in these instances, the delicate link between poverty and respect for the law is all too easily broken (Young, 1987: p. 343).

Thus this mode of analysis begins by taking 'black criminality' as given and then apologises for it on the grounds of racial deprivation.

There are two levels on which the debate about this line of argument takes place, one significantly more important than the other; left realism assessed as academic theory on the one hand and the ramifications of such 'theory' for the cultural representation of social practice on the other. Although the terms of the debate as construed by left realism have been shown to be incoherent and illegitimate (Gilroy, 1987), it is worth noting that the core assumption which ties police/black antagonism to the problem of 'crime' within their model is also no more than a logical tautology rather than empirically supportable fact. Left realism provides a field of discussion in which many different diagnoses can co-exist, united by a sympathetic apologia for black criminality. For the left realists black criminality is 'understandable'. Disproportionate involvement in crime is placed either at the source of, or else a major contributory factor in, generating police/black antagonism (Lea and Young, 1982a and b; Kinsey *et al.* 1986).

This type of view is not confined to any one paradigm. Characteristically Holdaway, a writer not associated with left realism, is able to write that by the late 1970s:

> The new emphasis, however, lay in the recognition by the police of high crime rates within areas with a large population of black British people, particularly those of Afro-Caribbean descent (Holdaway, 1987: p. 144)

Yet, there is simply no way that such a portrayal is verifiable (Solomos, 1988; Keith, forthcoming). The empiricist premise cannot be supported by evidence. To take just one of the more obvious flaws, the left realists regularly emphasise the role of the community in the detection and solution of crime. Most crimes are solved by the public reporting evidence or culprits to the police. In the crude theoretical terms with which left realism operates successful clear-up rates are a function of good 'police/ community' relations. Moreover, the left realists would acknowledge that whilst relationships between police and white working class communities may frequently be strained they would presumably not deny that there has historically been a qualitative difference between such strains and the nature of relations with British black communities. Given these two premises it is possible to posit the following positivistic hypothesis which there are strong *a priori* grounds to support. If it were possible to take two identical communities, one all white, one all black, with identical numbers of individuals carrying out 'street crime' it is more than probable that the 'crime rate' realistically defined will be higher in the latter than in the former. For if consensus policing has broken down further and more irrevocably within the black community few if any people are going to trust the policing institution enough to report crime, let alone to pass on their suspicions about perpetrators. It would simply be more difficult to solve those crimes that do occur in black communities because there can be no effective policing. The grounds for suggesting that perceptions of black involvement in street crime are exaggerations of the truth disappear.

Such apparently logically coherent generalisations can only be regarded as vague and dangerous. The point is that for left realist criminology disproportionate black involvement in street crime is the logical outcome of racial disadvantage. Yet within their own terms of debate their own premises can be used to highlight something completely different; that the black people committing street crime are simply more successful than their white peers.

More significantly, it is the terms of the debate itself that are illegitimate because they set clashes between police and the British black community exclusively in the context of real and (mis)perceived black crime rates. This is demonstrably untrue. One of the most striking features about the work of Lea, in particular, is the complete absence of any sense of history, a feeling that these 'relations' (crime after all is a social relation as the realists frequently maintain) occur in some neat social laboratory.

The flaws are essentially twofold. One is that the conflict between the police and black communities in Britain possesses a historical and geographical depth which is misrepresented by a focus on problems of crime. The second is the frequent assertion that this conflict involves only 'the youth'. This too is at best an extremely misleading portrayal of historical reality. Yet because of the attempt to suppress the past in the creation of criminological generalisations these two flaws remain irreconcilable with left realist explanation. Left realist explanation can only incorporate processes which take place at no place, always in the present (Keith, forthcoming).

A case in point can be taken from Lea's (1986) attempt to analyse the particular nature of police racism. Lea identifies a particular process, the manner in which societally derived racist notions of black criminality occupy a role in the institutional and cultural fabric of the police force to exaggerate minority crime rates. Lea highlights the significance of institutional practices rather than personal proclivities in identifying the particular construction of 'police racism'. The ensuing suspicion and attention paid to young black people is central to the reproduction of police/black antagonism.

But again by situating police/black conflict in terms of 'crime', left realist criminology suppresses history, amplifies the process of criminalisation and provides those who might need it with an explanation of confrontation which confirms the crisis of undisciplined British youth (Solomos, 1988). As always, at best left realism is partial. Only part of the story is told and then the part deceitfully masquerades as the whole.

Left realism and cultural pathology

If the antagonism between the police and black communities is, for the left realists, to be understood and explained through crime, the medium through which crime is to be understood is culture. Culture performs a crucial role in the organisation of left realist criminological explanation. It is the medium through which social injustice is transformed into delinquent behaviour. It is the means by which:

> The social psychology of urban decline and neglect is such that once set in motion there is a likelihood that a declining spiral of urban degeneration will continue (Matthews, 1987: p. 373)

'Crime' is seen as a cultural proclivity, a product of brutalisation by the vagaries of the economy (Lea and Young, 1984; Matthews, 1987). 'Culture' as an explanatory concept lies at the heart of left realist criminology yet there is little or no attempt to come to terms with its complexity, beyond attributing it as a personality characteristic to loosely defined groups of people. Their return to the search for the causes of crime revolves centrally around the production of cultural types based on generalities:

> Such a discussion is important because it is vital to ground generalisations in particular cultures and subcultures . . . It is a central task of the criminologist to construct generalisations between crime and wider material factors but these must be grounded in particular cultures and social groups (Young, 1987: p. 353).

What this amounts to in practice is a call for a return of the notion of *the criminal classes*, suitably refined by empirical investigation but explicitly theorised in terms of material conditions engendering collectivities endowed with particular cultural dispensations towards crime. There are several consequences which arise from the flawed use of generalisations. One is the sociological question about the nature of theory based on generalisation rather than abstraction. In the construction of generalisations it is not always easy to identify which academic projects follow on from such a focus (Matthews and Young, 1986) beyond the creation of diagnostic typologies.

A second consequence that logically follows from the first is that the generalisations that form the foundations of theory necessarily promote the use of vague descriptive categories as central constitutive elements of any explanation. The repeated confusion of typologies with theoretical foundations has more serious implications than straightforward error. At its best this sort of analysis produces trite truisms, at its worst it mass produces invidious stereotypes.

There are important questions to be asked about the utility and the use of such generalisations. It is not that generalisations are necessarily invalid. Rather it is of paramount importance to recognise that they are potentially dangerous. In a very specific context, that of the uprisings or riots of 1981, its common use to construct an identikit picture of 'the offender' as a 'black youth' is wholly misleading (Keith, 1987). The questions here revolve around the manner in which those same characteristics which are defined by demographic averages in objective criminological analysis become the salient characteristics in the social construction of perceptual maps of society which define particular groups as criminal.

The crass becomes offensive and dangerous when these stereotypes are used to suggest a marriage of the highly complex and parallel realms of morality and criminality in a manner that even charitably viewed resembles the deconstruction of a grandfather clock with a hammer and chisel. Typical of left realist cultural generalisation is the comment that:

> Occasionally, albeit rarely, the Criminal Justice System may take a lead in overcoming certain backward cultural practices which are regarded as unproblematic by substantial sections of the population. State criminalisation of purdah or cliterectomy in some third world countries would be an example (Lea, 1987: p. 361)

Leaving aside problems of moral relativism, such overgeneralisation is indicative of the truly impoverished analytical depth of this theory, whilst the suggestion that it is the Criminal Justice System that should perform the principal role of such moral arbitration is crudely and simplistically authoritarian. Perhaps most revealing of all though is that the two examples of contentious morality chosen summon up the foreign and the exotic. This can hardly be attributed to a lack of 'indigenous' backward cultural practices: would not examples of hare coursing, pit bull-terrier fighting or violence against women have served so well? Or are these not so much 'backward cultural practices' as part of an 'English cultural heritage'?

Perhaps the answer lies in an underlying feeling that 'multiculturalism' threatens some perverse notion of monolithic moral certainty that should be embodied in law through a process that Lea (1987) classifies as the criminalisation of 'problematic situations'.

Or can it just be a coincidence that in the examples he chooses there is a homologous relationship between one 'African cultural practice', one frequently associated with the Indian sub-continent and the historical roots of the two largest groups of the British black community? The fact that diverse cultural formations pose problems for the encoding of national moral protocols should not be avoided but as the alternatives suggest, such problems take on a nasty undertone of racism when the complex and contingent notion of culture is captured in the sort of crude stereotype so readily deployed in left realist criminology.

It is the very nature of over-generalisation *per se*, whether maliciously intended or not, that lends credence to the discredited notion of a single homogeneous British culture struggling to come to terms with an alien penetration of 'new' (im)moral practices.

It is very important to draw out this link as necessary rather than random and unfortunately incidental. Any theory that takes as central explanatory concepts terms that are not even slightly logically consistent and tries to produce generalised behavioural regularities will inevitably produce analysis that is stereotypical in implementation. The point here is not simply to what extent criminological pathologies that are verifiable at loosely defined low levels of statistical significance can amplify the reproduction of folk devils in a particular moral panic. As Hall *et al.* (1978) demonstrated, this form of moral panic did create a racist stereotype of the black mugger 'folk devil', and the left realists are quite prepared to acknowledge and reinforce it.

However, more profoundly, a series of racist practices have amplified this process and served to create a social definition of young black people (particularly young black males) whereby the term 'black youth' serves as a metonym which connotes lawlessness, disorder, 'alienation' and criminality. Rather than being the contingent product of a particular moral panic 'black youth' is a constructed social identity which results from a whole gamut of mutually reinforcing processes which range from state policy to the educational system (Solomos, 1988).

It is precisely because of its potential role in reinforcing these wider processes, well beyond the narrow realms of academic criminology, that left realism has aroused so much anger amongst those concerned with problems of 'race' and racism. With criminal actions divorced from politics the encounters of the British black community with the criminal justice system must be explained in terms of 'crime'.

The politics of left realism

We have argued so far that the left realist reliance on 'crime' to explain police/black antagonisms leads it into a cultural pathology which effectively ends up reinforcing and legitimating conceptions of 'riotous' and 'criminal' 'black youth'. We now turn to focus on why left realism is politically influential, both locally and nationally, and particularly the significance of its organic relationship with the similarly titled 'new realism' in the Labour Party.

The projects of the realists are political in two distinct senses. One, which is of less significance here is that from the time of the new deviancy conferences in the late 1960s and early 1970s, a group of sociologists have been explicitly concerned with the development of a left alternative to the dominance of crude positivism in criminology and, more recently, of the 'new administrative criminology' exemplified by the Home Office.

The second part of the realists' political project – and the issue we now want to focus on – relates to the institutional links between the group and the Labour Party. Our argument is that the importance of left realism is its relationship to, and legitimation by, the Labour Party.

The establishment of this link occurs through the connection between the left realists and local authorities, in particular through involvement in the controversial crime survey in Islington (Jones *et al.* 1986) and, latterly, the Broadwater Farm Estate survey as part of Lord Gifford's first inquiry (Stubbs, 1987). The surveys were central to establishing the veracity of left realist explanations and subsequently in laying the basis for the programme of the Labour Party in the 1987 General Election.

In understanding this development it is important to look back briefly at the events of the early 1980s to make two historical points. One which we have alluded to above is the importance, especially after the 1981 disturbances, of the politics of 'race' – and in particular the history of policing of black communities – in mobilising a section of the Labour Party into a programme of political activity such as the campaign for police accountability in

London, as well as the development of race equality and equal opportunities policies (Lansley *et al.* 1989).

We are not of course suggesting that these developments occur in a political vacuum. Rather, the response of London local authorities during the early 1980s developed out of and alongside the campaign of a determinedly monetarist government, the splits within the Labour Party, the 'new left' campaign to take control in local government and the Conservative's open play of the 'race card' in the 1979 General Election. This list is only meant to indicate some of the factors which were important at that particular period (Solomos, 1989).

The second historical point is that, in several areas of London, there was already an established basis of conflict between the police and black communities, long preceding the events of 1981. The agenda behind the political initiatives was then already established. The difference in 1981–2 was the explicit espousal of a political programme which sought to address itself to those issues.

The developments in London were led by the Greater London Council. The ruling Labour Group came in with manifesto commitments on 'race' and policing matters and, following the election of Ken Livingstone as leader, followed a series of policies which brought it into direct conflict with central government and eventually led to its abolition (Gilroy, 1987).

In May 1981 the GLC established its own Police Committee, with the central aim of campaigning for a new Police Authority for London, comprised wholly of elected councillors to replace the existing arrangements. In June 1981 the Chair of the Committee, Paul Boateng, wrote to Labour controlled authorities in London urging them to follow the lead set by the GLC and establish their own police committees. The 1982 Borough Council elections brought in a group of councillors who also had manifesto commitments on 'race' and policing. In the following period many Labour local authorities – predominantly the inner-city ones – established their own police committees and small support units. The GLC's Police Committee was largely hegemonic because of its command of an extra level of resource and its city-wide remit.

Despite the influence of the GLC, differences developed between the local councils in their approach to policing. Such differences are partly attributable to specific local historical circumstances (which for example dictated that Lambeth Council did not establish its own police committee until 1984) and partly to the ideological schisms within the Labour Party. There is some doubt about how substantive such differences were in anything other than rhetorical terms.

Despite all the recriminations which were to follow, most Labour local authorities continued to follow largely similar policies. The hegemony of the GLC Police Committee dictated that most local councils initially followed in their wake. It is after all as well to remember that this activity was a new and unfamiliar one to local councils. The GLC's principal concern was with what can loosely be described as police monitoring and the establishment and funding of a network of local police monitoring groups. While local authorities did, for a while, follow this model, it was relatively short lived. Changes in the political climate had begun to lead some councils away from their manifesto because of the reception they encountered. The important factors in the changing political climate included the storm of media activity which greeted the activities of the 'loony left' and 'anti- police' GLC, and the changes in the Labour Party (particularly after the general election debacle in 1983 and the election of the new leadership).

Within policing the important changes emanated form the police themselves, especially some of the initiatives of the Metropolitan Police under Commissioner Newman. In the early 1980s the Metropolitan Police launched initiatives in neighbourhood watch and multi-agency policing. The reaction of the GLC was strongly critical, but since some councils were already more concerned about crime itself rather than the politics of policing, it laid the basis for the rift between those local authorities which continued to follow the GLC line and those who wanted to respond positively to the police. The key differences which developed between councils was around their reaction to neighbourhood watch, crime prevention and multi-agency work and, later, involvement in local consultative groups. The GLC wanted the boroughs to retain a critical, pressure group approach to the police. Others argued that – until there was proper accountability – there was much to be achieved by a critical engagement with the police.

For our purposes we wish to encapsulate the latter tendency within the activities of the London Borough of Islington (LBI). Islington is particularly important because of its connection with the left realists and because within the London 'new left' authorities it charted a course which many were to follow. Its image as a 'market leader' was to be enhanced by a high-profile public stance, although it is arguable that many of the same policies were, in some form, being carried out by local authorities outside London.

In Islington the Council argued that while police-led Neighbourhood Watch was undemocratic and potentially dangerous, the correct response was not to argue against the idea *per se* (as the GLC and others did), but rather to institute a more democratic form of the same activity, based on the local council (which is at least democratically elected, unlike the police) and seeking to involve the police as one of the legitimate participants in the exercise. While the resulting 'LBI Crime Watch' scheme (LBI Police Sub-Committee, 1983) was unsuccessful, the crucial point is the argument advocating the organisation of quasi-policing activities around the leadership of the local authority (LBI Police Sub-Committee, 1984a and b). Contained within that, of course, is the acceptance that local government should actively engage in crime prevention activities – a position cemented by Islington's positive advocation of multi-agency crime prevention work and participation in consultation with the police in the police consultative group (Jones, 1988).

The development of such policies was integrally related to the emerging views of the left realists. Arguing that the fear of crime for working- class, inner city residents was based upon the 'rational kernel of experience' of victimisation consisting largely of intra-class and intra-racial crime (Young, 1987; Sim *et al.* 1987), the realists sought to establish that – in contrast to the Home Office – 'crime really is a problem' and that what is then required is to make the police more efficient at fighting it. For left realism the empirical basis for establishing the veracity of their beliefs about public demand for crime control and the extent of victimisation in the inner-city rests on the 'public audit' of crime, the victimisation survey. It is at this level that the links between Islington and Middlesex Polytechnic are cemented.

The sanctioning of the crime survey by the Council established its movement firmly along the realist road, marking (at that time) its separation from the other councils in London for whom being 'radical' had a rather different meaning. At the beginning of 1983 Middlesex Polytechnic approached three councils in North and East London with a proposal to conduct a criminal victimisation survey.

Although Islington initially accepted, they were forced to reconsider by consulting local community groups, after angry demonstrations had led the neighbouring boroughs of Hackney and Camden to refuse to support the survey. The principal object of the demonstrators anger were the writings of Lea and Young and in particular their theories of the cause of the 1981 disturbances *(Hackney Gazette*, 1983). Islington reconsidered for a period of a few months before sanctioning the crime survey in the autumn of 1983.

The findings of the crime survey and the prospect it held for the Labour Party to be seen as the party most concerned about the impact of crime can be gauged by Gerald Kaufman's – then the shadow Home Secretary – foreword to the published version of the crime survey. Calling it 'essential reading', he signs off with the conclusion that, 'the facts in this book are about Islington. The lessons are for Britain' (Jones *et al.* 1986). The lessons that Kaufman and the Labour Party drew were only too clear in the 1987 General Election campaign.

Crime and the Labour Party

The reforms we suggest are, of course, a matter for a future Labour government determined to tackle the problem of crime and its impact on working-class people (Kinsey *et al.* 1986: p. 212).

The results of the crime survey were used to proclaim the reality of the incidence of crime in the inner-city. Linked to it was to be a programme of crime prevention measures under the aegis of the local authority, but in partnership with the local police. The influence of the Islington approach led some other London councils – most notably Southwark and Newham – along the road to what became known as community safety programmes. Indeed today the extent to which crime prevention forms a standard part of the policing-related activities of local authorities can be regarded, in part, as the triumph of left realism. The other and more important part relates to the changes which were already underway in the profile of the Labour Party.

The proposal to conduct a criminal victimisation survey in 1983 ran alongside an incipient shift in the Labour Party's position on crime and policing. The Conservatives' play on the fear of crime and on 'mugging' had unsettled some of those in the Party who imagined that the bipartisan consensus still existed. In response, academics such as Taylor (1981) and Downes (1983) had begun to address questions about what Labour's response should look like. On the other hand the GLC's promotion of police monitoring represented another strand of the response within the Labour Party. The 'anti-police' storm of media interest which greeted the activities of GLC and the local councils became an increasing embarrassment to some in the leadership of the Labour Party. Even in 1982 Roy Hattersley was determined to distance himself from any 'anti-police' accusations:

> We have made it clear that we want an effective police force. . which is able to produce the more peaceful society that Mrs Thatcher promised at the last election but was unable to provide . . . We will not achieve that end if we allow ourselves to become the anti-police party, better known for our unfair attacks than our constructive criticism (quoted in Sim *et al.* 1987: p. 52).

The new realist Labour Party, following the 1983 leadership contest, was then clear in its intention to outdo the Conservatives as the party most concerned about the impact of crime, particularly on its 'natural' constituency: working class, white voters. The lesson was not to be lost on Hattersley's successor as shadow Home Secretary, Gerald Kaufman, who went to similarly great lengths to ensure that Labour was seen as the party which would support the police in fighting crime and against any unfair attacks. In 1986 Kaufman was speaking of Britain:

> Suffering from the worst crime wave ever known . . . despite all their best and most dedicated efforts the police cannot cope with this crime wave (quoted in Sim *et al.* 1987: p. 55).

Having grasped the bone of crime, Kaufman and the Labour Party were doggedly intent on holding on to it during the 1987 General Election. During that campaign Kaufman frequently placed an emphasis on the 'crime wave' which Labour saw as the legacy of the years of Thatcher rule. The purest expression of this came in April 1987 when speaking at the launch of Labour's document, Protecting Our People at Transport House. Kaufman's speech began:

By the time of the General Election, the 25 millionth victim of the Thatcher years will have been robbed, or mugged or burgled. Every three minutes and 48 seconds, someone is the victim of an act of violence. Every 48 seconds an act of criminal damage is carried out. Every 30 seconds someone is burgled. Every 14 seconds a theft takes place.

This theme is aptly symbolised by Labour's 'crime-o-meter' which displayed the total number of crimes committed under the Thatcher Government and adding to the total every seven seconds during a press conference. A sign of Labour's newly found confidence as the party of law and order is that the leader of the party himself got involved. While talking about the 'astronomical crime figures' on a Thames television programme, 'Reporting London' in May 1987, Neil Kinnock was asked what Labour would do. He replied:

I think we've got some models to build on. For instance in Islington, they've had great success with the partnership system, in the relationship that's been established with the police in providing people with support for making homes more secure and they've resulted in a crime increase, which is always too much, but of 2 per cent over a period of years in which crime has been going up in (the rest of) London by 30 per cent.

The new all-party consensus on law and order whereby they all bid to out-do one another in their concern about crime (Sim *et al.* 1987) was clearly not lost on the then Commissioner of the Metropolitan Police, Sir Kenneth Newman:

If you look at what the Labour Party are actually proposing on law and order – leaving the issue of accountability on one side – then it doesn't sound all that much different to me from what the Conservative Party is doing (quoted in Sim *et al.* 1987: p. 55).

Kinnock's comments and the document Protecting Our People marks the high tide mark of left realist legitimacy. The proposals – including more secure homes, better design of estates and improved street lighting – are precisely the measures which Islington had been arguing for in its crime prevention programme. In short then the policies and theories of left realism have become the political programme of the Labour Party. And in taking on board the explanations of the impact of crime and the need to make the police more effective crime fighters, the Party legitimates the pervasive racism which underlies left realist criminology.

Just as important to Labour's new realism was a conscious distancing between the 'respectable' Labour Party from those London borough councils regarded as the 'loony left' precisely because their concern with issues about the politics of 'race' and policing were seen as vote losers distracting public attention from Labour's 'traditional' political heartland. The manner in which questions of 'race' and racism can be written off the political agenda is clearly linked to the manner in which the politics of policing are identified as merely a 'sectional' issue.

Labour's attempt, *pace* left realism, to recast the issues of policing into the vocabulary of service delivery is a dangerous sleight of hand. The role of the police within the state raises fundamental questions about the enforcement of a particular social order. It will be clear then that we do not agree with the suggestion made by Ryan and Ward (1987) that the threat of left realism has declined in the late 1980s because the (ab)use of law and order politics has peaked. They support this assertion by citing the relatively low profile of these issues in the 1987 General Election. We interpret their point that it was only the Labour opposition who were keen to raise the issue rather differently, as representing Labour's confidence in its policy and as the institutional legitimation of left realism. In this sense, for all its theoretical and practical inadequacies, the left realists triumphed in one of their principal goals. Even though Ryan and Ward (1987) appear to see left realism as diminishing in significance, it is perhaps the costs of this Pyrrhic victory borne in the (non) commitment to racial justice that highlight why a hypocritical left law and order policy continues to be of primary importance in the evolution of British policing.

Realism and pragmatism

Within this changing local and national political environment it is perhaps not surprising that as we enter the 1990s the issue of race and policing has been put on the back burner. As in other areas of the local politics of race we have seen a marked retreat from the approach adopted by the GLC and other radical left authorities during the early 1980s. The views associated with the left realists and Islington council have become more dominant within the context of local Labour Party politics at a time when the left as a whole does not want to be seen as adopting a stance which is overtly critical of the police. At the same time in the period since the 1987 General Election the main premises from which left realist criminology begins have become clearly established. The starting point is the need to develop a marketable 'law and order' policy for the Labour Party, which distances it from the activities of the 'loony left'. This perhaps explains the increasing influence of left realism on the local politics of policing. Left realism provides a description of crime which fits well with current political priorities within the Labour Party.

As we have argued in this chapter, however, perhaps the main objection to left realist criminology and its treatment of 'race' is the confusion and conflation of political expediency with a theory of 'taking crime seriously'. Crime and the rule of law are, quite misleadingly, taken as unproblematic. At a broad level the result is a pathological and ahistorical form of explanation, relying heavily on stereotypical 'cultural generalisations' about black communities. Despite this, the tenets of left realism are affirmed and validated by a Labour Party which accepts the realist agenda about the primacy of 'crime control' and the role of the police.

In this context it is likely that concerns about the role of police racism and the tactics used in the policing of black communities will not have a major impact on the local political agenda. Even previously radical left local authorities are moving towards either adopting the 'left realist' stance associated with Islington or generally giving less priority to race and policing issues. Yet it is also clear that black communities across the country continue to see policing as a key issue of concern. This was shown recently in a study of Liverpool, which recommended among other things that there should be an official inquiry into the policing of the Toxteth area (Gifford *et al.* 1989: pp. 181–2). In this sense at least it is likely that questions about race and policing will remain part of the local political agenda during the 1990s, and therefore an essential element of any strategy which aims to achieve racial equality.

8 Resisting Institutional Change

Herman Ouseley

Introduction

Concern about the condition of the urban black and ethnic minority communities led to the development of race relations and race equality policies by some inner city councils from the late 1970s. These policies were varied, the programmes not always coherent and the actual equality outcomes were good in a few cases and relatively insignificant in many others. At the time of writing, however, genuine race equality programmes remain a high priority only on paper, with the exception of a very few local authorities. Indeed, it could be argued that in the context of the late 1980s racial equality initiatives are being pushed to the back of the local political agenda.

This is not a surprising development. Even during the high point of race equality developments in local government during the early 1980s a variety of experiences emerged which confirmed resistance to race equality initiatives (Ouseley, 1984). Obstacles were placed at many levels within local authorities to prevent effective change. In trying to implement effective race equality policies in local government it was common to hear statements such as: 'We have always done it this way'; 'We treat everyone the same'; 'We do not recognise colour'; 'We don't want to create a backlash or give special favours'.

Yet it should be remembered that during this time new central government legislation has restructured local government services

132

in a number of radical ways (there were over 50 legislative measures concerned with local government from 1974 to 1989). Government legislation has aimed to make local authorities more enabling bodies, rather than direct providers. This has been done partly by putting more services through the compulsory competitive tendering process, by reducing local government influence in the spheres of housing and education, by new financing arrangements (community charge/poll tax), and by giving local authorities a less prominent role in inner city regeneration, especially in areas where urban development corporations have been introduced.

Major changes within local government have therefore been carried out, and these have coincided with attempts to question the effectiveness, relevance and value of local authority race equality programmes (Stoker, 1988). Thus, without appraisal, assessment and critical evaluation, many local authorities have slipped race equality and anti-racism down the order of priorities or, in some cases, completely off the agenda. No new alternative strategies for providing race equality in employment, training, service delivery and access to resources and facilities have been put forward. Instead, local authorities are striving for respectability and credibility in the light of the Government's anti-local authority onslaught. Having anti-racist policies and positive action programmes aimed at redressing racial imbalances is not seen as compatible with the new 'enabling' role of local government in the 1990s.

The aim of this chapter is to address the key question of the possible lessons to be learned from the experience of the 1980s, and to explore ways in which resistances to radical change can be overcome. As the management of local government is redefined, the importance of anti-racist and race equality programmes should remain a high priority for any local authority agenda, but more so for councils in the urban inner city areas where the black and ethnic minority communities are concentrated. And there are examples of local authorities striving to involve and embrace their local black and ethnic minority communities, to devise policies and programmes to meet their particular needs, to support community self-help initiatives and to redress imbalances caused by racism and racial discrimination. There is also a wide range of experience now available to help local authorities to overcome the inherent obstacles within their institutions which prevent race equality from becoming a reality.

Background

Attempts by some local authorities to introduce and implement comprehensive race equality programmes have occurred only since the late 1970s (Ouseley, 1981). Since around 1979 local government has been bombarded by a plethora of new legislation which, if continued on the same scale and intensity over another decade of Thatcher-type government, could lead to the demise of local government. Some leading experts on local government are suggesting that local government in the 1990s could be unrecognisable and relatively insignificant (Stewart and Stoker, 1989). Organisations subscribing to this view include the Institute for Economic Affairs and the Chartered Institute of Public Finance and Accountancy.

Towards the end of the 1970s local authorities found themselves responding in new ways to the black and other ethnic minority communities in their localities, largely as a result of the exhortation contained in Section 71 of the 1976 Race Relations Act. Section 71 requires local authorities to make appropriate arrangements to ensure that their services and functions are carried out with due regard to the need to eliminate unlawful discrimination and to promote equality of opportunity and good relations between the various racial groups. For a limited number of councils more meaningful responses were generated by a combination of some or all of the following factors:

Black community pressure and more effective local organising;
black political consciousness and involvement in local mainstream political activity;
the black vote and the expediency of councils being seen to be responding to Black needs, demands and aspirations;
genuine concern by some local councillors to tackle endemic racism.

The increasing evidence of racial discrimination, both direct and indirect, was also a factor alongside Section 71, as were the urban uprisings of 1981 and 1985. The uprisings concentrated minds and injected a sense of urgency for a while (Benyon and Solomos, 1987).

These factors explain why local government over the 1980s took the lead in responding to black people and their particular needs. Certainly when put alongside the efforts of central government and private enterprise and, to a lesser extent, some parts of the independent voluntary sector, local authorities can be seen as playing a lead role during the 1980s.

Context of success and failure

Given this evidence of pressure for change why is local government commonly seen as having failed to achieve its equality targets? What have the initiatives taken by local authorities actually achieved? These are important questions.

The first point to make is that local government does not exist in a vacuum. The aggregate efforts of local authorities, while showing some undeniable and commendable successes in providing equality outcomes, have failed to make a significant dent in the level of disadvantage experienced by many black and other ethnic minority people. The evidence of continued racism and sustained racial discrimination suggest that the Race Relations Act and a decade of local authority positive action programmes have not significantly reduced the level of race inequality in British society or within local government.

There seem to be essentially five reasons which successive studies have shown to be central to any analysis of the limitations faced by local authorities in implementing racial equality policies:

1. Local government has failed because, for the most part, its efforts have been on a par with those of central government – as indeed the rest of organised society – pathetic. There has also been a distinct lack of any national strategy to tackle race inequality.
2. The Commission for Racial Equality (CRE) remains under-resourced and shackled by the Home Office.
3. The main political parties are powerless in opposition, cowardly when in power and the present Government continues to give succour to those who are most able to mount successful attacks

to prevent anti-racist policies and programmes from taking root.

4. A hostile media, particularly the sordid tabloid press, has launched its own assaults on anti-racism, so much so that the handful of local authorities who have embarked on comprehensive race equality programmes have introduced caution to their initiatives which means little or no prospect of altering the status quo.

5. Finally, and probably the most significant factor, has been the fact that local government has become a moving target with massive upheaval and changes which make restructuring race equality programmes for maximum effectiveness and impact an insignificant issue on the rapidly changing local political landscape.

In spite of these factors, some progress has been made. Whatever the failure in overall terms, the pockets of success cannot be dismissed, even though their significance may seem to be more local and parochial. There are important experiences to be shared from the innovations, experiments and programmes attempted. It is important to learn from previous mistakes and draw on the good practices which emerged from the equality programmes of the 1980s and overcome the obstacles experienced elsewhere.

There are many issues to be considered in such a context but the primary focus of this chapter is on that of how to use institutional change within local authorities to deliver race equality. An urban local authority, with all the trappings of environmental decay, economic decline, high unemployment, high crime rates, demographic upheaval and mobility and social and racial disadvantage, is caught in a pincer movement. It is being buffeted at one end by a community demanding better (sometimes even more) services and, at the other end, it is being squeezed by central government through cash limits, 'rate-capping', new legislation and privatisation. Institutional change in local government is therefore not being driven by one force, rather by several. Even before the enforced restructuring and reform of local government, only a few authorities genuinely attempted to address the issue of endemic institutional racism. Their efforts came largely after the 1981 uprisings and by the second term of Thatcherism were already showing signs of falling down the agenda and in some places are now completely out of sight.

The role model equality authority

The experience of the 1980s has provided an example of the model anti-racist local authority for this period. Anti-racist and race equality programmes emerged during the 1980s in a few local authorities which attempted to exorcise racism, and its concomitant discriminatory effects, from within their structures, their policies, procedures and activities.

By 1984 it was possible to describe the approach of a handful of local authorities as models for change (Ouseley, 1984). These authorities were characterised by the following three features:

(*i*) At a political level they would have clear and unequivocal manifesto commitments. These were translated into policy statements of intention through the decision-making machinery. Council meetings, committees, sub-committees, working parties and other advisory bodies were all given explicit race equality responsibilities.

(*ii*) Every policy activity and proposal had to be scrutinised to examine the race equality implication, to ensure no adverse impact on the black and other ethnic minority communities and to determine the benefits to be derived in equality and race relations terms.

(*iii*) Chief Officers and Heads of Departments were given unequivocal responsibility for drawing out the implications for race equality in their reports to committees and sub-committees which included race equality policy formulation and oversight of implementation within their terms of reference. The whole process in effect would work its way down the management and supervisory line and be reflected in the service delivery and other activities of the authority. In order to facilitate specialist advice, sharpen the focus of institutional change and to review and monitor progress, race committees were set up, race units supported their work, race advisers were either centralised in the units or based in directorates to provide the day to day advice and contribute to strategic policy development.

But this model for tackling institutional racism was based on a premise that local government would remain static as a body. It has not done so. While race equality policies were being implemented, and even after a reasonable period of their existence, the main programmes of service provision (that is housing, education, social services, and town planning, amongest others) were still largely run by the same people as before. Basic organisational structures remained unaltered and, although many procedures and practices changed, improvements and benefits in the form of fair and equal treatment often took a long time, sometimes years, to work their way through the system – a system increasingly under attack for other reasons by central government.

Not surprisingly, black and ethnic minorities became quickly frustrated by the lack of any visible substantial benefits. Because of raised, but reasonable expectations, as a result of the new and relatively radical approaches to tackling institutionalised racism and because of more open and accountable approaches, black and other ethnic minority communities were able to be much more critical of these authorities, even though they were generally among the most progressive. Quite remarkably, those authorities with no progressive policies on race remained relatively unscathed, giving no hint of a willingness to change things nor any encouragement to the victims of discrimination to complain or campaign for change; they were the 'do little, do nothing, no problems here' local authorities.

Alongside the intended institutional changes, and in order to create an appearance of positive action, local authorities had to be seen to be putting their money where their aims and objectives were. One more obvious way of demonstrating a commitment to race equality and to show immediate benefits was to offer grants to black and other ethnic minority groups. This was done in response to demands made by local voluntary organisations and, to some extent, more cynically as a way of buying off black disaffection. Over the last few years the fall-out from the consequences of hasty and ill-considered decisions without a clear strategy is being painfully experienced by both local authority and community groups, particularly also when the new resource constraints are beginning to result in the withdrawal of substantial cash help to such groups.

The Greater London Council

Perhaps the best way of illustrating the resistance to institutional change aimed at bringing about race equality through local government, is to sample a little piece of the experience of the final Greater London Council (GLC) administration from 1981–1986.

Obviously, as a case study, it is not without limitations because the GLC did not have responsibility for any of the main personal services (such as education, social services and most housing services) which impact significantly on people's lives. However, it was a large local authority, with a high public profile, a relatively unambiguous commitment to race equality, huge resources and considerable power. As an authority its pre-1981 existence made no positive impact whatsoever on black people's lives. Although it had major housing responsibilities prior to its transfer to the London Boroughs during the early 1980s, it also had a reputation, along with other local housing authorities, for channelling black households into the most deficient and least desirable public housing accommodation. As a large employer in London it had very few black people on the payroll, the vast majority of whom were in low grade and low status occupations.

The post-1981 race equality programmes were developed from a manifesto commitment to respond to the needs of London's ethnic minority communities (then about 150 different linguistic groupings but 181 by 1987) who were facing unacceptable levels of discrimination and disadvantage. In so doing, the programme's four main aims for the black and ethnic minority communities were to:

Make all services and resources accessible and relevant to their needs;
provide equal and fair share of jobs and training opportunities for them;
create a public image embracing all of London's racial groups;
pioneer and establish new initiatives to challenge racism in London.

An Ethnic Minorities Committee was established and chaired by the Leader of the Council. It was supported by an Ethnic Minorities Unit with race equality advisers shadowing each department and focusing specifically on employment, training, industrial and economic development, housing, planning, community grants and arts and recreation.

Between 1981–86 the GLC transformed London local government in a dramatic and highly publicised way (Ouseley, 1984; Gilroy, 1987). County Hall was continuously vibrant with excitement because of its new-found openness and sudden attractiveness for large numbers of people from the local communities. A previously uninviting building was to be dubbed the 'people's palace' but soon to be loathed by the Prime Minister and leading Conservative MPs across the River Thames. Some leading Labour MPs also resented the activities of the GLC because of its high public profile and its propensity for invoking controversy.

Every new GLC initiative was put under the media microscope to give maximum exposure to its costs, burden on the rate-payers, profligacy on minority causes and controversy because it was regarded as the 'loony left' at work. The race equality policies and programmes being initiated by the GLC were not reported as necessarily being any more controversial than any of the other widely reported programmes, but its media coverage was not only highly sensationalised but inevitably stirred up public hatred against local authorities such as the GLC whenever they attempted to do anything that was remotely designed to provide black people with access to fair treatment and resources by challenging racist policies, traditions and practices.

For example, when the GLC's first ever principal race relations adviser was appointed in 1981, he was described as political friend of 'Red Ken', i.e. Ken Livingstone, whom he had never actually met until three days after starting work at the GLC. He was also widely reported in one national newspaper as having led the youths on the front line of Brixton during the 1981 April uprisings – a myth and a fantasy which he enjoyed even though it had no relationship with reality. Similarly, when the race equality programme was first announced, the Ethnic Minorities Unit was bombarded with abusive telephone calls and vile correspondence, virtually all of which came from outside the Greater London area, demonstrating both the power of the media and the horrors of racism. This pattern was to be repeated when the anti-racist programme was announced in 1983 following the usual media hype and snide comments and by 1984 (the GLC's 'anti-racist year') the media attack was at fever pitch and the readership of the press were increasingly provided with their daily dosage of reported 'left loonyism' in the name of anti-racism.

Within the organisation itself, the established senior GLC bureaucrats were not at first jumping with joy to embrace the new race equality programmes. They had seen all that sort of razzmatazz before! After all, administrations usually come and then go but the officials are still there throughout. Race equality was regarded as 'the flavour of the day', an enthusiasm which would soon wear off. Those officers who were most astute and had a daily interface with elected members, were quick to pledge their support and soon developed a new vocabulary to suggest a commitment to the new policies. So long as those policies did not mean a great deal more than showing a willingness to write and present reports to committees differently (by spelling out the equality implications) and to introduce a black dimension here and an ethnic dimension there, senior officers would be able to live with the new race policies.

Most significantly, the GLC, with its reputation for having huge amounts of resources at its disposal, soon developed a reputation as a 'loads-a-money' council. 'Loads-a-money' attracting loads of attention, loads of people, loads of hangers-on, loads of controversy and loads of diversions. Grant aid to community groups became a major political commitment but was, in practice, a huge diversion. True, it provided much-needed resources direct to local communities in order to cushion them from the harsh effects of Thatcherism and the monetarist crisis. Black and ethnic minority communities entered into the competitive spirit and they were determined to secure their fair share. Not only were black groups competing against white groups and multi-racial groups, there was inter-ethnic competition, simply reinforcing divisiveness. The committees of the council were competing with each other to provide most grants annually and also ensure that they were top of the funding league. The huge workloads and intense pressure on the legal and finance departments led to their staff being defensive as well as resentful towards these burgeoning grant-aid programmes – when it came to black people and women's groups some officers would do as much as possible to stop them getting grants.

Thus, the grant aid programme was a huge diversion in spite of the considerable positive action which community groups generated in support of equal opportunities and increased opposition to racism from black and white people. The specialist race equality advisers were putting so much energy into the detailed administration of the grant aid programme that the rest of the institution remained relatively unscathed and broader consideration of the strategic issues facing black Londoners had to be shelved or re-prioritised. So, although the GLC espoused anti-racism on a grand scale, the main organisational structures and decision makers continued to reflect the status quo. The culture of tokenism had taken over without anyone really realising what was going on, such was the euphoria over the fact that new and radical initiatives were happening thick and fast.

Nevertheless, by 1985 the GLC had more than trebled the number of black staff, many of whom attained middle-ranking positions and raised consciousness about racism. It was as much the consciousness raising success of the anti-racist year in 1984 as the dabbling in international affairs that contributed to the ultimate demise of the GLC in 1986. The Government could not tolerate the scale of public resources going into anti-racism programmes. Nor could it be seen to fail to respond to a situation in which more black people were using the local government power machinery through the GLC, and an increasing number of other local authorities were being encouraged and influenced into trying to emulate the GLC by putting anti-racism on their own agendas. The Government's response was decisive.

The 'bandwagon effect' of equal opportunities policies

The GLC put equal opportunities on its agenda on a grand scale and developed anti-discrimination programmes to protect all groups of people experiencing discrimination of any kind. But what is also clear is that the process of eradicating racism from council structures, policies and procedures was significantly hampered by diversions such as the massive grants programme, on which most time and energy was invested. Media attacks, onslaughts from the Government and officer opposition also proved to be major obstacles to the eradication of racism from the GLC.

This can be illustrated by the negative effects of the 'bandwagon process' which was associated with racial equality policies. Whenever anti-racism is used as a process for change in any institution it becomes a challenge to all other unfair policies, practices and procedures that ultimately leads to a clean up of the whole discriminatory apparatus of the local state or the institution under scrutiny. For instance, this was so when the construction services department of Lambeth Council was forced to open up its craft apprenticeships to local black youth in and around the Brixton area. In so doing, new policies, practices and programmes led to the increased access and recruitment to these opportunities also from local white youth as well as young women for the first time. Thus, anti-racist approaches led to gains in the form of fair treatment for all potential job candidates. A similar effect and outcome was achieved when the GLC opened up the London Fire Brigade and made its jobs accessible to and obtainable by black people, other ethnic minority groups, women and other previously excluded white people.

The GLC first took on the challenge against racism and then realised quickly it had to take on all the other unforeseen challenges in respect of a whole host of other groups of people facing difficulties. The 'bandwagon process' evolved from responses made by institutions when challenged on the issue of racial discrimination and inequality. That response is usually 'Yes, that's okay for black people but what about other disadvantaged groups'.

Take the London borough council of Lambeth as an example. Back in 1979, when Lambeth Council started to pilot and develop race equality programmes in each of its directorates, senior town planners led an unsuccessful fight-back against the acknowledgement of a race equality dimension in planning processes. They claimed that as they did not plan directly for people they could not be accused of discrimination against people. This was probably true if you looked at the environmental decimation and the creation of modern slums in which local people have to live. More significantly, the planners said that if they were forced to consider the implications of their decisions for the local black community, they would also have to consider the needs of old people, young people, the disabled, and different-sized households and a whole range of other relevant human factors. Yes, at last they got the message: that of planning for people and their particular needs. Thus, race was, and still is, a trigger for other initiatives to eliminate inequalities.

The 'bandwagon process' in the GLC quite reasonably attracted all the 'usually excluded' groups of people. These included women, gay men and lesbians, young people, the elderly, people with disabilities, single-parent households, the homeless, the mentally handicapped, etc. If the black groups can get help, so can all the other groups. After all, that is what a real equal opportunity policy is about. Race equality policies and programmes, therefore had to compete along with other anti-discrimination programmes for survival and a share of the decreasing resources, even though evidence showed that the scale of deprivation and disadvantage warranted more extensive race equality programmes.

What the bandwagon effect seems to indicate, however, is that for race equality programmes to be meaningful they require an independent existence within the framework of an equal opportunities policy. It is the only way it can overcome the culture of tokenism. It cannot be effective if it is flattened out into an all-embracing equality programme with everyone in sight jumping onto the bandwagon while institutional racism remains alive under the veneer of the equality furnishings.

Process of managing change

What is also clear is that the process of managing change for race equality requires committed and effective managers who were capable of identifying, challenging and eradicating racism from the institution. Weak management was a contributory factor to non-achievement of race equality objectives in many local authorities. Deficient managers tended to have poor information and communication networks, and weak or non-existent evaluation and monitoring systems. Good management arrangements, where these existed, enabled race equality policies and programmes to be integrated into the day to day management processes and to be part of review and monitoring mechanisms. In such an environment, and in those rare situations where the genuine commitment to anti-racism existed, it proved easier to make progress systematically by placing ownership for equality policy implementation and the achievement of equality targets squarely on the shoulders of top management. Senior managers would be expected to take the lead and ensure that progress was being made at all levels throughout their departments, sections, depots, schools, centres and other places of work. Good communication systems, being synonymous with good management and sound leadership, would serve to ensure that all parts of the organisation were made aware of the new policies, its rationale, the aims and objectives, the basis for implementation, individual and collective responsibilities for implementation and action, changed ways of working and new ways of dealing with local communities, the equality targets and monitoring arrangements, lines of accountability and the consequences for non-compliance with the policy.

Suffice to say not all the local authorities, which were pursuing race equality policies and programmes, had sound or very good management arrangements. Therefore, weak and deficient management was and remains a major barrier to the effective implementation of race equality policies.

Responding to resistance

Reactions to the snail-like pace of change or the non-achievement of equality targets also often contributed to further resistance and recalcitrance on the part of a non-committed bureaucracy.

Because of the failure of local government to deliver changes to its expectant communities, the failure of the bureaucratic machinery to be sufficiently responsive and effective in meeting local needs, and known officer resistance to radical changes reflected in the incoming political party manifestos, an increasing proportion of elected members began to take on more active and full-time roles in their local authorities. Often roles became confused. Managerial and organisational failings led to some chairs of committees virtually taking on roles of managers, wanting to run the departments, negotiating direct with trade unions, trying to give instructions to middle managers and relatively junior officers and unwittingly sometimes even generally contributing to the chaos. Although well-meaning, only in very exceptional cases did these arrangements contribute positively to the race equality policies.

Of course, some members were extremely useful to race advisers in helping to unblock some situations and to take on recalcitrant and obstructive managers. They challenged managers on decisions which produced an adverse impact for black and other ethnic minority communities as well as taking up some individual cases. Such interventions were valuable when handled sensitively and dispassionately; in other cases they led to a diversion from the real priorities of establishing programmes and systems designed to guarantee fair treatment to all. The tendency was, at times, to harangue those transgressors, labelling them as racist and vilifying them as often and publicly as possible.

This rarely induced the required change and often led to an irretrievable hardening of attitudes. Instead of having a clear plan of action to achieve equality goals, setting out the tasks, apportioning the responsibilities and then ensuring that those with responsibilities actually delivered the goals on a systematic basis, members and some officers would engage in conflicts and confrontation which were always energy-sapping, and led to long drawn out disputes and wrangles but rarely, if ever, led to short, sharp action with positive outcomes for the intended beneficiaries of the race equality programmes.

One of the ways of 'dealing' with officer decision makers who were regarded as racist was to send them on racism awareness courses. This was seen as one way of cleaning up the organisation. Racism awareness training (RAT) exploded on the scene during the early 1980s with a growing posse of headhunters in search of public sector employees who needed to have their racism purged so that they could then be freed of this evil and have a clean bill of health for working in 'anti-racist' local authorities.

Yet what did it really achieve other than keeping many consultants in work? According to some recent analyses, it simply made white people feel guilty about racism, focused on individual attitudes and left the institution with all its power structures relatively untouched. In reality, people would come back with their RAT certificates and proclaim themselves as born again non-racist and yet behave in the same old discriminatory way as before, because the system, the procedures and the practices had not radically altered to change behavioural patterns and expectations so as to achieve equality outcomes (Gurnah, 1984; Sivanandan, 1985). In fact, it made them more sophisticated within their organisations for the purpose of boasting of their anti-racist credentials when seeking promotion and being near-impossible to pin down if challenged on racism.

In addition to RAT, the 'bandwagon processes' inextricably associated with equal opportunity policies and programmes meant that many people, including those who were already well-qualified, were going onto equal opportunities courses so that they could comply with the new codes of practice designed to ensure fair treatment. This soon had the effect of not only treating black people and other ethnic minority groups more fairly than ever before when being considered for jobs, promotion, access to services and facilities and other provision such as grant aid but it also made those already in the system even more sophisticated at projecting themselves and covering up deficiencies and prejudices. If you are intent on discriminating you learn not only how not to discriminate but, much more subtly, how not to be found out. You also acquire such skills as how to fill out an application form, how to impress selection panels, how to be better than the 'disadvantaged groups' of people seeking jobs or promotion so that fairness and equality triumphs in the notions of the 'best person for the job' or the 'best presentation in line with the specified criteria'. Thus, those already in the system help to change the system to make it fairer for black and ethnic minority people but at the same time make sure they acquire all the necessary tactics, tricks, subtleties and skills to keep beating the new system.

Limits to change

The present government has continuously introduced radical legislation and, in spite of its oppositional stance to anti-racism, it has also introduced radical anti-discrimination legislation. Alas, such legislation is seriously constrained by the fact that it is limited to Northern Ireland and restricted to religious discrimination. The 1989 Fair Employment (Northern Ireland) Act requires all employers with more than 10 workers regularly to monitor their workforce, submit annual reports to the Government and carry out systematic reviews of their recruitment, training and promotion policies every three years. Any employer who refuses will be committing a criminal offence. The Fair Employment Commission will be given new powers to audit the composition of workforces, issue directives and take recalcitrant employers to a Fair Employment Tribunal, which will have the unique power for a tribunal in the UK of being able to impose fines up to a maximum of £30 000. Employers, who have previously discriminated, will be encouraged to adopt affirmative action programmes. Other employers who refuse to change, will face losing all government subsidies and will be prohibited from tendering for any public authority contract.

Yet this piece of radical legislation in one part of the United Kingdom, compared with a lack of action on racism elsewhere, vividly reveals how racist the Thatcher Government appears to be. At the same time as the Government was legislating about religious discrimination in Northern Ireland, the 1988 Local Government Act launched an assault on the very same principles which some local authorities adopted in applying contract compliance programmes within their trading operations to secure goods and services from private contractors, rewarding those who actively pursue equality programmes. In England and Wales, black people will thus not experience the same sort of anti-discriminatory protection to be rightly afforded to the Catholic community in Northern Ireland.

For black people living in mainland Britain striving for equal treatment there is no statutory obligation on companies to monitor their workforces, no annual returns, no three-year reviews of company employment policies, no heavy fine on guilty companies, no likelihood of the loss of government subsidies and no prospect of companies being proscribed from 'approved lists' of contractors eligible to tender for any public authority contract.

Why has the Government resisted affirmative action programmes and opposed contract compliance in pursuance of race equality whilst promoting 'fair employment' for the religious minority in Northern Ireland? This is a question which remains unanswered, despite repeated criticisms of the Government's actions.

The fair employment programme for Northern Ireland sets out basic principles which could be applied in England, Scotland and Wales for outlawing and eradicating racial discrimination. A major programme of contract compliance led by central government, within an effective anti-discrimination legislative framework (with more enforcement powers and resources for the CRE and Equality Tribunals) and modelled along the lines of the contract compliance programmes developed initially by the GLC, the ILEA and a handful of other local authorities would provide an excellent framework for generating equality of opportunity. Linked to such contract compliance equal opportunity programmes could be a programme of contract procurement, in which black owned and run companies would be given positive encouragement to tender for contracts, particularly at local levels.

Given the push towards making more local authorities services competitive, it would also be important to ensure that voluntary organisations as well as local authority organisations (for example trading operations) operate within the context of anti-discrimination legislation, policies and programmes. Such a framework would enable fair and equal competition among local authorities bidding for contracts alongside private contractors and voluntary organisations (for example housing associations being encouraged to take on more local housing provision).

In the same way that companies would be rewarded (with subsidies and tendering opportunities) for having equality programmes, it would be beneficial to give recognition to individual employees who are able to demonstrate actual achievements in race equality targets and goals. Thus, assessment and appraisal schemes (for recruitment and promotion) should incorporate race equality performance-related goals, targets and bonus. Conversely, individuals who show a lack of commitment in this regard and who continuously fail to demonstrate any progress with the achievement of equality targets should be penalised by non-progression, non-promotion and no bonus-related rewards. There is no reason whatsoever for race equality targets to be excluded from the new performance-related criteria being developed for both the private and public sectors, particularly within local government. Race equality should be an integral part of all performance-related schemes figuring prominently in performance indicators and measures as part of the management tools in local government.

Conclusion

A number of conclusions can be drawn from the arguments developed in this Chapter.

First, race equality in Britain can never be achieved without a radical stance by central government of the day to eliminate racial discrimination. A plethora of evidence shows that racial discrimination remains rampant in virtually all aspects of life in Britain. Employment practices covering recruitment, selection training and promotion in both private and public sectors continue to be widely affected by racism a full two decades after racial discrimination was declared unlawful in the UK.

Second, race equality programmes and strategies for their achievement have to be revised to take account of the shape and role of local government in the 1990s. Its radical transformation during the latter stages of the 1980s, as enforced by a hostile central government, has not accorded any consideration to the race dimension. Central government has reserved more powers to itself without any local accountability, local functions are being passed on to a variety of non-elected bodies, voluntary agencies and private enterprise and local government has become more and more of an Aunt Sally. Already the black communities are having to readjust their sights in focusing on where the power has shifted or is shifting in order to build a new agenda for essential change, and, hopefully, one that can continuously be adjusted and adapted to keep abreast of the Government's own moving targets and markets.

Third, it seems clear that resistance to fundamental institutional change over the past decade to incorporate meaningful race equality programmes through local authority activities has derived from forces within the authorities themselves as well as external pressure.

Most of the external pressure has been through central government attacks on local government, particularly those in the urban areas pursuing or purporting to pursue anti-racist and race equality policies and programmes. Cash limits, rate-capping, power-eroding legislation, asset stripping and privatisation are some of the weapons used by central government to batter those local authorities into demonstrating their new realism – dropping race equality and radical anti-racist policies from the agenda. No longer wishing to be dubbed by the mass media as 'loony left', wanting to avoid blatant media lies about fantasies such as 'Baa Baa Green Sheep' nursery rhymes, and seeking to avoid creating their own martyrs such as Ray Honeyford and Maureen McGoldrick, these authorities have cut the programmes and commitment to race equality, if not the 'equal opportunity employer' slogans appearing on their job vacancy advertisements. Afraid of the gutter press and lacking a vision of how to embrace the 'usually excluded' groups of people from their local communities, it has become easier to embrace the survivalist culture and the 'new realism' with its familiar themes of cost effectiveness, value for money, rationalisation, efficiency, performance related reviews, output measures, cost indicators and decentralisation embodied in the populist enterprise culture being promulgated through Mrs Thatcher. 'Colour blindness' is a feature of this culture and the survivalist thrust extends into the community where everyone is expected to do more for themselves and free themselves from the shackles of the local 'nanny' state. Public service, the underprivileged, disadvantage, poverty and discrimination are shunned terminology, only to be associated with left-wing municipal socialism and lunacy.

Finally, it should be clear that the foundations for a nationally-led race equality strategy have been laid in a variety of piecemeal activities. There is evidence of success to be cultivated, models of good practice to be emulated, examples of difficulties and failure to be avoided and the experience of radical innovation to be built on. What is missing is a committed central government to lead this strategy with willingness and determination. Local government has shown the way. This is most vividly demonstrated by the London borough of Hackney, whose equality targets in employment have borne fruit. With a combination of active race advisers and management responsibility for achieving the targets, the following progress has been recorded:

Table 8.1

Year	Total Employees	Black and ethnic minority staff and percentage	
1980	4198	457	(11.5%)
1981	5705	772	(13.9%)
1982	6400	951	(14.4%)
1983	7303	1313	(17.9%)
1984	7417	1573	(21.0%)
1985	7582	1884	(24.8%)
1986	8034	2200	(27.0%)
1987	8836	2823	(32.0%)
1988	8816	3078	(34.9%)

Source: London Borough of Hackney.

Hackney is thus able to show a 300 per cent increase in eight years since setting its equality policy in 1980 and targets in 1981. It monitors progress on an annual basis, having set a target of 48 per cent to be achieved by the end of 1990. The above data hides the fact that more women than men are in employment and 20 per cent of all senior officers are from the black and ethnic minority communities.

That is undeniable and commendable progress. Unfortunately, there are very few other employers in England which come close to matching such achievements. There is no justifiable reason on the grounds of fairness, equality, justice, efficiency or effectiveness for the failure on the part of other employers to recruit and promote black and ethnic minority people at all levels in their organisations. Local government has demonstrated that a determination to remove obstacles and barriers to institutional change, a commitment to achieve fair treatment and equality outcomes for black and ethnic minority communities and a willingness to retain the principle of public service orientation as one of its highest priorities can lead to real and long-lasting success in the eradication of racism from institutional policies and practices. Alas, only a few local authorities have attempted to go far enough.

III RETHINKING RACIAL EQUALITY

9 Race Policies in Local Government: Boundaries or Thresholds?

Phil Nanton and Marian Fitzgerald

Introduction

> Local government is confronting both a major threat to its traditional role and the challenge and opportunity to redefine its functions. . . The function of local government will shift from a provider of services to that of stimulator, adviser and enabler. The new opportunities for local government are large. . . Local government is on the defensive but in reality significant opportunities have opened up which will relieve it of the burden of day-to-day management of services to focus on broader policies affecting the local community (Noel P. Hepworth, Director, Chartered Institute of Public Finance and Accountancy, August 1988).

High on any list of 'broader policies affecting the local community' must, surely, be policies developed by local authorities in furtherance of their duties under Section 71 of the 1976 Race Relations Act – and, in particular, the responsibility to promote 'good race relations'. Yet, even in the optimistic scenario painted by the CIPFA paper, it is by no means guaranteed that local authorities would give these policies such priority in future as they now have. Moreover, that priority already varies considerably from one authority to another. Some are still fixed in the state of 'colour blindness' where Young and Connelly (1981) found them eight years ago while others have become targets of vilification in the popular press for the high profile they have given to their race equality initiatives.

Within this spectrum, there now lies a wealth of experience of which it is timely to take stock. Local government itself may profitably do so if it is to seize the initiative in its new, strategic role. And the lessons of that experience need constructively to be learned by central government and by the range of quasi-public and private bodies who are beginning to assume many of the former powers and functions of local government.

This chapter provides an overview of that experience, a critical examination of the premises on which it has developed and an analysis of the consequences of these in practice. By way of concrete illustration, it draws on the experience of developing and implementing policies to deal with racial harassment in local authority housing. It concludes by suggesting that a broader, more flexible approach is needed if race equality policies are effectively to address the seemingly intractable problems of racial discrimination, disadvantage and hostility.[1] Such an approach would need to recognise the essentially dynamic character of these problems, to apprehend the localised aspects of their manifestation and to understand and accommodate the ways in which both race-specific and non-race specific factors combine variously to produce them.

As well as other published work, we shall draw on an empirical study of racial harassment in local authority housing undertaken on behalf of the Department of the Environment between late 1986 and early 1988 as the basis of its Good Practice Guide for local authorities (Department of Environment, 1989). The project looked broadly at policy development and implementation in this area and the main reports on which these have been based, as well as examining them more concretely in in-depth studies of a limited number of local authorities taking such initiatives.[2]

The origins of 'race' policies and structures

In his book, *There Ain't no Black in the Union Jack*, Paul Gilroy claims that the primary problem for the analysis of racial antagonism must be the manner in which racial meanings, solidarity and identities provide the basis for action (Gilroy, 1987). The 'racial meanings' which have pervaded the action envisaged by local authority policies have, we would contend, been characterised by a 'reified' concept of 'race'. That is, a nebulous, shifting political idea has been conceptualised in the form of a number of circumscribed, discrete categories. These categories have been variously grouped by nationality, geographic area of origin, religion and ethnicity and have been imbued by local government with a sense of permanence. At least in part, this must be seen as a consequence of the ways in which the policies themselves have developed and of the forms in which they have been implemented.

The years 1976–1980 provide an important watershed in the development of race equality policies in British local government. The principle of local authorities catering separately for the 'special needs' of black people had already been established in 1966 with Section 11 of the Local Government Act;[3] but, with the exception of one or two London authorities who had tentatively begun to take a more self-conscious approach, the development of services catering for a multi-racial public was department based, professional, and 'colour blind'. It was after 1976, for the most part, that a new emphasis was patchily added. This *additional* focus was on the development of a structure for the management of race relations within local authorities.

Assimilationist assumptions after the wave of immigration to Britain in the late 1950s and early 1960s had begun to be replaced by a glimmering recognition of Britain as a plural society during the second half of the 1960s and in the early 1970s. Along with the recognition of pluralism in Britain can be traced, particularly in urban areas of black concentration, the early development of a form of 'expertise' on race issues among a limited range of white, public services professionals. This development was a predominantly individual and informal process, based on experience both in Britain and abroad.

Notions about the type of expertise which was needed were exemplified by the range of travel bursaries made available around this time for teachers and social workers to visit the immigrants countries' of origin to find out 'how they do things'. From such visits, there developed among professionals, concepts of difference which derived from implicitly static notions of culture as a *product* of historically lived experience. These then became a cornerstone of future policy development.

In Britain, as the black population began organising to negotiate with local power structures in the public sector, individual white officers as well as a few councillors associated with service committees took informal responsibility for regular contact and negotiations with local Afro-Caribbean and Asian 'leaders' of voluntary and religious organisations. Pressures from black[4] communities for funds, premises and planning permission for change of use of buildings, led directly to the formalisation of links between council representatives and representatives of these organisations. In these negotiations, a high value was commonly placed on the maintenance of a culturally distinct environment in responding to particularised needs.[5] There were frequent debates between individual groups and local authority departments about the form of the relationship which should exist between them; was the organisation supplementing, opposing or operating a parallel but distinct service to that provided through the department?

Absent from these contacts was any officer or member with specific responsibility for race issues. That is, there was at this stage no person, unit or committee within the department or council claiming special knowledge with the formal, corporate responsibility to supervise council provision, collate or interpret demands and who was formally interposed between the black organisation, the department or the council.

From 1976 onwards, the pace of local authority developments had gathered momentum under the influence of a range of factors. Section 71 of the 1976 Race Relations Act provided an opportune lever (inside the authorities and out) to press for more specific and more formal initiatives. Black people themselves came to assert greater political influence, not least as the parties absorbed the message of a study in 1975 which argued that black voters in certain areas might hold their electoral fortunes in the balance (CRC, 1975). And the anti-racist movement of the late 1970s swept many politicians – particularly among the rising generation – along in its brief but powerful tide. Against this background, increasing numbers of councils came to develop formalised race advice either at departmental or corporate levels and both types of provision have become commonplace in urban areas (especially those with significant black populations).[6]

At the corporate levels, two distinct models began to be developed. In 1979 Lambeth employed a principal race adviser with a unit of advisers reporting to the chief executive of the council. This centralised model can be contrasted with that developed rather earlier in Lewisham. The latter eschewed a corporate formal structure for one focused on community representation in council committees and service department advisers, reflecting the preoccupation of the time with eliminating discrimination in service delivery.[7]

The centralised model gained the ascendancy, bringing with it an increasing shift of emphasis onto employment policies within the authority. In the early 1980s it received a major boost when it was adopted by the trail-blazing Greater London Council and was taken up, in turn, as the blueprint for a new wave of Labour-controlled authorities elected from 1982 onwards. By 1986 some 41 corporate race advisers were employed.

By no means all local authorities were similarly affected, though. Many policy makers and administrators persisted in an almost purblind refusal to recognise the fact of racial discrimination and the disproportionate extent to which black people, as a whole, were affected by particular types of disadvantage. Young and Connelly, in one of the first publications to describe the response of local government, noted that, in the late 1970s, 'colour blindness' was the major obstacle to progress, arguing: 'Apprehension about racial explicitness is the invisible barrier to the development of equal opportunity policies' (1981: p. 65).

Among authorities which had by then abandoned colour blindness, however, they noted a variety of administrative and bureaucratic arrangement. Since then, as increasing numbers have taken initiatives and even as the centralised model has gained the ascendancy, this diversity has persisted. By the late 1980s, the national pattern of race advice could be represented along a continuum from inaction to the development of small departments.[8] While there is an obvious connection between the size of an authority's local black population and the likelihood of its having highly developed race structures, the correlation is by no means exact; nor does it appear immutable for the future. At the time of writing, many Welsh authorities and those in East Anglia had shown no formal bureaucratic response to the requirement to promote race equality. The single officer post remained the norm in five Scottish authorities and among a number of authorities which tended to favour a less specific focus on 'ethnic minorities' or 'equal opportunities'. In the 41 predominantly urban authorities where corporate race structures had developed, some units have begun to negotiate for the control of race adviser posts which had already been established in individual departments, while some started from scratch by setting up new departmental posts with line management responsibility to the unit. But more recently, some units had begun to be closed down or amalgamated: at least one authority which operated a race relations committee had subsumed its activities under the more conventional personnel committee. Further along the spectrum, Hammersmith and Fulham has created a department of ethnic minority interests. An estimate in 1988 of the total number of race advisers (either corporate or department based) suggested a national minimum of 685 posts.

By the early 1980s race advisers were involved in recruitment and selection procedures, the review of services, the establishment of equality targets, various forms of training associated with issues of 'race', and consultation procedures between the black communities in a locality and the council. An important feature of the work also involves monitoring and analysing department and council policy and records as a guide to possible discriminatory practices or to areas where 'positive action' is required.

Problems of current policies and practice

Authorities which have crossed Young and Connelly's threshold have, for the most part, adopted a form of racial explicitness which is also racially exclusive. This treats the problems of discrimination in terms of discrete (and static) racial groups rather than in terms of the relationship between them; and it takes racial disadvantage out of the context of the wide range of other disadvantages with which it is inextricably linked.[9]

Both service delivery and formal structures for the attainment of racial equality appear to assume that it is possible and necessary to apprehend directly a race dimension in the provision and development of services. It appears that the meaning of race which informs local government action contains two assumptions. The first is that there exist fundamental differences between black groupings and the white British population. These differences appear to be determined either by cultural traits or as a result of the experience of racism by the numerically smaller and politically subordinate groups. The second assumption is that it is possible to quantify the extent of racism and the extent of racial inequality through the use of identifiable categories and to utilise this information as a basis for action to attain racial equality.

This has had four main consequences which give rise to concern; for, whatever the immediate gains attributed to the initiatives to date, they must seriously be questioned if, in the long-term they effectively militate against equality of opportunity and fuel animosities based on perceptions of 'racial' difference.

Firstly, it has now become so commonplace to address race issues as a discrete collective of problems that a number of difficulties which inhere in such a reification have been overlooked. As a result of the panoply of race advice from specialists a presumption has entered the mainstream of *fundamental* differences between black and white. Where needs may exist in common, they may be falsely dichotomised or ignored in favour of the emphasis on difference. Thomas (1986) identifies just such a pattern in his analysis of community work in working class neighbourhoods. He argues that work focused predominantly against institutionalised racism has resulted in the neglect of the common features of everyday life which can serve to unite black and white neighbours. More generally, at the level of welfare provision, 'black' problems are routinely assumed to be separate from those of homelessness, old age and youth. The growth in number of black public service professional sub groupings may serve to reinforce such assumptions.

A second problem is the limited dimensions within which black issues are apprehended by the state. The black population appears to become of special interest to local government when they are present in sufficient numbers to affect the outcome of elections. The unquestioned acceptance of this view of the black voting public as a unitary collective in British politics has acted as a major contributor to the reified thinking which has affected the management of local government. Although this may be changing in areas of significant black concentration, the outcome has for many years been the simplistic view of the black population as victims of racism; and it is on this above all that local race equality and anti-racist concepts appear to be premised. As Gilroy (1987) has noted, this view of the black person, reinforced by the simplistic formula 'power plus prejudice equals racism' – can inhibit analysis which attempts to assess the diversity of power relations and 'reduces the complexity of black life to an effect of racism'.

Thirdly, the cultural assumption of race policies also reveal static conceptualisation. Such assumptions provide no scope for the *process* of adaptation and change and ignore any possible influence of material or environmental conditions on the migrant population and their descendants. Rapid decline in fertility rates of the black population between 1971 and 1985 to rates more comparable with the white population suggest a process of growing similarity of family size. It has become commonplace for Hindus and Sikhs to readopt sub-caste names for the purposes of fitting in to the British naming system. There is evidence of relatively high levels of intermarriage between the Afro-Caribbean and white population, with nearly one third of Afro-Caribbeans under 30 by now married or cohabiting with white partners. These indicators suggest, at a minimum, the *prima facie* existence of a differentiated pattern of adaptation with which those who support a static concept of racial analysis based on fundamental differences have failed to come to terms.

Finally, ethnic monitoring when stripped of its managerialist pretensions, may be seen to contribute both to the reification of race and the furtherance of static cultural relativism. The willingness of job applicants to classify themselves under a variety of cultural, religious, racial or geographic groupings is one indication of the way in which convenient racialised identities are becoming widespread. A substantial number of people are currently employed in collecting and analysing these statistics. The willingness to attribute meaning to the results by local government personnel departments and to provide these with the protection of confidentiality adds a spurious importance to what are at best *prima facie* indicators of a likely source of racism. When these categories remain unaltered year after year, it becomes a small step for local government officers to make concrete an oversimplified racialised identity for the black population in a locality.

The cumulative and self-reinforcing process described here has resulted in a local government 'model' in which group boundaries are clearly identifiable and fixed. Such a model not only fails to accommodate, but actively precludes recognition of constant evolutionary processes and the dynamic quality of human relations. By the same token as groups observed and categorised at a moment in time are the outcome of these forces in the past so, in the future, they will continue to change and regroup and the boundaries between them constantly shift. Yet it is to this local government model that other public service managers have already started to turn and which, in the future, may be adopted without question on an increasing scale.

The case of racial harassment

Racial harassment, as an issue in local government race policies, has come relatively late onto the agenda. First raised in the 1970s, it has been the subject of a number of highly publicised reports since that time.[10] Of itself a matter of service delivery, it has, in fact, arrived on the agenda at precisely the time when the emphasis was shifting to creating equality in local government employment. It has also coincided with the rapid expansion in race specialist posts in the 1980s, with an escalating rate of council house sales, with cutbacks in local authority services, with the curtailment of local authority powers generally and with a marked party political polarisation around race equality issues in local government (Fitzgerald, 1987a and b).

For these reasons alone, the local government response to the issue of racial harassment would already highlight many of the tensions and dilemmas now facing local authorities. But it is, of its nature, symbolically important also. For it is an issue which presents 'at the sharp end': racial harassment happens 'out there', on the streets, in the everyday interaction between ordinary black and white citizens. As such, it is an important indicator of the likely future of Britain as a plural society.

The broad pattern which emerged from the DoE study well illustrates the four major problems identified in the previous section as the consequences of reified assumptions about 'race'. Inevitably, that broad pattern was patchy: many local authorities had made little or no formal provision for dealing with racial harassment.[11] Inevitably also, among those authorities which had them, many of the formal statements, policies and practices could be traced back to a core of orthodoxy established by a few 'pace setters'. Four main characteristics of this core are:

1. Racial harassment is perceived as a quite distinctive and serious manifestation of racial hostility perpetrated by white people on black people;
2. The primary response advocated is punitive legal action against the perpetrators, beyond which a variety of measures are ideally expected to be taken on the basis of formal inter-agency co-operation;
3. The fact of harassment may equally well be established on the victim's perception as on the basis of objective evidence of racial motivation;
4. The wishes of the victim are to be the overriding consideration in the course of action to be pursued.

On the ground, however, the reality of racial harassment and the response to it is very different, for a variety of reasons. Local authority staff 'at the sharp end' remain confused about what racial harassment actually is. While many are resistant to the policy '*per se*' others who are committed to it find it difficult to respond effectively because the individual cases they come across do not square neatly with policy. The scope for legal action against perpetrators is in practice very limited.[12] And the Holy Grail of a meaningful multi-agency response remains elusive, even where formal structures exist: in practice responsibility falls to the housing department and the police who – if they accept that responsibility – may act quite independently of (and even at variance with) each other. In practice, the most common response has been either to sweep the harassment under the carpet or to transfer the victim at their request.

It is in this context that the local authority response is illustrative of the four main problems deriving from the reification of race.

Firstly, an effective response to racial harassment is constrained by the emphasis on the distinctiveness of 'race' issues and on treating them discretely from others. In reports and in the political language used on the subject, racial harassment is depicted as an extreme form of naked hostility manifest, for example, in unprovoked attacks on people and property. But the daily reality consists in 'low level' verbal abuse and insults, most of which go unreported. And, in practice, it is rarely encountered by estate-based housing officers in forms which are as clear-cut as policy suggests. They may have to deal with a neighbour dispute where one of the parties throws racial abuse into the pot.[13] Or they may be faced with groups of teenagers and even younger children whose anti-social behaviour – of which racial harassment is only one manifestation – is causing problems for everyone on the estate.

On the one hand, the non-racial elements which come into play in these situations are often used by officers as a pretext for playing down or ignoring the seriousness of racial harassment. On the other hand, ironically, when the racial element in these situations is isolated and given prominence, this may actually increase the potential for harassment. One of the most telling findings of the tenants' survey conducted during the project[14] in areas of reportedly high racial harassment was that between a quarter and a third of white tenants believed that black people were better treated by the council than whites. However false this perception, it stood only to be fuelled by some aspects of racial harassment policy. Thus, the policy of transferring victims of racial harassment on request often caused resentment among white tenants. These were themselves often desperate to move but – as they saw it – lacked the additional lever of being able to claim racial harassment. And on estates characterised by high levels of nuisance, the insertion of a specific clause in tenancy agreements to ban racial harassment might be seen as the authority giving priority to the nuisance experienced by black tenants.[15]

In the case of officers themselves a further perceived cause of grievance was often the role of 'race specialists' in cases where harassment was alleged. Finding themselves challenged - and even overruled - in what, to them were matters of professional judgement made many who were not 'race specialists' feel at best inadequate and self-conscious in dealing with cases involving black tenants. At worst, it could create serious resentment.[16]

Secondly, racial harassment policies, *par excellence* treat black people in general as victims. Two important corollaries of this are: policy implies strongly that officers should not consider black people to be in the wrong; and white people *en masse* are considered as perpetrators – if not in fact, at least by implication. It is thus very difficult even for black housing officers to suggest that black people may, in some instances, be responsible for racial harassment or that a claim of racial harassment may occasionally be made in order to secure a transfer. Yet in some areas (see also below), black victims themselves were clear that those responsible for the harassment might be members of other black groups.[17] Moreover, where transfer was the chief response to racial harassment, inevitably there was occasional cases of abuse. Even though the numbers involved might amount to only a handful, officers were literally scandalised if forced to comply with the dishonesty because policy made 'victim definition' paramount. This then became an obstacle to their ability to respond to the majority of genuine cases.

Two consequences of implicating all whites in harassment further undermined the chances of an effective response. On the one hand, support to victims was expected to come from their 'own' community groups and organisations – even though these might be virtually non-existent (especially in predominantly white areas). Not only did more immediate sources of meaningful support from whites (such as neighbours) tend to be overlooked, so, by the same token, did the further potential for bridge-building implicit in this approach. On the other hand, some white officers were so overwhelmed by their own sense of inadequacy – because, as white people, they could not hope to understand the victim's experience or because they actually shared the guilt for the harassment – that it was impairing their ability to respond.

The third consequence of reification – a static view of race – was epitomised in the underlying assumption of policy that relations between different ethnic groups were fixed in a mode of white hostility towards black people. Using the formulation 'racism equals prejudice plus power', it was taken as a given that black people, lacking power, could not be racist and could not, therefore, be responsible for racial harassment.[18] The research, by contrast, offered insights into the dynamic situation of black people and the changing nature of their relations with each other and with whites. Most telling was the finding that relatively isolated Afro-Caribbeans in one area were the main victims of racial harassment, while in another – where they had been established nearly as long as whites – they were as likely as whites to harass Vietnamese newcomers. And another telling note was struck by the extent to which the literature, the rhetoric and the policy itself conspired to ignore the harassment of mixed-race children or of whites in mixed-race households. Although these are growing in number and may be particularly vulnerable to harassment,[19] policy was failing to accommodate them because they did not fall within the established 'ethnic' categories.

Fourthly, the experience of racial harassment illustrates the wide range of pitfalls associated with interpreting ethnic monitoring data. Indeed, the tenants' survey itself already threw up examples of *prima facie* racial differences where the explanation was as likely to be non-racial. Thus, in one area, Asian respondents were far more likely to have had their windows broken deliberately; but they were also more likely to be living in ground floor accommodation. And local authority statistics on racial harassment present further problems of explanation, being, of themselves, almost certain to give a false impression.

There are two major difficulties associated with the 'meaning' of figures on racial harassment reported to local authorities:

Racial harassment is inevitably under-reported, especially in the 'low level' form in which it is most commonly experienced. So the figures will not represent accurately either the scale or the pattern of harassment;
higher levels of reported incidents in one part of the authority may reflect a higher proportion of black residents and/or higher levels of confidence in reporting as much as a higher real incidence of harassment.

Yet, because the figures are hallowed with the notion that they represent an objective, scientific measure, they strongly influence the thrust of the policy response and may consume a lot of time and energy in attempts to increase their sophistication and 'accuracy'. Policy derived from them, however, is likely to be geared to less representative forms of racial harassment and to target identifiable 'problem' areas at the expense of those where black people may suffer worse because they are more isolated and/or because those who should respond to them are failing to do so.

Racial harassment policies, then, and the practices associated with them may not only fail effectively to tackle the very real problem they seek to address; they may actually set in train a process which further heightens the perception by white tenants and officers alike of black people as 'different', existing primarily or only in the dimension of their colour. At the same time, they may eclipse the potential for increasing mutual understanding and co-operation which derives from tenants' shared experience. As such, they have parallels in many other policies and practices which have developed piecemeal, uncritically but, in a sense also, inevitably

from the seeds which began to germinate in the late 1970s but which
were sown as early as 1966.

The future

The future of local race equality initiatives is currently very
uncertain; and two broad scenarios might be painted.

In the first – negative – scenario, race equality issues would
wither on the vine, with local authorities retreating from the
initiatives taken to date, while other agencies fail to include race
equality in the responsibilities they take over from them. There are a
number of portents for this, not the least of which are indications
that local authorities are, indeed, already in retreat and that the
reasons for this constitute strong disincentives to others.

The political climate is very different from that which obtained
during the initial and main phases of local authority policy
development. Politicians have by now concluded that in many
(even most) areas the voting power of black people is much less than
they had once believed. Moreover, the white support which they
need to secure is hostile to race equality initiatives which can be
equated with 'loony leftism' and which are perceived as giving
special treatment to black people. Some, by now, are also scarred by
the experience of trying to implement policies which have
occasionally provoked severe political, organisational and managerial problems and this has undoubtedly added to the impetus for
retreat. For other agencies, electoral considerations do not come
into play at all, but the 'loony left' tag which such initiatives now
carry is bound to be influential. Not only are they starting out in a
different political climate from that in which local authority
initiatives developed, they are swayed by different (primarily
economic and commercial) considerations. Above all, they are not
under the same pressure from central government to take the race
dimension of their work into consideration: they are not dependent
on the type of grant aid (such as Section 11 funding and urban
programme monies) which require local authorities to do so; nor are
they subject to Section 71 of the 1976 Race Relations Act.

An alternative, more positive, scenario is posited on the
assumption that the clock cannot be put back. Quite simply, the
level and breadth of awareness of race equality issues has developed

beyond recognition over the last 10 to 15 years and has begun to take root in the consciousness of policy makers and administrators. Particularly among the rising generation, it has become a matter of professionalism, such that even people working in areas with very few black people may find it necessary to develop a certain level of awareness if they are to be eligible to compete for jobs in areas with a different ethnic mix. Moreover, it could be argued that the momentum will be sustained in two specific ways. One is that, with extensive 'pruning' in local government, many local government staff – imbued with an 'equal opportunities' ethos and experienced in developing and implementing race equality policies – will move into posts in the new agencies and elsewhere, ensuring that these values permeate more widely and offering models for action. The other is that central government – albeit with a fairly low profile – is indeed sustaining some pressure: it has, for example, accepted the CRE's Code of Practice in Housing and has made some concessions in local government legislation on contract compliance in respect of race equality conditions. Added to these (and connected to the latter point) is the possibility that local government, while less directly involved in the delivery of services, will continue to play a significant *strategic* role in local provision and will do so in accordance with its Section 71 responsibilities. Finally, the counter-argument to the absence of electoral considerations is that, in this context, where commercial considerations obtain, they may actually prove both more powerful and more abiding. Arguably, this could give black people a better chance of equal treatment in new, private sector initiatives (certainly in areas of high concentration) than they received from public sector services which were established without reference to their needs. And, ironically, within local authority provision, as services come to be increasingly determined by commercial considerations, the consumer power of black people may prove more influential than their votes.

In practice, however, the future is unlikely to conform neatly to either scenario. Rather, as with local authorities to date – albeit in a less conducive climate – developments are likely to be patchy and unco-ordinated. Where initiatives are taken, however, it is important that those taking them should learn from the experience of local government and avoid replicating some of the mistakes of the past. Significant among these, as the foregoing analysis has argued, has been the reinforcement of static assumptions of race.

The simplistic and reified concepts with which policy makers have come to operate – as the illustrations from racial harassment show – are inadequate to address the everyday reality faced by practitioners and fail to accommodate either changes over time or locally specific situations. The problem has been compounded where crude and inadequate bureaucratic structures for the attainment of racial equality have been superimposed on the mainstream of local government structures and where, in part as a result of this, mechanisms for change have themselves become impediments to effective intervention.

Local government itself, then, and other agencies who might learn from its experience need to look afresh both at the thinking which underlies race equality policies and at the ways in which these are developed and implemented.

The first task, from which all else flows, is to establish a new conceptual framework for 'race' policies. In this chapter we have argued that the policy response to both discrimination and disadvantage has been based in a direct apprehension of a reified concept of 'race' which has become commonplace among certain social policy analysts. Yet other social analysts, whose work has tended to be ignored outside academic circles, have approached the discussion of race *indirectly*, applying to their analyses of race and ethnicity a broader conceptual framework based on ethnic boundaries, ethnic competition, class analysis and a view of race as a process of political formulation and reformulation. Policy makers, in short, have to date drawn on only a minute fraction of the possibilities available in their approach to establishing an analytical framework for the conceptualising of race and the attainment of racial equality.

In the context of this new conceptual framework those developing, adapting and initiating or simply recommending race equality strategies will need to be guided by three key considerations.

First, the strategies adopted and the ways in which they are administered must be appropriate. That is, they must be appropriate to the functions of the agency concerned, with the emphasis on equality in service delivery as much as on the numbers of black staff employed. They must also be appropriate to the agency's local circumstances, bearing in mind both the particular ethnic mix of the area and the roles being played by other local agencies. And, finally, they must be appropriate to the agency's capacity to deliver what it promises. This may vary considerably and will depend on a number of factors including the size and length of experience of the agency and the resources available to it. But the danger must be recognised that raising false expectations creates disappointment and, ultimately, cynicism.

Secondly, the strategies need to have clear goals. An overarching and comprehensive set of goals is already established by Section 71 of the 1976 Race Relations Act, viz. eliminating unlawful discrimination, promoting equality of opportunity and promoting good race relations. Specific initiatives (which are both consistent with the new conceptual framework and appropriate to the agency concerned) should be developed under each of these heads. Each initiative in turn should have its own clearly stated goals and provision should be built into the initiative for measuring progress towards achieving those goals. Care will be needed to ensure that these goals are consistent with each other: in particular, the dangers need to be recognised of promoting equality of opportunity in ways which unnecessarily damage race relations.

Thirdly, the role of race specialists needs to be thought through carefully. A principal organisational goal must be that the mainstream should operate on the basis of equality of opportunity. There is undoubtedly still a major task to be undertaken in opening the eyes of the colour blind and fostering awareness, sensitivity and – importantly – confidence in the mainstream of the agencies' work; and this suggests an on-going role for race specialists for some time to come. However, if this goal is to be achieved, their role will need to be strategic – that is, enabling or catalysing developments rather than hiving off mainstream functions that have a 'race' dimension; and – to the extent that this is compatible with securing change – their 'style' will need to be collaborative with the mainstream.

Finally, it may appear that local initiatives to foster race equality have reached their limit and that many have failed, if they have not actually been counter-productive. Rather, it is important that those who remain committed to the principles underlying these initiatives perceive in the changed circumstances of the late 1980s openings for new developments in the future. These openings exist even within the least optimistic of the scenarios described in this chapter; but they are likely to be seized most effectively by acknowledging the lessons of the past.

Notes and references

1. *Black and White Britain: The Third PSI Survey* concludes: 'For the most part. . . Britains's well-established black population is still occupying the precarious and unattractive position of the earlier immigrants. We have moved, over a period of 18 years, from studying the circumstances of immigrants to studying the black population of Britain only to find that we are still looking at the same thing' (Brown, 1984: p. 323).

2. Philip Nanton was a member of the project steering group. Marian Fitzgerald was the project co-ordinator and undertook half of the case studies. Both are grateful to DoE for allowing material from the project to be used in this way.

3. Section 11, enabled local authorities to claim back 75 per cent of salary costs incurred over and above their normal expenditure because of the 'special needs' of immigrants from the New Commonwealth and Pakistan.

4. The term 'black' refers to people of African, West Indian and Indian subcontinent origin and reflects accepted usage at the time of writing. There are, however, important differences between these groups; and there has been growing controversy over the application of the term to Asians. See, for example, Modood, 1988.

5. Examples of such particularised need were the problems of homeless black young people and requests for facilities to run supplementary schools.

6. Thus, the more comprehensive approach to local authority policies which the Community Relations Commission began to promote in 1977 began to be reflected in Camden in the same year, in Wandsworth in 1978 and in Greenwich in 1979. These early developments are traced in Robinson, 1980.

7. Some 'pioneering' resulted from actual or apprehended investigations of discrimination in individual service areas (particularly in housing allocation). And the Commission and others, in targeting policy recommendations on individual departments, tended to reflect the structure of local government at that time. The subsequent move to more centralised arrangements for race equality matters parallelled the move to greater corporatism in local government; and the increased emphasis on employment issues may be viewed in the context of the strengthening of local authority personnel functions which coincided with the move to corporatism.

8. Local Authorities Race Relations Information Exchange (LARRIE), forthcoming.

9. Thus, the classic definition in the Home Affairs Committee report on *Racial Disadvantage*: Racial disadvantage is a particular case of relative disadvantage within society. With the exception of racial discrimination, the disadvantages suffered by Britain's ethnic minorities are shared in varying degrees by the rest of the community. Bad housing, unemployment, educational underachievement, a deprived physical environment, social tensions - none of these are the exclusive preserve of ethnic minorities . . . But the ethnic minorities suffer such disadvantages more than the rest of the population and more than they would if they were white (Home Affairs Committee, 1981, Volume 1: x, para.12)

10. Racial Harassment on Local Authority Housing Estates, CRE, 1981; *Racial Attacks*, Home Office, 1981; *Racial Harassment in London*, GLC, 1984; *Racial Attacks and Harassment*, House of Commons Home Affairs Committee, 1986; *Racial Violence and Harassment*, Runnymede Trust, 1986; *Living in Terror*, CRE, 1987; *Racial Harassment*, Association of Metropolitan Authorities, 1987.

11. Occasionally the original aggrieved party to a dispute reacts in a manner which constitutes racial harassment. But it is also possible that grievances are likely to be pursued more aggressively where the parties are of different ethnic origins.

12. A survey of 200 tenants was conducted by MORI in each of the six case study authorities.

13. Even the few successful cases which have been brought to date have used the general 'nuisance' provisions of tenancy agreements rather than rely on racial harassment clauses. The latter would require not only the nuisance to be proved, but the racial motive also.

14. In one specific case, which we came across in our research, a housing officer was very suspicious of a tenant's claim of racial harassment in view of her past history. Advisers in the central race unit intervened, however, and insisted she be given the transfer she had asked for. Once this had been agreed, she admitted to one of the officer's colleagues that she had herself painted the letters 'KKK' on her wall.

15. Afro-Caribbean, Asian and white tenants were asked who they thought was mainly responsible for racial harassment and who they thought were the main victims.

16. Ironically, those responsible for racial harassment appear sometimes to be the least powerful of whites, as the Burnage Inquiry into the racist killing in a Manchester high school argued.

17. Not infrequently, such children were living with white single parents who were ill-equipped to respond supportively to their experience of harassment.

18. For the most part, respondents to the tenants' survey held very similar views on the estates, including the main problems they faced. Racial harassment was low on black tenants' negative perceptions; and on estates where they were more likely than whites to be seeking a transfer, this was most often because they were more likely to need a different size of accommodation.

19. Under Section 18.2 of the 1988 Local Government Act, local authorities are permitted to ask private firms up to six prescribed questions in respect of racial equality policies and to add terms covering equal opportunities to the contracts they let.

10 A Dirty War: the New Right and Local Authority Anti-Racism

Paul Gordon

Introduction

By the time Margaret Thatcher entered Downing Street for her second term as Prime Minister in 1983, far-reaching reform of British local government had been firmly established on the Conservative agenda. The Party's manifesto for the 1983 General Election promised action to deal with the 'excessive and irresponsible rate increases' imposed by 'high-spending councils' and the abolition of the 'wasteful and unnecessary tier of government' represented by the Metropolitan County Councils and the Greater London Council (see Stewart and Stoker, 1989). These moves had little to do with the race equality or anti-racist policies of local authorities for the simple reason that few local authorities had done anything serious in this respect. The arguments for reform of local government which had been put forward by free market think tanks such as the Adam Smith Institute and the Centre for Policy Studies were more that local administrations were inefficient, costly and politically motivated and were failing to provide decent services. However, as an increasing number of local authorities began to adopt race equality policies, largely as a consequence of the 1981 urban rebellions, race became an important focus for Conservative attacks on local government. Race equality and anti-racist policies, it was argued, constituted a further reason for restrictions on local government. This was so, the arguments went, for a number of reasons. Not only were they a waste of rate-payers' money, they fostered divisions along racial lines, they interfered with freedom, they promoted left-wing ideas, they undermined British culture and they amounted to a form of racism against white people.

The attack on anti-racism was one of the most striking features of the period of the Conservatives' second term of government and within the space of a few years, municipal anti-racism had been largely discredited. If the arguments put forward by the New Right opponents of anti-racism had not killed it, by the start of the Conservatives' third term of office they had seriously curtailed it, both by influencing government policy and legislation and, equally important, by creating a climate in which anti-racism was a dirty word and an embarrassing concept to many of those who had previously espoused it.

This undermining of municipal race equality policies – and of anti-racism in general – was one of the key achievements of the Conservative 'New Right' in the 1980s and opposition to municipal anti-racism united, as few other issues did, the different tendencies generally regarded as constituting the 'New Right' (Gordon and Klug, 1986). The economic liberals primarily concerned with the freeing of market forces deplored the local state interventions in social and commercial life and saw in municipal anti-racism disincentives to free enterprise and a waste of rate-payers' money. For their part the social authoritarians seeking the re-establishment of traditional Conservative values saw in municipal anti-racism nothing less than attempts by the far left to subvert British culture and values and to constrain individual freedom.

The target of the New Right attacks was not just anti-racism in a strict sense, that is policies which addressed the question of unequal relations of power between black people and white people, but also multi-cultural policies which simply acknowledged the existence of different ethnic or racial groups and sought to meet the specific needs of particular ethnic or racial groups or equal opportunities policies which attempted to end discrimination and give individuals equal access to services and, especially, to jobs. For some on the right, anti-racism was the real threat with its belief in equality and the need for intervention to achieve it, along with its implied critique of the existing social, economic and political order. For others, all race policies were a threat either in their own right for reasons which are discussed in this chapter or because they were seen as the thin end of an anti-racist wedge.

The New Right onslaught against anti-racism was, like so many others, waged at different levels. At one level were the attempts to challenge anti-racism on an intellectual plane, through the publications of New Right organisations such as the Centre for Policy Studies which had been set up in 1974 by Keith Joseph and Margaret Thatcher as a radical Conservative alternative to the Conservatives' own Heathite-dominated research department, the Social Affairs Unit set up in 1980 as an offshoot of the monetarist Institute of Economic Affairs, and the traditionalist Salisbury Group and through the writings of the individuals associated with them. Equally important, however, was the attempt, ultimately successful, to discredit municipal anti-racism at a popular level through the press. What emerged from these two strands taken together was, in effect, not just a campaign against anti-racism, but a campaign which used as its means a fertile mixture of intellectual dishonesty, fabrication, smear, innuendo, half-truth and selection. This is not to say that everything done in the name of anti-racism or race equality was beyond reproach or criticism. That, unfortunately, was far from true. But the attacks on local authority policies were not concerned with constructive criticism. They did not distinguish between the good and the bad but were, rather, aimed at anti-racism as such, in almost whatever form it took.

It is important when looking at the new right attack on anti-racism to think of the 'New Right' not just as a range of organisations and the individuals associated with them, but in a much broader sense, as referring to a constellation of *ideas* adopted and espoused by a wider range of people and institutions. In this chapter, therefore, I want to look at the emergence of a wide-ranging Conservative opposition to local authority race equality policies and at the interaction of politicians, the press and New Right thinkers and writers.

Anti-racism as interference with freedom

One of the most powerful tactics adopted by the New Right in its campaign against anti-racism was to portray anti-racist policies as an interference with individual freedom of thought, choice and action and to present itself, on the other hand, as the true defender of individual liberty. Thus, anti-racism was described by Andrew Alexander, *Daily Mail* political commentator, as nothing less than a 'new inquisition' (*Daily Mail*, 24 October 1983), while for Ray Honeyford writing in the *Salisbury Review* it was a 'new and insidious form of intolerance', a 'latter-day inverted McCarthyism' (Honeyford, 1983). Paul Johnson too claimed that it was a 'McCarthyite witch-hunt' which would eventually lead to race relations inspectors entering homes and libraries to censor books and to the censorship of newspapers (*Daily Mail*, 17 June 1985). Johnson also compared anti-racism to fascism claiming that the 'secondary racism' of the 'race relations fanatics' was more insidious than the racism of the fascist National Front (17 June 1985) and similar sentiments were expressed by Peregrine Worsthorne in the *Sunday Telegraph* less than two weeks later (30 June 1985). A few months later government ministers joined in these denunciations. At the Conservative Party conference, Home Secretary Douglas Hurd described council leaders Bernie Grant and Ted Knight as 'just as surely as the National Front . . . the high priests of race hatred' while Party chairman Norman Tebbit attacked the 'divisive racism preached by the black power merchants of the extreme left' which was, he said, 'as objectionable and destructive as that preached by the white racists of the National Front'.

Local education authority policies in particular were the target of such smears. These required teachers to purge and 'sanitise' school libraries, Ray Honeyford claimed (Honeyford, 1983), while the Inner London Education Authority's campaign against racism in textbooks (or 'campaign of censorship') provided *Salisbury Review* editor Roger Scruton with evidence to compare the anti-racist movement to the 'Nazi movement whose habits of vilification it imitates'. Quoting the Greater London Council's anti-racist poster, 'If you are not part of the solution, you are part of the problem', Scruton warned that, 'as before, the solution is to be final' (*The Times*, 16 April 1985). The following year the London Borough of Brent's policy for racial equality in schools was denounced for its recruitment of '180 Thought Police' (*Mail on Sunday*, 19 October 1986) and for its drafting 'an army of race spies' into its schools (*Daily Mail*, Today, 20 October 1986). Woodrow Wyatt simply claimed in his *News of the World* column that 'Hitler would cheer' (26 October 1986). In the wake of such reports another borough, Ealing, was also revealed to be creating 'a new army of race snoopers' who would go into schools and into council departments to 'report on officials' (*Daily Mail*, 29 October 1986).

Such stories were entirely without substance – Brent had sought and obtained central government assistance for a programme for racial equality in schools which involved the recruitment of extra advisory teachers – but they led directly to the Department of Education setting up an inquiry into Brent's plans (under former Home Office Minister, Sir David Lane) and ordering the inspectors into Brent schools.

Local authority contract compliance policies were also denounced as evidence of such creeping totalitarianism. When the Greater London Council began to implement its contract compliance policy whereby council contractors would have to show that they were taking steps to implement equal opportunities, the Confederation of British Industry saw in it an abuse of power and evidence, not of the 'Anti-Racism Year' which the Council had announced, but 'Anti-Business Year'. And in the press the Council was accused of being 'the Thought Police of the race relations industry' (*Daily Express*, 4 April 1985), of subjecting contractors to an 'inquisitorial approach' (*Daily Telegraph*, 6 April 1985) and of being 'nosy parkers' (*Sun*, 4 April 1985). All these papers supported the confectionery company Rowntree Mackintosh in its refusal to answer a GLC questionnaire.

At the level of individuals, it was claimed, local authority race policies intimidated 'decent people' who were now not only afraid of voicing certain thoughts but were 'uncertain even of their right to think those thoughts' (Honeyford, 1984). Councils were accused of being run 'like miniature totalitarian states' in which 'kangaroo courts' tried workers for racism (*Daily Mail*, 25 October 1985). Even everyday language was subject to censorship. According to stories which surfaced at various times in *The Times*, *Sunday Telegraph* and *Daily Mail* and even *The Guardian*, several anti-racist councils had ruled that it was no longer permissible in council canteens and dining rooms to ask for black coffee; one had to ask for coffee without milk. Camden Council, another story had it, had banned workers from calling each other 'sunshine'; Hackney had banned the use of the rhyme 'Baa Baa Black Sheep' in its nurseries;

and Lambeth had banned the use of the road safety symbol, Tufty the Squirrel, because he was 'racist and sexist'.

Like the claims about Brent's 'race spies', most of these claims about race equality policies were either complete fabrications or gross distortions of the truth, but they had the effect of discrediting anti-racism in the eyes of the public, particularly when repeated in more than one newspaper (Media Research Group, 1987). They also, it would appear, influenced government policy. A few weeks after the first press stories about Brent's 'race spies', Environment Secretary Nicholas Ridley spoke in the debate on the Queen's speech of 'the stink emanating from the Labour town halls'. People living and working under Labour councils, he said, 'live in fear . . . they think they are being watched like spies. They are afraid that chance remarks might lose them their jobs and their livelihood on the grounds of racism.' Britain, he said, was becoming a 'nation of race and sex snoopers and informers; and people could not believe it was happening here: 'It is more like Poland and East Germany: they knock on the door in the middle of the night. It is totalitarian, it is intolerant, it is anti-democratic and it employs fear to control people.' Legislation would be introduced to curb local authorities attaching 'non-commercial' clauses to their contracts, Mr Ridley said (*Hansard*, 17 November 1986).

Anti-racism as subversion

While comparing anti-racism to the extreme right, as something akin to fascism, the New Right has also sought to depict anti-racism as inextricably linked to the political left – what *Salisbury Review* author Geoffrey Partington has described as 'Rastafarian–Marxism' (Partington, 1982a and b) – and to a project of socialist insurrection. It has claimed that what lies behind anti-racism is no simple humanitarian concern for the status and situation of black people but, rather, attempts to manipulate the issue of race for revolutionary ends. In this way it hopes, presumably to alienate from the anti-racist cause those who might support its belief in racial equality but who would not consider themselves of the left, far less want to be associated with subversion or the promotion of conflict. Thus traditionalist Tory writer Ronald Butt told readers of his *Times* column following the 1981 urban disorders, that anti-

racism was a cover for the pressure groups active in schools who
were stirring up 'black hatred of white society' (*The Times*, 10 July
1981). Peregrine Worsthorne, alluding to prominent local black
political figures, warned of 'unscrupulous black and brown
politicians' who had a vested interest in exacerbating race hatred
since it promoted their political interests (*Sunday Telegraph*, 30
June 1985) while Charles Moore, editor of *The Spectator* and
Salisbury Group author, accused British anti-racists of promoting
apartheid in order to create a political force from a 'large,
disaffected ghetto' (*Daily Telegraph*, 15 July 1985). Similarly,
Honeyford, identifying the underlying ideology of anti-racism as
Marxism, ('proving' his case by identifying three Marxist
intellectuals 'who have provided the theoretical basis of the
movement') claimed that anti-racism was 'an attempt to create a
new and disaffected proletariat in our volatile inner cities'
(Honeyford, 1988a). The urban rebellions of 1985 provided the
New Right with the evidence they needed. Butt cited the Broadwater Farm disturbances in support of his claim that race had
become a weapon in a 'new class war', in which 'class warriors'
manipulated blacks, seeing in them a class politics which had
otherwise disappeared from Britain (*The Times*, 17 October 1985),
while educationist John Marks saw in the Handsworth and London
'riots' proof of the anti-racists' aim of generating 'insurrectionary
confrontations' (Marks, 1986).

Among the 'new class warriors' identified by Butt were left-wing
local authorities. These had earlier been accused of funding
'politically motivated and mischievous activists' (*Daily Express*, 8
March 1984) or using grants to create a 'revolutionary
consciousness' (*Daily Telegraph*, 11 April 1984), claims supported
by the free market pressure group Aims of Industry which alleged
that the effect of the GLC's funding policy was to 'heighten ethnic
and racial consciousness and to identify the enemy as the non-left'.
Aims director Michael Ivens told would-be applicants that the best
way to get a grant was to 'become an ethnic minority group' and
Alfred Sherman, one-time speechwriter for Margaret Thatcher and
founder director of the Centre for Policy Studies, accused local
authorities of 'legalised forms of robbery' and of giving money to
'revolutionary groups, prostitutes, sexual deviants and organisations whose aim is to incite immigrant communities against their
host society' (Aims of Industry, 1984).

Examples of such subversive funding have been identified particularly in the funding of police committees, local police monitoring groups and individual campaigns such as the Roach Family Support Committee which was awarded a grant by the GLC to assist its campaign for a public inquiry into the death of Colin Roach who died from shotgun wounds in Stoke Newington police station in 1983. This elicited from the *Daily Mail* reports that 'black activists' were to receive the money, quoting 'furious opponents' of the GLC's 'left wing leaders' who accused the GLC of 'fostering discontent' between black people and the police (27 January 1983). In a similar vein, a video on policing produced by the Greater London Council's police unit and a cartoon book on racism produced by the Institute of Race Relations were adduced by the *Daily Mail* in the immediate aftermath of the Broadwater Farm disturbances as evidence of 'the torrent of lies and twisted truths that is indoctrinating our society today' (8 October 1985).

But it is in the schools that the New Right has discovered the most insidious local authority subversion. Writing in the aftermath of the 1981 riots, *Salisbury Review* contributor Geoffrey Partington claimed that schools had taught black pupils that they were 'victims of British injustice to whom the British state owed every possible restitution and whose justified anger could hardly ever be rightfully assuaged' (Partington, 1982a). Since then the New Right has spawned a range of books, pamphlets and articles claiming that anti-racism is but one aspect of the 'political indoctrination' now taking place in schools. Honeyford has accused multi-racial education of confusing education with propaganda (*TES*, 19 November 1982), while Salisbury Review editor Roger Scruton and his colleagues identified 'indoctrination' not just in peace studies and women's studies, but in anti-racist education too (Scruton *et al.* 1985). From the Social Affairs Unit it was argued that anti-racist education was an aspect of the 'wayward curriculum' where a campaign had been waged to 'subvert the teaching of history and to preach contempt and hatred for the central political and cultural traditions both of Britain and of western civilisation' (Partington, in O'Keeffe, 1986). For the *Salisbury Review* authors who contributed to a 1986 collection, anti-racism was nothing less than a form of 'racial mischief', an 'assault on education and value' (Palmer, 1986). And for the Hillgate Group (Scruton, Marks, Caroline Cox and others), anti-racist and multi-racial teaching are part of the 'politicisation' of education to which they are opposed (Hillgate Group, 1986).

Such claims of anti-racist subversion were in harmony with the notion of the 'enemy within' which was a hallmark of the second term of Thatcherism and which encompassed not just striking miners, but as Margaret Thatcher made clear, 'the Hard Left, operating inside our system, conspiring to use . . . the apparatus of local government to break, defy and subvert the laws.' (*The Guardian*, 26 November 1984). The allegations made by the New Right had their effect at the highest level of government. In 1986, Tory Party chairman, Norman Tebbit, launched the Party's manifesto for the ILEA election by accusing ILEA of 'driving children to truancy' by teaching 'anti-sexist, anti-racist, gay, lesbian and CND rubbish' in schools (*The Guardian*, 4 March 1986) and two years later, Margaret Thatcher signalled the abolition of ILEA when she expressed her concern at the authority's 'political indoctrination' of its pupils. In his last official statement as Education Secretary, Sir Keith Joseph made a stinging attack on those he called the 'self-appointed apostles of anti-racism' who wanted nothing less than to 'subvert our fundamental institutions and values'. And in June 1987, his successor Kenneth Baker, together with senior officials from the Department of Education and Science, attempted to prohibit the use of the IRR cartoon book in ILEA schools claiming that it was ideologically aggressive, likely to increase racial division and that it did not promote respect for others.

That anti-racism was counter-productive and led to increased racial tension and polarisation was, for the New Right, borne out in the playground of Burnage High School, Manchester, when in 1987, a 13 year old Asian pupil, Ahmed Iqbal Ullah, was murdered by a white pupil, Darren Coulbourn. An independent inquiry set up by Manchester City Council concluded that the anti-racist policy pursued by the school had led to polarisation along racial lines. The New Right found in their reading of the report a complete vindication of what they had argued. Anti-racism *did* divide black from white and it did so with what, in this case at least, had proved to be fatal consequences. The *Daily Mail* gleefully reported the report as 'the autopsy of an obsession' with race (26 April 1988) and the following day carried a lengthy article by leader-writer Russell Lewis who claimed that anti-racist policies such as those at Burnage had created racial tension 'where none had existed before' (*Daily Mail*, 27 April 1988). The *Sun* crowed that the 'dream to bring racial understanding' to the school 'had led to so much hatred that it cost 13 year old Ahmed Ullah his life' (28 April 1988). In the so-called quality press too, anti-racism was linked to the killing. As the *Daily Telegraph* reported, the atmosphere which had led to the killing had been 'promoted by the school's anti-racist policies' (26 April 1988), while *The Times* claimed that responsibility lay with senior school managers who had 'over-zealously interpreted racial harmony guide-lines' laid down by the education authority (27 April 1988). The same paper linked the problems at the school to the 'left-wing nature' of the local education authority, as its headline put it, 'Left ideas 'engendered tension'' (27 April 1988), while the *Daily Mail* warned its readers that the Burnage headteacher was not alone in his 'blinkered and self-defeating creed' but that it was one 'endemic to certain left-dominated education authorities' (26 April 1988).

Yet, despite such reporting of the inquiry's conclusions from which few newspapers departed, the committee of inquiry had *not* concluded that anti-racism had led to the tragedy. Nor had it suggested that racism was a creation of left-wing authorities. Indeed, so distorted was the coverage of its work that the committee called a press conference to repudiate any suggestion that anti-racism had led to Ahmed Iqbal Ullah's death and to repeat that what it was criticising was the 'senseless and counter-productive way' in which anti-racist policies had been applied at one particular school. This disclaimer did not prevent Ray Honeyford publishing the following year a pamphlet arguing that the 'lesson' of Burnage lay in the nature of anti-racist education itself which could generate feelings of deprivation and resentment in the white majority, 'feelings that can so easily, in the rough and tumble of school life . . . be displaced onto ethnic minority children' (Honeyford, 1988a).

Nor, for the New Right, was Ahmed Iqbal Ullah the only black victim of anti-racism. When Tyra Henry, a 21 month old black child who had been in local authority care was murdered by her father, the scene was set for questions to be raised about the application of anti-racism to social work practices. 'Are black power politics costing the lives of children?', asked the *Daily Express* which claimed that the child had suffered from policies which were supposed to help the black community (27 July 1985) and in his weekly column in the *Sun*, Professor John Vincent claimed that Tyra Henry had died because of Lambeth Council's belief in 'separate treatment' for blacks. The anti-racist 'mumbo jumbo about black identity', Vincent wrote, had overridden the safety of the child and had led to disaster (31 July 1985).

Anti-racism as a form of racism

A further important argument of the New Right has been that anti-racism is itself a form of racism – against white people. Roger Scruton has described the anti-racists as the 'real racists', terrorising the white population (*The Times*, 30 October 1984) and, as we have seen, people such as Paul Johnson have seen in the 'racism' of the anti-racists something much more dangerous than the racism of the fascist right. Others such as Salisbury Group author Charles Moore have likened British anti-racism to apartheid. Others have focused on specific anti-discrimination measures, claiming that these represent discrimination against white people. So, for instance, Conservative philosopher and *Salisbury Review* contributor Antony Flew argued in a pamphlet for the Centre for Policy Studies (its first on the subject of race) that what he called 'positive discrimination' was nothing less than 'institutionalised discrimination' against white people (Flew, 1984). Similarly a pamphlet from the Social Affairs Unit warned that 'positive discrimination', far from reducing discrimination promoted racial discrimination – against whites – as well as racial disharmony, as well as fostering 'undesirable group images', 'inferior self images' and a 'welfare dependency' among minority groups (Parkins, 1984). A major feature the following year in the *Daily Mail* claimed that affirmative action in the United States had precisely the opposite effect to that intended: 'Whites ended up as victims of discrimination and blacks complained that it perpetuated a system that granted them second class status'. Yet in Britain, the article went on, 'the GLC and other militant left wing councils still eye it as a model to be added to the already ponderous and often counter-productive racial equality regulations' (22 August 1985).

In attempting to discredit anti-discrimination measures, these and other accounts not only present arguable accounts of the effects of affirmative action. They also confused the issue by eliding the distinction between 'affirmative action' programmes and those of 'positive discrimination'. The former, which usually take the form of providing special training for minorities who are under-represented in a workforce or targeting advertisements of vacancies, are perfectly lawful in Britain. But discriminating in favour of black people and the fixing of quotas are quite unlawful.

Claims that anti-racism is a form of racism have been applied in particular to the multiracial education policies adopted by many local education authorities. Thus Flew in the pamphlet cited above claimed that the policies adopted by the Inner London Education Authority and Berkshire Education Authority amounted to a 'revolution of destruction' against traditional 'colour blind' education while another *Salisbury Review* contributor, Geoffrey Partington, described the ILEA policy as not only 'monstrous' but 'deeply racist' (Partington, 1986) and in his contribution to a Social Affairs Unit book, *The Wayward Curriculum*, he claimed that anti-racists had fostered a 'new racism' which involved a hatred of British institutions, values and beliefs. Similar sentiments have been expressed in the press. The ILEA's policies for race, gender and class equality were described by the *Daily Mail* as 'reverse discrimination' (2 October 1983), while the *Daily Express* went further saying they amounted to 'School apartheid' and that they were 'racist, patronising, divisive' (2 October 1983).

The *Daily Mail* has been quick to highlight other instances of municipal 'anti-whites racism', claiming in 1984 that 'apartheid in reverse' was being 'preached and practised here in Britain' (24 February 1984). The evidence for this was that Lambeth Council was considering creating a separate home for black youngsters in care, that the GLC was considering negotiating separately with black employees unless they were treated better by the unions and that several councils were considering, wherever possible, that black children be adopted and fostered by black families. Even something as apparently innocuous as an advertising campaign to encourage black people to enrol for evening classes was seen as further evidence of this creeping menace (17 May 1985).

Defending British culture

At the heart of the New Right attack on anti-racism is a defence of traditional British values and British culture. Again education is seen as one of the key sites of contestation, for according to Ray Honeyford, the advocates of multi-racial education have among their aims 'the elimination of a distinctive English culture from the schools' (Honeyford, 1988a). Roger Scruton has parodied the ILEA's concept of multi-racial education as meaning that an equal emphasis must be placed on reggae and Shakespeare (*The Times*, 17 January 1984), while fellow *Salisbury Review* contributor Geoffrey Partington has bemoaned as 'utterly wicked' that there should be no consideration of 'British achievements' in the 'one sided and unbalanced diatribes against our colonial past' now presented as history in many schools (Partington, 1982a and b).

Behind the New Right defence of British culture is a denial of the idea that all cultures may be equally valuable, an issue which exercised many of the contributors to the 1986 collection, *Anti-Racism: an assault on education and value*. Thus Antony Flew derides the notion that cultures are equally good or equally valid and claims that some are more 'instrumentally valuable' (although he does not say which). Caroline Cox went further, seeing cultural relativism as reducing everything to an intellectual quicksand and producing a climate in which 'Western civilisation is now the target of constant attack'. So too Roger Scruton has denounced the 'myth of cultural relativism' and argued that it is a prime duty of schools to transmit British culture (Palmer, 1986).

But it is not just high culture which the New Right sees as under threat from local authority anti-racist policies. Aspects of 'popular culture' too are under threat and the 'popular' press has leaped to the rescue. So for instance in 1985 several newspapers reported that Hackney Council in east London was about to change the name of Britannia Walk to Shaheed-E-Azam Nhagot Singh Avenue, ridiculing the plan and claiming that local people were being made 'foreigners in our own country' (*Sun*, 7 September 1985). The truth was that Bhagot Singh's name was one of 40 being considered for a new extension of Britannia Walk. There never was any question that Britannia Walk would disappear. And when Lambeth Council was considering changing the names of some local landmarks to commemorate black political figures, the story in the *Sun* was headed, 'Lefties do the Zephanie Mothopeng Walk' and an editorial commented, 'They have finally flipped their lids in Lambeth' (8 February 1986).

Similarly, newspapers invariably rally round whenever that symbol of racist popular culture, the golliwog, is under attack. In

1984, several newspapers rounded on Merseyside County Council when it tried to prevent a giant golliwog castle and other golliwog objects being used to advertise Robertson's jam at the International Garden Festival. The council was a 'bunch of sourpusses' according to one paper (*Daily Star*, 1 May 1984), while another accused 'the loony left-wingers' as being 'simply out to incite hysteria' over the toys which were 'enormously popular with children of all colours' (*Daily Mail*, 2 May 1984).

In a sense the golliwog was a symbol for the Britain which the New Right saw itself as defending from the anti-racists. Just as it was not racist in any way so, the New Right argues, Britain is not racist. What exists is not institutional racism but personal racism, the behaviour of individuals who may behave in a discriminatory way. Thus, the argument continues, there is no legitimate need or basis for anti-racism. Furthermore, the position of black people cannot be explained by recourse to racism but rather, as Flew among others has argued, in the group itself (Flew, 1984). In this he echoes Honeyford who has asserted that the 'roots of black educational failure' are to be found in 'West Indian family structure and values' (Honeyford, 1984).

New Right achievements

Within the space of a few years, the New Right, whether in its intellectual garb or wearing its populist guise, had successfully established that anti-racist policies were inextricably part of the ideological baggage of the far left and had created a whole new demonology of municipal anti-racism – of loony left councils, banana republics, Barmie Bernie, in which councils vied for the title of Britain's barmiest borough, where rate-payers' money was used for brazenly political – as well as ludicrous – ends. As already indicated, many of the stories about local authority anti-racism were untrue, as a study by researchers at Goldsmiths' College showed. For example, the *Mail on Sunday* reported that Haringey Council in north London had banned the use of black rubbish sacks because they were 'racially offensive'. Yet when it became clear that this was completely without foundation, the paper simply reported that the Council had decided not to ban them after all. So too the

Sun claimed that 'a loony left council' was 'splashing out at least £9 000' to send a group of black teenagers to 'communist Cuba'. In fact, the trip was organised by a group called Caribbean Exchange which was quite independent of Brent Council which had only allowed the group to use Council premises for fund-raising events (Media Research Group, 1987; see also Murray, 1986 and Gordon and Rosenberg, 1989).

Such allegations helped to secure support for government policies and influenced others and helped achieve a number of victories: the abolition of the Greater London Council, a pioneer in municipal anti-racism and a hate figure of the New Right; the restriction of local authority powers to pursue contract compliance policies; the abolition of the Inner London Education Authority; and the restrictions on the curriculum and local education authority powers represented by the Education Act 1986 and the Education Reform Act 1988. And to these must be added the fiscal restrictions, such as rate-capping, and the replacement of rates by the poll tax.

Equally important, however, the New Right campaign against anti-racism succeeded to a significant degree in creating a climate of opinion which was hostile to race equality initiatives and policies. This has led to several Labour authorities to question their work in this respect and to the downgrading of anti-racist work as race equality units are cut, merged or scrapped and race equality policies abandoned as councils try to shake off their 'loony left' images and jettison policies believed to be electoral liabilities.

It would, however, be a grave mistake to ascribe the collapse of much municipal anti-racism solely to the activities of the New Right. Too much that passed for anti-racism or racial equality policies left itself open to the kinds of attacks which appeared. Too often, local authorities indulged in gestural politics, engaging with appearances, rather than dealing with material realities, elevating relatively minor issues to major ones. So too the ways in which policies were implemented often left local authorities open to serious charges of autocratic and high-handed behaviour and served only to alienate the support which was necessary for the policies to succeed. Racism became personalised and individualised, providing the New Right with 'race martyrs' such as Brent headteacher Maureen McGoldrick, an avowed and respected supporter of multiculturalism, suspended on the basis of hearsay, while anti-racism became bureaucratic.

That said, even at its best and most thought out, municipal anti-racism faced a dirty war waged by the New Right and its supporters in the press who were not interested in truth or in seeking the best ways to improve the situation of the population, black or white, but in defending the status quo and its entrenched racial inequality.

11   The End of Anti-Racism

Paul Gilroy

Introduction

The task of developing a radical critique of the moralistic excesses practised in the name of anti-racism is an urgent task today. The absurdities of anti-racist orthodoxy have become a target of critique by the right (Honeyford, 1988; Lewis, 1988), and have formed a back-drop to the bitter debates that have surrounded the publication of *The Satanic Verses*.[1] The dictatorial character of anti-racism, particularly in local government, has itself become an important theme within the discourse of popular racism.

These assaults on the fundamental objective of anti-racism and the attendant practice of multi-culturalism in education, social work and other municipal services have passed largely unanswered and vocal political support for anti-racism has been hard to find. This is partly because the cadre of anti-racism professionals which was created during the boom years of radicalism on the rates has lost its collective tongue: its political confidence has been drained away. There has been little support from independent black defence organisations and authentic community groups whose actions go far beyond the narrow categories in which anti-racism can operate. Meanwhile, many of the ideological gains of Thatcherite Conservatism have dovetailed neatly with the shibboleths of black nationalism – self-reliance and economic betterment through thrift, hard work and individual discipline. The impact of this resolutely Conservative and often authoritarian political ideology can be felt right across the field of social and economic policy where an idealised and homogenised vision of 'The Black Community' is the

191

object of a discourse that urges it to take care of its own problems and assume the major burden of managing its own public affairs. This is not a wholly negative development, but in the new atmosphere it creates, anti-racist initiatives can only appear to be a patronising and unacceptable form of special pleading. Apart from these important changes, specialised anti-racist work within the local state has been increasingly identified as an embarrassment by the Labour Party for whom political commitments to anti-racism and multi-culturalism are apparently a vote loser.

These developments have created political inertia in what was once an anti-racist *movement*. The political forces which once made that movement move are now enveloped in a catastrophe that has two distinct dimensions. Firstly, there is a crisis of organisational forms. In the absence of mass mobilisation around anti-racist aims, it has been impossible to construct structures that could span the gulf between the elements of the movement which are outside the local state and the residues which are dedicated to remaining within it. This problem is also conveyed in the considerable rift that has opened up between those sections which are ideologically committed to the Labour Party and those which are indifferent if not actively opposed to it. Secondly, and more importantly for what follows, there is a crisis of the political language, images and cultural symbols which this movement needs in order to develop its self-consciousness and its political programme. This problem with the language of anti-racism is acutely expressed by the lack of clarity that surrounds the term anti-racism itself. It includes the difficulties involved in producing a coherent definition of racism[2] as well as the tension that appears from the need to link an account of the racialisation of social and political structures and discourses with an understanding of individual action and institutional behaviour.

For all its antipathy to the new racism of the New Right, the common sense ideology of anti-racism has also drifted towards a belief in the absolute nature of ethnic categories and a strong sense of the insurmountable cultural and experiential divisions which, it is argued, are a feature of racial difference. I have argued elsewhere that these ideological failures have been compounded firstly by a reductive conception of culture and secondly by a culturalist conception of race and ethnic identity (Gilroy, 1987). This has led to a position where politically opposed groups are united by their view of race exclusively in terms of culture and identity rather than politics and history. Culture and identity are part of the story of racial sensibility but they do not exhaust that story. At a theoretical level 'race' needs to be viewed much more contingently, as a precarious discursive construction. To note this does not, of course, imply that is any less real or effective politically.

It is possible then, that the idea of anti-racism has been so discredited that it is no longer useful. It is certain that we have to devise ways to move beyond anti-racism as it is presently constituted. I must emphasise that I am thinking not of anti-racism as a political objective, or a goal which emerges alongside other issues from the daily struggles of black people, from the practice of community organisations and voluntary groups, even from the war of position which must be waged inside the institutions of the state. I am not talking about the ongoing struggle towards black liberation, for there is much more to the emancipation of blacks than opposition to racism. I am thinking instead of anti-racism as a much more limited project defined simply, even simplistically, by the desire to do away with racism.

The anti-racism I am criticising trivialises the struggle against racism and isolates it from other political antagonisms – from the contradiction between capital and labour, from the battle between men and women. It suggests that racism can be eliminated on its own because it is readily extricable from everything else. Yet in Britain, 'race' cannot be understood if it is falsely divorced from other political processes or grasped if it is reduced to the effect of these other relations. Anti-racism in this sense is a phenomenon which grew out of the political openings created by the 1981 riots. In the years since then, anti-racists have become a discrete and self-contained political formation. Their activism is now able to sustain itself independently of the lives, dreams and aspirations of the majority of blacks from whose experience they derive their authority to speak.

To criticise anti-racism necessitates understanding racism and being able to locate the politics of 'race' from which it springs. Analysing what racism does in our society means, first of all, claiming 'race' and racism back from the margins of British politics. Racism isn't epiphenomenal. Yet just as racism itself views black settlers as an external, alien visitation, anti-racism can itself appear to be tangential to the main business of the political system as a whole.

The apparent marginality of race politics is often an effect of a fundamental tension inherent in anti-racist organising. A tension between those strands in anti-racism which are primarily anti-fascist and those which work with a more extensive and complex sense of what racism is in contemporary Britain. This simplistic anti-fascist emphasis attempts to mobilise the memory of earlier encounters with the fascism of Hitler and Mussolini. The racists are a problem because they are descended from the brown- and black-shirted enemies of earlier days. To oppose them is a patriotic act; their own use of national flags and symbols is nothing more than a sham masking their terroristic inclinations.

The price of over-identifying the struggle against racism with the activities of these extremist groups and grouplets is that however much of a problem they may be in a particular area (and I am not denying the need to combat their organising) they *are* exceptional. They exist on the fringes of political culture and for the foreseeable future are destined to have only tenuous and intermittent relationships with respectability. They are a threat but not the only threat. There is more to contemporary racism than the violence they perpetrate. We shall see in a moment that there are problems with the nationalism which goes hand in hand with this outlook.

A more productive starting point is provided by focusing on racism in the mainstream and seeing 'race' and racism not as fringe questions but as a volatile presence at the very centre of British politics actively shaping and determining the history not simply of blacks, but of this country as a whole at a crucial stage in its development.

The importance of racism in contemporary politics betrays something about the nature of the painful transition this country, and the overdeveloped world as a whole, is undergoing. The almost mystical power of race and nation on the political stage conveys something about the changing nature of class relations, the growth of state authoritarianism, the eclipse of industrial production, the need to maintain popular support for militarism and exterminism and the end of the nation state as a political form.

The highly charged politics of national identity that has been occasioned by these developments has been transposed into a higher, shriller key by current concern over the appeal of a wide pan-European disposition tailored to the new range of possibilities that flow from tighter political and economic integration of the European Economic Community. This potentially post-national European consciousness has racial referents of its own. It is however, felt by elements of both left and right to pose a threat to the sovereignty and cultural integrity of the United Kingdom. Whether it is possible to generate a political discourse capable of articulating the distinctive needs and historical experiences of black Europeans remains to be seen. Though the rich legacy of an extensive black presence on this continent suggests that it may be possible, for many commentators, the terms 'black' and 'European' remain categories which mutually exclude each other.

Racism and the ideology of anti-racism

The first question I want to ask of contemporary anti-racism is whether it doesn't collude in accepting that the problems of 'race' and racism are somehow peripheral to the substance of political life. My view, which locates race in the core of politics, contrasts sharply with what can be called the coat of paint theory of racism (Gilroy, 1987). This is not in fact, a single theory but an approach which sees racism on the outside of social and political life – sometimes the unwanted blemish is the neo-fascists, sometimes it is immigration laws, other times it is the absence of equal opportunities – yet racism is always located on the surface of other things. It is an unfortunate excrescence on a democratic polity which is essentially sound, and it follows from this that with the right ideological tools and political elbow grease, racism can be dealt with once and for all leaving the basic structures and relations of British economy and society essentially unchanged.

Though not always stated openly, the different permutations of this view underpin much of contemporary anti-racism. I think there are particular problems posed by the fact that this type of theory is intrinsic to equal opportunities initiatives. The coat of paint approach is doubly mistaken because it suggests that fundamental issues of social justice, democracy and political and economic power are not raised by the struggle against racial subordination.

Seeing racism as determining rather than determinate, at the centre rather than in the margins, also means accepting that

Britain's crisis is centrally and emphatically concerned with notions of race and national identity. It has been held together, punctuated and periodised by racial politics – immigration, the myriad problems of the riotous 'inner city' and by the loony left. These terms are carefully coded and they are significant because they enable people to speak about race without mentioning the word. The frequent absence of any overt reference to 'race' or hierarchy is an important characteristic of the new types of racism with which we have to deal. This kind of coded language has created further strategic problems for anti-racism. It is easy to call Mr Honeyford a racist and to organise against him on that basis but less easy to show precisely how and why this is the case.

We must be prepared to focus unsentimentally on anti-racism's inability to respond to other distinctive aspects of these new forms of racism. Apart from the way that racial meanings are inferred rather than stated openly, these new forms are distinguished by the extent to which they identify race with the terms culture and identity, terms which have their own resonance in anti-racist orthodoxy. The new racism has a third important feature which enables it to slip through the rationalist approach of those who, with the best will in the world, reduce the problem of racism to the sum of power and prejudice. This is the closeness it suggests between the idea of race and the ideas of nation, nationality and national belonging.

We increasingly face a racism which avoids being recognised as such because it is able to link 'race' with nationhood, patriotism and nationalism. A racism which has taken a necessary distance from crude ideas of biological inferiority and superiority and now seeks to present an imaginary definition of the nation as a unified *cultural* community. It constructs and defends an image of national culture – homogeneous in its whiteness yet precarious and perpetually vulnerable to attack from enemies within and without. The analogy of war and invasion is increasingly used to make sense of events.

This is a racism that answers the social and political turbulence of crisis and crisis management by the recovery of national greatness *in the imagination*. It's dreamlike construction of our sceptred isle as an ethnically purified one provides a special comfort against the ravages of decline. It has been a key component in the ideological and political processes which have put the great back in Britain. The symbolic restoration of greatness has been achieved in part through the actual expulsion of blacks and the fragmentation of their households which is never far from page three in the tabloids.

The shock of decline has induced Britons to ask themselves a question first posed by Enoch Powell 'What kind of people are we?' The emphasis on culture and the attendant imagery of the nation composed of symmetrical family units contributes to a metaphysics of Britishness which has acquired racial referents. I can illustrate this by reading you a poem which was part of a racist leaflet circulated in Haringey during the last election. It was illustrated by a picture of Bernie Grant with the hairy body of a gorilla. It read:

> Swing along with Bernie its the very natural thing
> He's been doing it for centuries and now he thinks he's king
> He's got a little empire and he doesn't give a jot
> But then the British are a bloody tolerant lot
> They'll let him swing and holler hetero-homo-gay
> And then just up and shoot him in the good old British way.

These lines signify a powerful appropriation of the rights and liberties of the freeborn Briton so beloved of the new left. The rhyme's historical references demonstrate how completely blackness and Britishness have been made into mutually exclusive categories, incompatible identities. The problems which Bernie represents are most clearly visible against the patterned backdrop of the union jack. The picture of him as a gorilla was necessary on the leaflet because the words make no overt mention of his race. The crime which justifies lynching him is a form of treason not racial inferiority.

This culturalist variety of racism and the cultural theory of 'race' difference linked to it, hold that the family supplies the units, the building blocks from which the national community is constructed. This puts black women directly in the firing line. Firstly, because they are seen as playing a key role in reproducing the alien culture, and, secondly, because their fertility is identified as excessive and therefore threatening.

It has become commonplace to observe that the precious yet precarious Churchillian, stiff-upper-lip culture which only materialises in the midst of national adversity – underneath the arches, down in the air raid shelters where Britannia enjoyed her finest

hours – is something from which blacks are excluded. The means of
their exclusion is identified in the colourful deviancy which is
produced by their pathological family forms. Pathology and
deviancy are the qualities which define distinct and insubordinate
black cultures. This apples in different yet parallel ways to both
Afro-Caribbean and Asian populations, whose criminality violates
the law – the supreme achievement of British civilisation.

Deviancy, so the argument runs, has its roots in generational
conflict which appears along cultural lines. The anti-social activities
of the 'Holy Smokes' in west London's Asian gangland are, in a
sense, parallel to the barbarous misdemeanours of the Afro-
Caribbean Yardies on London's proliferating frontlines. The
'racial' criminal subcultures of each group are seen to wantonly
violate the laws and customs which express the civilisation of the
national community and in so doing provide powerful symbols
which express black difference as a whole. To be a street criminal is
therefore to fulfil cultural destiny.

For a long while, the crime question provided the principal
means to underscore the *cultural* concerns of this new nationalist
racism. Its dominance helped us to understand where the new
racism begins in Powell's bloody nightmare of the aged white
woman pursued through the streets by black children. However,
crime has been displaced recently at the centre of race politics by
another issue which points equally effectively to the incompatibility
of different cultures supposedly sealed off from one another forever
along ethnic lines. This too uses images of the black child to make
its point – the cultural sins of the fathers will be visited on their
children. Where once it was the main streets of the decaying inner
city which hosted the most fearsome encounter between Britons and
their most improbable and intimidating other – black youth – now
it is the classrooms and staffrooms of the inner city school which
frame the same conflict and provide the most potent terms with
which to make sense of racial difference.

The publication of *Anti-racism: An Assault on Education and
Value*, the book of essays edited by Frank Palmer, confirmed the
fact that the school has become the principal element in the
ideology with which the New Right have sought to attack anti-
racism (See the paper by Gordon in this volume). While it is
important not to be mesmerised by the gains and strengths of the
New Right – as many radicals are – it is essential to understand *why*

their burgeoning anti-anti-racism has focused upon education. From their perspective, schools are repositories of the authentic national culture which they transmit between generations. They mediate the relation of the national community to its youthful subjects – future citizens.

Decaying school buildings provide a ready image for the nation in microcosm. The hard fought changes which anti-racists and multi-culturalists have wrought on the curriculum mirror the bastardisation of genuine British culture. Anti-racist initiatives that literally denigrate educational standards are identified as an assault on the traditional virtues of British education. This cultural conflict is a means through which power is transposed and whites become a voiceless ethnic minority oppressed by totalitarian local authority anti-racism. The racists are redefined as the black racists and Mr Honeyford, dogged defender of freedom, is invited to Number 10 for consultation. In *The Independent* of 23 July 1987 Baroness Cox is arguing that black parents are motivated to demand their own separate schools not by dissatisfaction or frustration with the way that racism is institutionalised in state education but because they want 'a good old fashioned British education' for their children.

I think we have to recognise that the effect of these images and the conflicts from which they spring in Brent or Bradford has been to call into question any anti-racist or multi-cultural project in education and indeed the idea of anti-racism in general. The new racism's stress on cultural difference and absolutist conception of ethnicity have other significant effects. It is now not only a feature of the relationship between blacks and whites. It enters directly into the political relations between the different groups which, in negotiating with each other, promise to construct a unified black community from their diversity.

The potentially unifying effects of their different but complementary experiences of racism are dismissed while the inclusive and openly politicised definitions of 'race' which were a notable feature of the late 1970s have been fragmented into their ethnic components, first into Afro-Caribbean and Asian and then into Pakistani, Bangladeshi, Bajan, Jamaican and Guyanese in a spiral. This boiling down of groups into their respective ethnic essences is clearly congruent with the nationalist concerns of the right. But it is also sanctioned by the anti-racist orthodoxy of the left and by many voices from within the black communities themselves which have needed no prompting to develop their own fascination with ethnic differences and thus reduce political definitions of 'race' to a narcissistic celebration of culture and identity.

I have argued that anti-racism has been unable to deal with the new forms in which racism has developed. In particular, it has been incapable of showing how British cultural nationalism becomes a language of race. The power of this patriotic political language is there for all to behold. It puts the vital populist force into those processes for which 'Thatcherism' serves as a reasonable shorthand term. However, it does not appear to be the exclusive property of the right. Its magical populist appeal will tempt political pragmatists of all hues. I'm afraid there are segments of the left who are especially envious of its capacity to animate the groups which were once regarded as their traditional supporters. Unfortunately, Labour's blustering 'patriotism of freedom and fairness' like its recent attempts to 'take crime seriously' are not less saturated with racial connotations than the Conservative versions of these arguments (see the paper by Keith and Murji in this volume). This is not to say that the right and left are necessarily the same but rather that they converge at key points and share an understanding of what is involved in the politics of 'race'.

The Bernie poem seamlessly knitted together images invoking empire, sovereignty and sexuality, with a concluding exhortation to violence. There is nothing about this combination of themes which marks it out as the exclusive preserve of the right. It is another example of how the racism which ties national culture to ethnic essences, which sees custom, law and constitution, schools and courts of justice beset by corrosive alien forces, has moved beyond the grasp of the old left/right distinction.

This populist character of the new racism works across class lines as well as within them. It can link together disparate and formally opposed groups leading them to discover the morbid pleasures of seeing themselves as 'one nation'. It transmits the idea of the British people as the *white* people. While Labour seeks to simply snatch the language of one nation from the Tories, the danger here can only grow and it is compounded because it is by no means clear how far a re-constituted and emphatically 'un-loony' socialism may go in negotiating its own language of toughness on immigration and nationality even perhaps on humane socialist repatriation. The French left has not had any qualms about this.

It is particularly difficult for blacks to resolve our relation to Labourism and the Labour Party when it is not clear precisely what Labour stands for. The party's ideological and political problems are so severe in my view that we may never see another Labour government in this country. This means that we must at least ask the question of what role the party that passed all the race relations legislation can be expected to play in the racial politics of the bleak years ahead. It is clear that anti-racism as a political project may be identified as a vote loser – as an example of the 'London Effect' which is supposedly so disastrous among 'the pensioners'. Whatever the impending Conservative legislation does to equal opportunities initiatives, the dangerous radicalism involved in them and in contract compliance schemes may be among the first political baggage cast out of the Labour balloon if it is to rise once more.

The recent outcome of the by-election in Vauxhall, South London, provides an example. There, you may remember, an independent black 'People's Candidate' ran against the officially endorsed Labour aspirant – Kate Hoey – after a dispute between the local party and the national executive. The independent black hopeful, the Rev. Hughie Andrews polled only 300 odd votes, while the nominee imposed by the party's National Executive was elected to Parliament with an increased majority. Taking a hard line against blacks inside the party whose demand to organise autonomously is identified as racial separatism, has become a significant sign of the general rehabilitation of the Labour leadership. It would appear that a party which is able to impose a white MP on an inner city constituency that desires a black representative is truly a party fit to govern. This sorry episode certainly suggests that as far as communities of Afro-Caribbean descent are concerned, Labour has calculated that it can manage without that historic enthusiasm for racial equality which has been misrecognised by many of its traditional supporters as an agenda of special treatment for blacks. After the crisis of cultural relativism provoked by the mass movement against *The Satanic Verses*, the *realpolitik* of electing Labour in Sparkbrook or Bradford may be rather different from the challenges posed by the studied indifference of South London's black electorate.

If Labour has calculated that it can do without its commitment to blacks (whatever that commitment may mean) the steady detachment of blacks from Labour may be an inescapable, indeed inevitable fact. From a historian's point of view, it is by no means certain that we were ever firmly attached to Labour. The idea of our attachment seems to be a recent development, a product of the post-1981 period in which anti-racism drifted off the streets and into the warm, dry atmosphere of municipal buildings where many of its activists – socialists and feminists – went in search of funds for their subversive activities. I think we should discuss not simply whether anti-racism became too reliant on Labour but whether the belief that anti-racism can be a separate and cohesive political project has been almost entirely a creation of Labour local authorities. It is certainly worth recording that *The Journal*, an independent black nationalist newspaper, advocated a Tory vote at the last election on the extraordinary grounds that blacks had benefited from the enterprise culture inaugurated by Mrs Thatcher:

> Black people have made gains from the Thatcher years, because of the right to buy housing legislation, privatisation, the expansion of higher education and increasing training opportunities. A Labour Party would of course expand the employment of anti-racist advisers, inhibit wealth creation in our community and will be so obsessed with the comprehensive system of education that our children will continue to be education failures ... Let us be responsible. Let us be honest and open. What is best for black people? Vote Conservative for a stronger, self reliant and proud black community. There is no alternative.

The manifest absurdity of this editorial should not detract from the seriousness of the issues it attempts to raise in such an idiotic manner. To deal with them seriously requires looking beyond our historic association with Labourism at the relationship between blacks and the institutions of formal electoral politics, at the crisis of representation in the political system. This is signalled in several ways:

1. By the changing relationship between national and local politics;
2. by the level of abstention from electoral politics in some areas;

3. by significant changes in the geography of class and party political affiliation. We do now speak of two nations north and south, of Scotland and Wales as in a sense separate because of the absence of a Conservative mandate. Why not try and situate the experience of blacks in this general crumbling of the nation as a political unit?

The destruction of local government which is underway can only entrench the radical sense of powerlessness we experience and which is too readily dismissed as apathy. An antidote to it cannot be found in attempts to bargain with the black vote as some, though not all, of the black sections activists have suggested. It is not simply that this vote is not in their gift, not theirs to deliver, but also that the logic of economic and political fragmentation of poverty and dispossession as well as the concentration of black settlers in particular areas all mean that it is quite possible that we can be overlooked by electoral politics altogether.

The gulf which is being opened up between many blacks and the electoral system cannot be discussed without careful attention to the issue of class relationships within the black communities. Further research has to be done here, but it would appear that the complexity of class and cultural relationships is far more complex than any crude polarisation into proletarian 'Afro-Caribbeans' and petit bourgeois 'Asians' would allow. The 'Asians' do not have a monopoly of entrepreneurial impulses, and these catch-all terms of anti-racist language mask a huge diversity of cultural and economic experiences. A small but significant illustration of the uneven coming together of class, ethnicity and culture is provided by the conflict over the organisation of the Notting Hill Carnival in 1989. Here, the Carnival Enterprise Committee under the leadership of 'Buppie' lawyer Claire Holder sought, in opposition to the anarchy apparently inherent in the Caribbean cult of spontaneity, to make 'Europe's biggest street festival' into a successful commercial event. It is significant that the respectable, orderly and cleaned up conception of what the Carnival should be, emphasised the supposedly 'traditional' activities of Pan, Mas and Jump Up at the expense of the modernist intrusion of the Sound Systems. In this conflict, it is possible to find echoes of a wider antagonism over what the culture of the nascent black middle class is to be.

Racial justice and civil society

I think it is important to concede that what we can loosely call the anti anti-racist position associated with sections of the New Right and with populist politics has fed on crucial ambiguities in anti-racist and multi-cultural initiatives.

The definition of racism in the sum of prejudice and power can be used to illustrate these problems. Power is a relation between social groups not a possession to be worn like a garment or flaunted like an anti-racist badge. Prejudice suggests conscious action if not actual choice. Is this an appropriate formula? The most elementary lessons involved in studying ideas and consciousness seem to have been forgotten. Racism, like capitalism as a whole, rests on the mystification of social relations – the necessary illusions that secure the order of public authority.

There are other aspects of what has become a multi-culturalist or anti-racist orthodoxy which can be shown to replicate in many ways the volkish New Right sense of the relationship between race, nation and culture – kin blood and ethnic identity. I have already mentioned how the left and right distinction has begun to evaporate as formally opposed groups have come to share a sense of what race is. These problems are even more severe when elements of the black community have themselves endorsed this understanding. Here I am thinking of the definition of race exclusively in terms of culture and identity which ties certain strands in anti-racism to the position of some of the New Right ideologues.

By emphasising this convergence I am not saying that culture and identity are unimportant but challenging the routine reduction of race to them alone which obscures the inherently political character of the term. The way in which culture is itself understood provides the key to grasping the extraordinary convergence between left and right, anti-racist and avowedly racist over precisely what race and racism add up to.

At the end of the day, an absolute commitment to cultural insiderism is as bad as an absolute commitment to biological insiderism. I think we need to be theoretically and politically clear that no single culture is hermetically sealed off from others. There can be no neat and tidy pluralistic separation of racial groups in this country. It is time to dispute with those positions which, when taken to their conclusions, say 'there is no possibility of shared history and no human empathy'. We must beware of the use of ethnicity to wrap a spurious cloak of legitimacy around the speaker who invokes it. Culture, even the culture which defines the groups we know as races, is never fixed, finished or final. It is fluid, it is actively and continually made and re-made. In our multi-cultural schools the sound of the steel pan may evoke Caribbean ethnicity, tradition and authenticity yet they originate in the oil drums of the Standard Oil Company rather than the mysterious knowledge of ancient African griots.

These theoretical problems are most visible and at their most intractable, in the area of fostering and adoption policy. Here, the inflated rhetoric and culturalist orthodoxies of anti-racism have borne some peculiar fruit. The critique of the pathological views of black family life that were so prevalent in Social Services during the late 1970s and early 1980s has led directly to an extraordinary idealisation of black family forms. Anti-racist orthodoxy now sees them as the only effective repositories of authentic black culture and as a guaranteed means to transmit all the essential skills that black children will need if they are to 'survive' in a racist society without psychological damage. 'Same-race' adoption and fostering for 'minority ethnics' is presented as an unchallenged and seemingly unchallengeable benefit for all concerned. It is hotly defended with the same fervour that denounces white demands for 'same race' schooling as a repellent manifestation of racism. What is most alarming about this is not its inappropriate survivalist tone, the crudity with which racial identity is conceived nor even the sad inability to see beyond the conservation of racial identities to possibility of their transcendence. It is the extraordinary manner in which the pathological imagery has simply been inverted so that it forms the basis of a pastoral view which asserts the strength and durability of black family life and, in present circumstances, retreats from confronting the difficult issues which result in black children arriving in care in the first place. The contents of the racist pathology and the material circumstances to which it can be made to correspond are thus left untouched. The tentacles of racism are everywhere, except in the safe haven which a nurturing black family provides for delicate, fledgeling racial identities.

The forces of anti-racism

I want to turn now to the forces which have grouped around the anti-racist project and to the question of class. There is a problem here in that much of the certainty and confidence with which the term has been used have collapsed along with the secure life-time employment which characterised industrial capitalism. Today for example, I think it means next to nothing to simply state that blacks are working class when we are likely to be unemployed and may not recognise our experience and history in those areas of political life where an appeal to class is most prominent. Class politics does not, in any case, enjoy a monopoly of political radicalism. Obviously people still belong to classes but belief in the decisive universal agency of the dwindling proletariat is something which must be dismissed as an idealist fantasy. Class is an indispensible instrument in analysing capitalism but it contains no ready-made plan for its overcoming. We must learn to live without a theological faith in the working class as either a revolutionary or an anti-racist agent.

There is a major issue here but I want to note it and move on to consider a different aspect of how race and class intersect. A more significant task for class analysis is comprehending the emergence of a proto-middle class grouping narrowly constituted around the toeholds which some blacks have been able to acquire in the professions, mostly those related directly to the welfare state itself – social work, teaching, and now anti-racist bureaucracies. A Marxist writer would probably identify this group as the first stirrings of a black petit bourgeoisie. I don't think this grouping or grouplet is yet a class either in itself or for itself and it may never become one. For one thing it is too small, for another it is too directly dependent on the state institutions which pay its wages. But it is with this group that anti-racism can be most readily identified and we need to examine it on its own terms and in its relationship to other more easily identifiable class groupings. It is obviously in an uncomfortably contradictory position – squeezed between the expectations of the bureaucracies on which it relies and its political affiliation to the struggles of the mass of blacks which it is called upon to mediate, translate and sometimes police. It is caught between the demands of bureaucratic professionalism and the emotive pull of ethnic identification.

This not-yet-class plays a key role in organising the political forces of anti-racism centred on local authorities. It involves three opposed tendencies which have evolved an uneasy symbiosis. They are not wholly discrete. The black sections campaign for example, involves elements of each of them.

1. The equal opportunities strand, which has its roots in the social democratic 'race' interventions of the 1960s. It has also borrowed heavily from the experience of Afro-America's shift into electoral politics – the black mayors' movement and so on. This tendency is proud and secure in its bureaucratic status and it identifies equality (anti-racism) with efficiency and good management practice. Policy questions dominate political ones and anti-racism emerges from the production of general blueprints which can be universally applied. Of course, equal opportunities afford an important interface between struggles around race and gender and they can be a locus of possible alliances. However, in the context of local authorities these initiatives can also host a competition between different political forces over which of them is going to take immediate priority. We should therefore be wary of collapsing anti-racism let alone black emancipation into equal opportunities.

2. The second tendency is what used to be called black nationalism but is now fragmented into multiple varieties each with its own claim to ethnic particularity. It is now emphatically culturalist rather than political, each ethnic or national group arguing for cultural relativism in the strongest form. Very often, these mutually unintelligible and exclusive ethnic cultures just happen to be the same as the groups which common sense tells us are 'races'. Perversely and ironically, this tendency has happily co-existed with old style Labourism for which ethnic absolutism and cultural relativism have provided an obvious means to rationalise and balance its funding practices.

3. The third tendency is the most complex. It unendingly reiterates the idea that class is race, race is class and is both black and white. Its spokespeople have sought refuge from inter-ethnic conflict in some of the more anachronistic formulae of socialist class politics. For them class is the thing which will unify the diverse and end the polyphonic ethno-babble in the new municipal tower of babel. Class remains synonymous with organised labour regardless of the fact that in the context of

local authorities organised labour isn't always very radical. This tendency overlooks the role which the bureaucratic hierarchy plays in coercing the actually existing working class into anti-race line. So far its class-based line has been almost exclusively animated by a critique of race awareness training – a practical strategy which has been thrown up in the grating between the first two tendencies. This is an important issue but it is nonetheless the most gestural and superficial aspect of deeper problems namely, culturalism and ethnic absolutism. This tendency has mistaken the particular for the general – racism awareness training is a symptom, not a course in its own right.

Apart from their conceit, these diverse yet inter-dependent groupings share a statist conception of anti-racism. In making the local state the main vehicle for advancing anti-racist politics they have actively confused and confounded the black community's capacity for autonomous self-organisation. Here, we must make an assessment of the politics of funding community organisations and the dependency which that creates.

There is every likelihood that the versions of anti-racism I have criticised will wither away as the local state structures on which they have relied are destroyed by the conflict with central government. But anti-racist activities encapsulate one final problem which may outlive them. This is the disastrous way in which they have trivialised the rich complexity of black life by reducing it to nothing more than a response to racism. More than any other issue this operation reveals the extent of the anti-racists' conceptual trading with the racists and the results of embracing their culturalist assumptions. Seeing in black life nothing more than an answer to racism means moving on to the ideological circuit which makes us visible in two complementary roles – the problem and the victim.

Anti-racism seems very comfortable with this idea of blacks as victims. I remember one simplistic piece of GLC propaganda which said 'We are all either the victims or the perpetrators of racism'. Why should this be so? Suffering confers no virtue on the victim, yesterday's victims are tomorrow's executioners. I propose that we reject the central image of ourselves as victims and install instead an alternative conception which sees us as an active force working in many different ways for our freedom from racial subordination. The plural is important here for there can be no single or homogeneous strategy against racism because racism itself is never mogeneous. It varies, it changes and it is *always* uneven. The recent history of our struggles has shown how people can shrink the world to the size of their communities and act politically on that basis expressing their dissent in the symbolism of disorderly protest while demanding control over their immediate conditions. However you feel about the useless violence of these eruptions, it was the riotous protests of 1981 which created the space in which political anti-racism became an option.

We must accept that for the years immediately ahead, these struggles will be essentially defensive and probably unable to make the transition to more stable, totalising forms of politics. But the challenge we face is the task of linking these immediate local concerns together across the international division of labour, transcending national boundaries, turning our back on the state and using all the means at our disposal to build a radical, democratic movement of civil society. This kind of activity could be called the micro-politics of race though in practice, as where we align ourselves with the struggles of our brothers and sisters in South Africa, it is more likely to prove the micro-politics of race's overcoming.

Notes and references

An earlier version of this paper was given as the Runnymede Lecture in July 1987.

1. Fay Weldon, the muddle-headed spokeswoman for 'leftish humanist feminism' has not only announced that 'our attempt at multi-culturalism has failed' but has assumed a posture of absolute cultural superiority. See *Sacred Cows* (Chatto, 1989).

2. Robert Miles *Racism* (Routledge, 1989) is indicative of these difficulties. His undoubted intellectual rigour leads to a definition of racism exclusively in terms of ideology. The links between this and what he calls 'exclusionary practice' remain obscure. There is little comparable rigour in Miles's account of the problems which cluster around the Marxian notion of ideology which makes his definition plausible and attractive.

12 New Initiatives and the Possibilities of Reform

John Solomos and Wendy Ball

Introduction

As the various chapters in this volume have shown innovations in policy and practice were a recurrent feature of local authority practice in relation to racial equality during the 1980s. Such innovations were the product of both local and national political tendencies, and no doubt we shall see further changes during the 1990s. Certainly as we enter the 1990s there is every sign that the issue of race will in one way or another remain part of the local political agenda.

At the same time it is by no means clear that there will be a consensus about the best way in which local authorities can effectively intervene in this field. This is particularly the case because local government as a whole is clearly in a period of transition (for a variety of perspectives on the future of local government see Stewart and Stoker, 1989).

In this concluding chapter we want to address the question of prospects for the 1990s by examining the role and impact of some of the most radical initiatives aimed at promoting racial equality which emerged in the local political context during the 1980s. This will then allow us to reflect back on both the achievements and limitations of existing policy initiatives, and to look forward at alternative courses of action.

During the 1980s perhaps the most publicised innovations were the development of a number of new initiatives by radical left

Labour local authorities which were presented as an attempt to use
to the full the powers given to local authorities by Section 71 of the
1976 Race Relations Act and related legislation. The most
important of these initiatives were:

1. Positive action initiatives: which aim to remove discriminatory
   barriers to full equality of opportunity and to encourage
   minority group participation in education and the labour force
   by means of additional training or education.
2. Contract compliance programmes: which require companies
   that tender for contracts from local authorities that they
   undertake to adhere to an equal opportunity policy.
3. Training strategies: which are designed to increase awareness of
   processes of discrimination and to encourage the implementation of equality policies.

For the purposes of this concluding chapter we shall focus our
attention on these initiatives and their role and impact.

In one way or another these initiatives have attracted criticism
from New Right, liberal and even radical writers (Palmer, 1986;
Edwards, 1987). It has been argued, for example, that such
measures are not necessarily a means by which local authorities
can tackle racial inequalities more effectively. They have been
presented as a form of interference in the workings of the market
and as perhaps leading to forms of 'positive discrimination' against
the white majority. Before discussing these wider political
dimensions, however, it is necessary to look more deeply into the
origins and development of these initiatives.

Initiatives based on the principles of positive action and contract
compliance, as Herman Ouseley makes clear in an earlier chapter,
originated in the political and ideological climate of the early 1980s.
They were perceived by a number of radical local authorities as an
effort to go beyond the limits of existing racial equality and equal
opportunity policies. Amongst the main innovators in this field
were the now abolished Greater London Council and Inner London
Education Authority, Lambeth, Hackney and Brent.

This chapter looks critically at the history and impact during the
1980s of these three sets of initiatives. The central questions we shall
ask are: What impact have they had on practices within local
authorities? How have they influenced the agenda of racial equality
policies? How can effective measures be taken by local authorities to
promote racial equality in their employment and service functions?

By exploring the role of these initiatives in detail this chapter will link up with the discussion in Ouseley's chapter about the limits faced in the implementation of race equality initiatives within specific institutional contexts. We shall look at the development and impact of these initiatives and explore the controversies which have arisen in those local authorities that have sought to use them as part of their race equality strategies.

Equal opportunity or positive action?

In common sense usage the notion of positive action has come to be associated with giving preferential treatment to black and ethnic minority groups, or with the imposition of quotas and 'positive discrimination' (*Equal Opportunities Review*, 10, 1986: pp. 6–10; Institute of Personnel Management, 1987). This perhaps explains why over the past decade it has been the subject of an intense debate and attracted regular media attention. Such conflict is perhaps not surprising. Terms such as equal opportunity, racial equality and related notions are essentially contested. Although they have gained wide currency over the past decade, there is still much confusion about what each of them means, and perhaps more fundamentally, about what kind of objectives they are supposed to fulfil (Young, this volume). Even within the confines of this collection it should be clear that researchers and practitioners do not concur on what they mean by such terms as equality of opportunity and racial equality, or what they consider as evidence of a move towards the stated goals of policies. Some writers see the development of equal opportunity policies as the outcome of a process of political negotiation, pressure group politics and bureaucratic policy making (Ben-Tovim *et al.* 1986; Young and Connelly, 1981). Others have, however, emphasised the need to look beyond the stated objectives and public political negotiations and explore the ways in which deeply entrenched processes of discrimination may be resistant to legal and political interventions while inegalitarian social relations structure society as a whole (Solomos, 1989; Smith, 1989). From this perspective promises of equal opportunity can easily become largely symbolic political actions which can do little to bring about real changes in discriminatory processes.

In Britain, unlike the United States, there is no intellectual and political tradition which gives support to the view that 'affirmative action' is a legitimate policy tool in attempts to tackle the effects of past and present racial and other social inequalities. Rather the basis of successive policies on racial inequality since the 1960s have been held together by the notion that the main objective of state intervention in this field is (a) to secure free competition between individuals and (b) to eliminate barriers created by racial discrimination. These objectives have been pursued through the twin mechanisms of legislation aimed at outlawing discrimination and administrative intervention by quasi-governmental bodies such as the Commission for Racial Equality. Yet, a wealth of official reports and academic research findings have shown that in practice the impact of public policy in this field has been limited even within the limits of this narrow definition of equal opportunity. Recent research on employment, for example, indicates that equal opportunity policies have had little effect on levels of discrimination in employment, though they have reduced its more direct forms. Similar arguments have been made about the impact of equal opportunity policies in the areas of housing and education (Brown and Gay, 1985; Jenkins and Solomos, 1987).

It is against this background of disappointment about the achievements of past policies that in the past few years we have seen a growing interest in the use of positive action measures as a way of improving the likelihood of race equality policies bringing about effective changes in the employment and service delivery practices of local authorities. In practice positive action as it has been practiced in Britain during the 1980s consisted mainly of the following two kinds of measures:

(*i*) efforts to remove discriminatory barriers to full equality of opportunity, such as rethinking job qualification requirements, placing job advertisements in the ethnic minority press;

(*ii*) attempts to facilitate and encourage minority group participation in education and the labour force by means of additional education and training, the use of Section 11 of the 1966 Local Government Act to create new posts and related actions.

The general principle behind such measures is that action should be taken to overcome the effects of past discrimination in order to allow certain sections of the community to 'catch up' with the experience of other employees or applicants, and to remove those barriers which have the effect of excluding some people from employment opportunities (*Equal Opportunities Review*, 14, 1987: pp. 13–18). Part of the rationale of positive action is thus the argument that even if racial discrimination could be removed overnight, employment opportunities would not be immediately equally available to all members of the community. Further steps are needed to make up for past disadvantage and discrimination experienced by minority groups. It is thus not meant to be a means of providing direct benefits to minority groups, but an opportunity to encourage the promotion of equal opportunity in a more effective manner. The Commission for Racial Equality definition of positive action is clear on this point:

> Positive action is a series of measures by which people from particular racial groups are either encouraged to apply for jobs in which they have been under-represented or given training to help them develop their potential and so improve their chances in competing for particular work. The element of competition remains paramount. The Act does not provide for people to be taken on because they have a particular racial origin, except in very limited circumstances where racial group is a genuine occupational qualification (CRE, 1985: p. iv).

It is within these limits that authorities such as Hackney, Lambeth, ILEA and others have attempted to develop positive action initiatives. As yet, and this is a point discussed in a number of the chapters in this volume, it is not clear how effective such initiatives have been. There is some preliminary evidence that some limited success has been achieved in relation to some of the broad objectives which guided the initiatives, particularly in relation to the development of training and the reform of recruitment procedures.

But what is also clear is that within the limits imposed by the 1976 Race Relations Act and the present political climate those local authorities that want to develop positive action strategies are forced to work within very narrow limits. These limits do allow for some radical initiatives to be taken, but those authorities that have attempted to go down this path have found themselves criticised for going too far in the direction of 'positive discrimination'. This can be illustrated more clearly if we look at the experience of perhaps the most radical form of positive action attempted so far, namely contract compliance.

Contract compliance

Contract compliance as a strategy adopted by local authorities attempting to develop positive action programmes to promote racial equality is largely the product of developments during the 1980s, though it has a longer history in the United States and in the context of Northern Ireland. Its main advocate during the early 1980s was the Greater London Council and the Inner London Education Authority, although the idea was also taken up by other left wing local authorities in London and elsewhere (Hall, 1986; Carr, 1987; IPM, 1987). It attracted much attention in the early 1980s, and a number of local authorities saw it as a way in which effective reforms in this field could be institutionalised.

The first major initiative came in 1983, when the GLC/ILEA amended their Code of Practice on Tenders and Contracts to include an equal opportunities clause. This required companies that tendered for contracts from the authority to undertake to adhere to an equal opportunity policy and to develop strategies for implementing these policies. To implement this initiative the GLC/ILEA set up the Contract Compliance Equal Opportunities Unit to ensure that companies with which it was trading understood the equal opportunity policy and were prepared to put them into practice. Those companies that failed to comply with an equal opportunity policy were threatened with the sanction that they would be removed from the Council's list of approved contractors. Similar initiatives were made at around this time by a number of other local authorities.

Another more recent form of contract compliance is the idea of 'local labour contracts', which would require that companies in receipt of government grants to carry out capital works in inner city areas should undertake to employ mainly or only labour from the local area, thus ensuring that some inner city residents at least would benefit. Such initiatives have been developed in areas such as Birmingham and London in the aftermath of the urban unrest of 1981 and 1985. The unrest was seen as partly related to the employment situation in inner city areas and 'local labour contracts' were seen as one kind of positive action that could help to remedy the situation (CRE, 1987b).

From an early stage contract compliance initiatives such as this proved to be controversial with some major employers and with the

Thatcher Government. Additionally, they became a subject of controversy in the popular media and attracted negative publicity regularly. One famous example of this occurred in 1985 with the news that the GLC/ILEA had decided to ban Kit Kat bars from its schools. This was on the grounds that Kit Kat's manufacturers, Rowntree Mackintosh, refused to supply information about how it complied with the Sex Discrimination and Race Relations Acts *(Equal Opportunities Review*, 8, 1986: pp. 9–15). This case, along with some others, helped to politicise the issue of contract compliance and link it to the broader moral panic about the role of the 'loony left' in local government.

At the same time the Government itself was attacking the use of contract compliance as yet another example of the work of 'loony left' local authorities, and as an attack on the workings of the market. Nicholas Ridley, then Minister for the Environment, expressed this view directly when he argued in October 1986 that:

> Conditions in contracts which have nothing to do with the contractor's ability to carry out work or supply goods ignore a local authority's duty to its rate-payers to obtain value for money, and are merely an attempt by some councils to impose their own social policies on firms who wish to carry out business with them. Such actions have no place in the contractual processes of local government, and early steps will be taken to stamp them out (*DoE Press Notice*, 21 October 1986).

This criticism of the role of contract compliance initiatives was maintained even after the abolition of the GLC, and the fact that only a small number of radical authorities were interested in implementing meaningful contract compliance programmes. Part of the reason for this may have been that contract compliance fell outside of the Government's avowed programme of rolling back the boundaries of the state and increasing the role of market forces. Perhaps the main reason, however, was the official concern with the actions of radical left local authorities in the field of race relations.

After the stormy debate during the early 1980s about contract compliance it came as no surprise when the 1988 Local Government Act sought to effectively prohibit contract compliance as it has been practiced by some of the more radical local authorities. The Act prevents local authorities and other specified public bodies from taking account of 'non-commercial' matters in drawing up approved lists of contractors, inviting tenders and making or terminating contracts (*Equal Opportunities Review*, 18, 1988: p. 31). However, during the passage of the Bill through Parliament, the legislation was amended to permit local authorities to operate a limited and defined form of contract vetting so as to carry out their duties under Section 71 of the 1976 Race Relations Act as long as they did not take into account 'non-commercial' criteria (*Equal Opportunities Review*, 19, 1988: pp. 24–7; *Equal Opportunities Review*, 24, 1989: pp. 26–31).

It is too early to assess how this arrangement will work out in practice, though it will clearly reduce local authorities' room for manoeuvre in developing an active policy stance on contract compliance in relation to racial equality. This seems to fit in with the Government's concern to make sure that local authorities do not get involved in implementing controversial social policies on issues such as race. But it is already clear that the Commission for Racial Equality and some of the radical local authorities are attempting to see how to continue a weak form of contract compliance even under the terms laid out by the 1988 Local Government Act (*Equal Opportunities Review*, 28, 1989: pp. 32–5). What this will achieve remains to be seen, but the signs are not at all promising.

Training and racial equality

Race related training has grown at a fast rate during the 1980s, particularly in the aftermath of the growth of local race equality policies. Whether under the rubric of 'race awareness training' or of 'equal opportunity training' local authorities, employers and other agencies have introduced courses on race issues as part of their training activities (*Equal Opportunities Review*, 3, 1985: pp. 8–14 and 18, 1988: pp. 34–5). Such courses have been around for some time in the United States, but in the British context they are basically a phenomenon of the 1980s. They have been conceived as a means of informing decision makers, employers, employees and other important actors of (a) the problems facing black and ethnic minority communities and (b) challenging individual prejudices and values.

Within local authorities such courses have generally been introduced only in the past decade in most cases, but they have already led to much public and media controversy about both the content and use of such courses (Gurnah, 1984; Sivanandan, 1985). Perhaps the most controversial form of race related training during the 1980s has been what is commonly referred to as 'race awareness training' (RAT).

Such training programmes take a number of forms but they generally start from the basic assumption that an essential part of policies in this field should be training courses that aim to challenge and change racist attitudes. Following from the work of Judy Katz (1978) which argued that the root cause of racism was the inherent prejudice of white people, combined with power, the proponents of race awareness training have argued that the development of initiatives to deal with racism needs:

(i) to challenge the individual prejudice on which racism is based;
(ii) to develop in the people who take part in such courses attitudes which challenge their racism.

The proponents of such training programmes argue that by challenging racial prejudice they could help to change the institutional practices that discriminated against black and ethnic minority communities. It was perhaps this claim, along with the promise of quick results, that helped to push many local authorities along the road of introducing such courses in the early 1980s.

Yet what became clear from the earliest stages of the introduction of race awareness training was that the claims on which it was based were by no means universally accepted. Indeed opposition to race awareness courses came from a broad spectrum of political opinion, ranging from avowedly anti-racist groups and individuals to the spokespersons of the New Right (Sivanandan, 1985; Palmer, 1986; Gilroy, 1987 and chapter in this volume).

Criticisms from anti-racists centred particularly on the assumed link between changes in attitudes and changes in practice, the 'guilt complex' on which the courses relied and the determinism of seeing all white people as inherently racist. Sivanandan's critique of race awareness training argues, for example, that its proponents ignore the role of socio-economic, cultural and historical factors, and therefore construct a deterministic view of racism as an individual problem. He argues:

Racism, according to RAT, has its roots in white culture, and white culture, unaffected by material conditions goes back to the beginning of time. Hence, racism is part of the collective unconscious, the pre-natal scream, original sin . . . It is a circular argument, bordering on the genetic, on biological determinism: racism, in sum, is culture and culture is white and white is racist (Sivanandan, 1985: p. 29).

For Sivanandan, and other critics, such an analysis of racism is at best superficial and at worst counter-productive, since it ignores the material social and political conditions which help to reproduce discrimination and racialist ideas.

For the New Right the imposition of RAT courses, along with broader anti-racist initiatives, is seen as yet another example of attempts by left-wing local authorities to restrict the freedom of the individual to express certain opinions and to impose multi-cultural values as against traditional 'British' values (Palmer, 1986; Honeyford, 1988b). Along with sections of the popular media they have attempted, with some popular success, to portray the role of RAT courses as akin to a form of 'race brainwashing'. Over the past few years the actions of numerous local authorities, ranging from Lambeth, Haringey, Brent, Birmingham to Bradford, have attracted critical comment from sections of the press and from New Right commentators.

Part of the problem is that although in the early 1980s numerous local authorities, along with the police and other bodies, went down the path of including forms of racism awareness training as part of their policies on race there is surprisingly little information about the actual impact of these courses on the implementation of equal opportunity policies. Much attention has been given to the publicity which RAT courses have received but we still know relatively little about how such courses have affected employment and service delivery practices. This lack of concrete evidence about their effectiveness has in turn contributed to the controversy which surrounds race training courses.

Some local authorities have attempted to respond to criticisms of race awareness training and related courses by locating race-related training within a broader strategy for achieving organisational change. According to Valerie Amos, who was involved in the development of this approach in the London Borough of Hackney, the objective of race related training in this context is to make clear to staff the objectives of the equal opportunity policies and to allow them to gain the skills necessary for implementing them. While she rejects the idea that training on its own can be effective as a means of bringing about organisational change, she argues that it can play a role in developing the right conditions for the implementation of equal opportunity policies (CRE, 1987a; *Equal Opportunities Review*, 20, 1988: pp. 26–7).

The future of race-related training is still a matter of debate and controversy within local authorities. It remains an issue which attracts regular attention from the media. But what already seems clear is that the controversy that has surrounded the development of RAT courses has forced local authorities to rethink the kind of race related training that they provide.

Racial equality and recent local government legislation

The only major initiative undertaken to promote equal opportunity by the Thatcher administrations is the 1989 Fair Employment (Northern Ireland) Act, which deals as Herman Ouseley eloquently reminds us not with racial discrimination but with the question of discrimination against Roman Catholics in Northern Ireland (McCrudden, 1988; *Equal Opportunities Review*, 27, 1989: pp. 27–9). In fact it is clear that this piece of legislation actually goes against the thrust of Government legislation in relation to racial discrimination on the mainland, by allowing in Northern Ireland forms of positive action and contract compliance which have been severely restricted in the rest of the United Kingdom by recent legislation.

Far from encouraging new initiatives to tackle racial discrimination legislation on local government by the Thatcher administrations during the 1980s has been based on the principles that there will in future be a considerable reduction in (a) the role of local authorities as direct service providers in education, housing and related fields, and (b) in the ability of local authorities to develop alternative policies and practices to those that are part of the national political agenda. Within this broad ideological framework the pursuit of egalitarian social objectives does not even make first base on the Government's political agenda.

The Government has, for example, set itself apart from local authorities in the development of inner city policy and local economic regeneration. This was a key theme in the aftermath of the 1987 General Election when Mrs Thatcher undertook a short tour through Britain's inner cities, with the aim of declaring her Government's commitment to regenerating these areas (Robson, 1989). As we enter the 1990s and the lead up to the next General Election such symbolic initiatives about 'those inner cities' are likely to become part of the war of words between Conservative and Labour politicians.

Despite such symbolic gestures, however, it is now almost a decade since Lord Scarman called for urgent action to tackle racial discrimination and the social conditions which underlay the disorders in Brixton and elsewhere, and during that period there has been little evidence of positive changes for the populations of those areas. Whatever the merit of the particular programme proposed by Lord Scarman, and this has been the subject of some debate, the one consistent response that has been evident since 1981 has had little to do with the pursuit of social justice: rather than dealing with the root causes of racial disadvantage and urban unrest the government has chosen to give more resources, more training and more equipment to the police in order to control the symptoms of urban unrest. The Government's overall objective has been to decrease public expenditure, for the sake of lower taxation and to encourage an 'enterprise culture' in the inner cities (see the various papers in Stewart and Stoker, 1989). In this context aid for the inner cities has been dwarfed by the financial cuts applied to inner city local authorities.

The present political climate gives one little cause for optimism that a radical change in governmental priorities in this field is likely. During both the 1981 and 1985 outbreaks of urban unrest central government promised to help those inner city areas particularly hard hit by economic restructuring and urban decay. The impact of such promises in practice has, however, been limited and their role in promoting equal opportunity has been minimal to say the least (Benyon and Solomos, 1987; Robson, 1988).

Conclusion

Two general conclusions can be derived from the account of the fate of positive action, contract compliance and training programmes over the past decade. First, it seems to indicate that it is inherently difficult for local authorities to institute radical changes in a context in which central government is unsympathetic to the pursuit of racial equality. Second, it is important to be aware that the development of radical initiatives in this field is likely to lead to opposition and resistance, and to develop strategies that can help overcome resistance.

This argument links up with the theme which Herman Ouseley argues forcefully in his chapter, namely that the failure to implement radical race equality policies at the local level during the 1980s was the result of inadequate attempts by national and local politicians to tackle the problems of institutional resistance and bureaucratic inertia within local authorities. He also cites the negative attitude of central government to attempts to develop positive action and contract compliance initiatives as a major factor in limiting the impact of local authority initiatives.

Indeed one of the central themes that recurs throughout this volume is the question of what conditions inhibit or encourage the development of effective programmes to tackle racial inequality in the local political context. At both the local and national policy levels the experience of the past decade has shown that the pursuit of racial equality in societies such as Britain is an inherently contradictory process. The translation of policies into practice has been hampered by a weak legal framework, organisational marginality and a lack of political legitimacy. This lack of political legitimacy has become increasingly evident during the past decade in relation to the actions of local authorities.

Within the present political climate there is little cause for optimism that local government can become a channel for radical measures to tackle the roots of racial inequality. Under a different political and legislative context it may be possible to use initiatives based on the principles of positive action and contract compliance to initiate radical change in this field. But recent legislation on various aspects of local government has constrained local authorities to such an extent that it is impossible to be optimistic about the role of such initiatives at the present time. Changes in the role of local government envisaged by the present Thatcher Government may constrain local authorities further in the next decade.

Whatever the actions of local authorities at the level of national politics it is clear that the concern with promoting a greater role for the market fits uneasily with the pursuit of equity for racial minorities through administrative and judicial channels. It is perhaps for this reason that the Thatcher Governments have sought to rein in the more radical authorities and circumscribe their ability to act independently in this area. In this context the ability of local authorities to develop radical initiatives to promote racial equality is becoming increasingly constrained. The need for radical reforms is clear, but the eventual outcome of current debates will depend on political struggles and actions to reshape the local and national political agendas. The lessons learned from the 1980s may help to bring about a more positive political environment during the 1990s.

But there is no necessary guarantee that this will happen. Even as we write the debate in the media and in Parliament about the possible arrival during the 1990s of a sizeable number of Chinese migrants from Hong Kong has evoked images from earlier debates about immigration, and both Conservative and Labour politicians have seen the electoral value of taking a hard or at least ambiguous line on immigration. In one of the most controversial interventions in the debate about Hong Kong Norman Tebbit went as far as to claim 'most people in Britain did not want to live in a multi-cultural, multi-racial society, but it has been foisted on them' *(Evening Standard*, 21 December 1989). Additionally he reiterated his agreement with Mrs Thatcher's warning in 1978 that white British people were fearful of being 'swamped' by migrant communities from different cultures and values. In the context of the debate about Hong Kong the Labour Party has also been keen to show that they are not a party which favoured immigration, no doubt with one eye on the next General Election (*The Guardian*, 21 and 22 December 1989) So the question of immigration and 'race' remains a live and controversial issue in party politics and may become even more so as the next General Election moves closer.

Given this broader political context the pursuit of racial equality, whether through local or national initiatives, is likely to remain on the back burner politically. There may even be pressure to reduce the role of local authorities in this field even further. As long as the realities of racial injustice remain, however, there will remain a need to examine how local political initiatives can help to overcome racism. As we enter the 1990s the need for radical thinking and action on these issues remains as clear as ever. We hope that the various chapters in this volume have contributed to this.

Bibliography

AIMS OF INDUSTRY (1984), *How to Get Money from the GLC and other Left-wing Authorities*, London: Aims of Industry.

ALIBHAI, Y. (1988), 'The reality of race training', *New Society*, 29 January, 17–19.

ASSOCIATION OF DIRECTORS OF SOCIAL SERVICES AND COMMISSION FOR RACIAL EQUALITY (1978), *Multi-Racial Britain: the Social Services Response*, London: CRE.

BALL, W. and TROYNA, B. (1989), 'The dawn of a new ERA? The Education Reform Act, "race" and LEAs', *Educational Management and Administration*, 17, 1: pp. 23–31.

BANTON, M. (1983), 'Categorical and statistical discrimination', *Ethnic and Racial Studies*, 6, 3: pp. 269–83.

— (1985), *Promoting Racial Harmony*, Cambridge: Cambridge University Press.

— (1989), 'Minority Rights and Individual Rights', paper presented to CRE–PSI Seminar on Freedom of Speech, 28 September 1989.

BARTHES, R. (1967), *The Fashion System*, New York: Hill and Wang.

BEETHAM, D. (1970), *Transport and Turbans*, London: Oxford University Press.

BENFIELD, C. (1986), 'Get Stringer', *The Guardian*, 29 November: p. 23

BEN-TOVIM, G., GABRIEL, J., LAW, I., and STREDDER, K. (1986), *The Local Politics of Race*, London: Macmillan.

BENYON, J. and SOLOMOS, J. (eds) (1987), *The Roots of Urban Unrest*, Oxford: Pergamon Press.

BHAT, A., CARR-HILL, R., and OHRI, S. (eds) (1988), *Britain's Black Population*, Aldershot: Gower.

BLACK HOUSING, Volumes 1 to V, 1985–89.
BOX, S. (1981), *Deviance, Reality and Society*, London: Holt, Reinhart and Winston.
BRIDGES, L. (1983), 'Policing the urban wasteland', *Race and Class*, XXV, 2: pp. 31–47.
BRIDGES, L. and GILROY, P. (1982), 'Striking back: race and crime', *Marxism Today*, June: pp. 34–35.
BROGDEN, M. (1988) , *Introducing Policework*, London: Allen and Unwin.
BROOKS, D. (1975), *Race and Labour in London Transport*, Oxford: Oxford University Press.
BROWN, C. (1984), *Black and White Britain*, London: Heinemann.
BULLIVANT, B. (1981), *The Pluralist Dilemma in Education*, Sydney: Allen and Unwin.
CAMPBELL, J., LITTLE, V. and TOMLINSON, J. (1987), 'Multiplying the divisions? Intimations of educational policy post-1987', *Journal of Education Policy*, 2, 4: pp. 369–378.
CARR, J. (1987), *New Roads to Equality: Contract Compliance for the UK?*, Fabian Tract 517, London: Fabian Society.
CHEETHAM, J. (1981), *Social Work Services for Ethnic Minorities in Britain and the USA*, University of Oxford, Department of Social and Administrative Studies.
COMMISSION FOR RACIAL EQUALITY (1984), *Race and Council Housing in Hackney: report of the formal investigation*, London: CRE.
— (1985) *Positive Action and Equal Opportunity in Employment*, London: CRE.
— (1987a) *Training: The implementation of equal opportunities at work*, London: CRE.
— (1987b) *Principles of practice for contract compliance*, London: CRE.
COMMUNITY RELATIONS COMMISSION (1975), *Participation of Ethnic Minorities in the General Election, October 1974*, London: CRC.
COYLE, A. (1989), 'The limits of change: local government and equal opportunities for women', *Public Administration*, 67, 1: pp. 39–50
CROSS, M. (1982), 'The manufacture of marginality', in Cashmore, E. and Troyna, B. (eds) *Black Youth in Crisis*, London: Allen and Unwin.

CROSS, M. ,JOHNSON M. and COX, B. (1988), *Black Welfare and Local Government: Section 11 and Social Services Departments*, Policy Papers in Ethnic Relations No 12, Centre for Research in Ethnic Relations, University of Warwick.

DALE, R. (1988), 'Implications for progressivism of recent changes in the control and direction of education policy', in Green, A. G. and Ball, S. J. (eds) *Progress and Inequality in Comprehensive Education*, London: Routledge.

DANIEL, W. (1968) *Racial Discrimination in England*, Harmondsworth: Penguin.

DAVID, T. (1988), 'The funding of education', in Morris, M. and Griggs, C. (eds) *Education – The Wasted Years? 1973–1986*, Lewes: Falmer Press.

DEAKIN, N. (1972), 'The Immigration Issue in British Politics', Unpublished PhD thesis, University of Sussex.

DEPARTMENT OF EDUCATION AND SCIENCE (1985), *Education for All, Committee of Inquiry into the Education of Children from Ethnic Minority Groups*, Cmnd. 9453, London: HMSO.

DEPARTMENT OF THE ENVIRONMENT (1987), *Housing: The Government's Proposals*, London: HMSO.

— (1989) *Tackling Racial Violence and Harassment in Local Authority Housing: A Guide to Good Practice for Local Authorities*, London: Department of the Environment.

DEPARTMENT OF HEALTH (1989), *Working for Patients*, London: HMSO.

DORN, A. (1983) 'LEA policies on multiracial education', *Multi-Ethnic Education Review*, 2, 2: pp. 3–5.

— (1985), 'Education and the Race Relations Act', in Arnot, M. (ed) *Race and Gender: Equal Opportunities Policies in Education*, Oxford: Pergamon Press.

DORN, A. and HIBBERT, P. (1987), 'A Comedy of errors: Section 11 funding and education', in Troyna, B. (ed) *Racial Inequality in Education*, London: Tavistock.

DORN, A. and TROYNA, B. (1982), 'Multicultural education and the politics of decisionmaking', *Oxford Review of Education*, 8, 2: pp. 275–85.

DOWNES, D. (1983), *Law and Order: theft of an issue*, London: Fabian Society.

EDWARDS, J. (1987), *Positive Discrimination, Social Justice and Social Policy*, London: Tavistock.

EDWARDS, J. and BATLEY, R. (1978), *The Politics of Positive Discrimination*, London: Tavistock.

EMPLOYMENT GAZETTE (1988), 'Ethnic minorities in the labour market', *Employment Gazette*, December: pp. 633–646.

EQUAL OPPORTUNITIES REVIEW, Numbers 1–27, 1985–89.

FIELD, S. (1987), 'The changing nature of racial disadvantage', *New Community*, XIV, 1/2: pp. 119–122.

FITZGERALD, M. (1987a), 'Immigration and race relations: political aspects', *New Community*, XIII, 3: pp. 442–9.

— (1987b), *Black People and Party Politics in Britain*, London: Runnymede Trust.

— (1988), 'Different roads? The development of Afro-Caribbean and Asian political organisation in London', *New Community*, XIV, 3: pp. 385–96.

— (1989), 'Legal approaches to racial harassment in council housing: the case for reassessment', *New Community*, 16, 1: pp. 93–105.

FLEW, A. (1984), *Education, Race and Revolution*, London: Centre for Policy Studies.

FULTON, O. (1987), 'Categorical funding and its limitations: the experience of TVEI', in THOMAS, H. and SIMKINS, T. (eds) *Economics and the Management of Education: Emerging Themes*, Lewes: Falmer Press.

GAY, P. and YOUNG, K. (1988), *Community Relations Councils: Roles and Objectives*, London: CRE.

GIFFORD, Lord., Chairman, (1986), *The Broadwater Farm Inquiry*, London: Karia Press.

GIFFORD, Lord, BROWN, W. and BUNDEY, R. (1989), *Loosen the Shackles: First Report of the Liverpool 8 Inquiry Into Race Relations in Liverpool*, London: Karia Press.

GILROY, P. (1981–2), 'You can't fool the youths: race and class formation in the 1980s', *Race and Class*, XXIII, 2/3: pp. 112–120.

— (1982a), 'Police and thieves', in CCCS Race and Politics Group, *The Empire Strikes Back*, London: Hutchinson.

— (1982b), 'The myth of black criminality', *Socialist Register 1982*, London: Merlin.

— (1987), *There ain't no black in the union jack*, London: Hutchinson.

GILROY, P. and SIM, J. (1985), 'Law, order and the state of the left', *Capital and Class*, 25: pp. 15–21.,

GORDON, P. and KLUG, F. (1986), *New Right/New Racism*, London: Searchlight.

GORDON, P. and ROSENBERG, D. (1989), *Daily Racism: the press and black people in Britain*, London: Runnymede Trust.

GRIFFITHS, Sir Roy, (1988), *Community Care: Agenda for Action. A Report to the Secretary of State for Social Services*, London: HMSO.

GULAM, W. (1988), 'LEA policy and implementation in race related matters', in Allen, S. and Macey, M. (eds) *Race and Social Policy*, London: ESRC.

GURNAH, A. (1984), 'The politics of Racism Awareness Training', *Critical Social Policy*, 11: pp. 6–20.

GUTZMORE, C. (1983), 'Capital, 'black youth' and crime', *Race and Class*, XXV, 2: pp. 13–21.

HACKNEY, LONDON BOROUGH OF (1981), 'Review of Hackney Council for Racial Equality', Policy Committee, 1 July.

— (1988a), 'Commission for Racial Equality Investigation', Housing Services Committee, 17 January.

— (1988b), 'Housing Race Relations Sub-Committee', 11 July.

HACKNEY GAZETTE (1983), 'Black crime victims survey is rejected', *Hackney Gazette*, 20 May.

HALL, S., CRITCHER, C., JEFFERSON, T., CLARKE, J., and ROBERTS., B. (1978), *Policing the crisis: mugging, the state, and law and order*, London: Macmillan.

HALL, W. (1986) 'Contracts compliance at the GLC', *Local Government Studies*, 12, 4: pp. 17–24.

HALSTEAD, M. (1988), *Education, Justice and Cultural Diversity: An Examination of the Honeyford Affair*, London: Falmer Press.

HAMNETT, C. and RANDOLPH, B. (1988), 'Ethnic minorities in the London labour market: a longitudinal analysis, 1971–81', *New Community*, XIV, 3: pp. 333–46.

HARINGEY, LONDON BOROUGH OF (1985), 'Haringey's Minority Ethnic Communities: Equal Opportunities in Housing', by Tim Davis, Consultation Paper No. 10.

HARLAND, J. (1987), 'The new inset: a transformation scene', *Journal of Education Policy*, 2, 3: pp. 235–244.

HATCHER, R. (1987), 'Education for racial equality under attack', *Multicultural Teaching*, 5, 3: pp. 4–7.

— (1989), 'Antiracist education after the act', *Multicultural Teaching*, 7, 3: pp. 24–27.

HENDERSON, J. and KARN, V. (1987), *Race, Class and State Housing: Inequality and the Allocation of Public Housing in Britain*, Aldershot: Gower.

HILL, M. and ISSACHAROFF, R. (1971), *Community Action and Race Relations*, London: Oxford University Press.

HILLGATE GROUP (1986), *Whose Schools?: a radical manifesto*, London: Hillgate Group.

HOGWOOD, B. W. and GUNN, L. A. (1984), *Policy Analysis for the Real World*, Oxford: Oxford University Press.

HOLDAWAY, S. (1987), 'Themes and issues in police/race relations policy', *New Community*, XIV, 1/2: pp. 142–150.

HOME AFFAIRS COMMITTEE, Sub-Committee on Race Relations and Immigration (1981), *Racial Disadvantage*, London: HMSO.

HOME OFFICE (1988), *Probation Service Policies on Race*, Home Office Circular 75/88.

HONEYFORD, R. (1983), 'Multi-ethnic intolerance', *Salisbury Review*, 4: pp. 12–13.

— (1984), 'Education and race: an alternative view', *Salisbury Review*, 6: pp. 30–2.

— (1988a), *Multi-Ethnic Education: the Burnage High School Lesson*, York: Campaign for Real Education.

— (1988b), *Integration or Disintegration*, London: Claridge Press.

INSTITUTE OF PERSONNEL MANAGERS (1978), *Towards Fairer Selection*, London: IPM.

— (1987), *Contract Compliance: The UK Experience*, London: IPM.

ISLINGTON, LONDON BOROUGH OF (1977) 'Allocation of Islington Housing to Ethnic Minorities', Directorate of Housing, Research Report 12.

— (1983), 'LBI Crime Watch', Police Sub-Committee, 22 September.

— (1984), 'Crime Prevention – A Multi Agency Approach', Police Sub-Committee, 15 March.

JENKINS, R. (1982), *Managers, Recruitment Procedures and Black Workers*, Working Paper No 18, Centre for Research in Ethnic Relations, University of Warwick.

— (1986) *Racism and Recruitment*, Cambridge: Cambridge University Press.

JENKINS, R. and PARKER, G. (1987), 'Organisational politics and the recruitment of black workers', in Lee, G. and Loveridge, R. (eds) *The Manufacture of Disadvantage: Stigma and Social Closure*, Milton Keynes: Open University Press.

JEWSON, N. and MASON, D. (1984–5), 'Equal opportunities at the workplace and the concept of monitoring', *New Community*, XII, 1: pp. 124–36.

— (1986a), 'Modes of discrimination in the recruitment process: formalisation, fairness and efficiency' *Sociology*, 20, 1: pp. 43–63.

— (1986b), 'The theory and practice of equal opportunities policies: liberal and radical approaches', *Sociological Review*, 34, 2: pp. 307–334.

— (1987), 'Monitoring equal opportunities policies: principles and practice;, in Jenkins, R. and Solomos, J. (eds) *Racism and Equal Opportunities in the 1980s*, Cambridge: Cambridge University Press.

— (forthcoming), *Ethnic Minorities and Employment Practice: The Experience of Six Organisations*, Department of Employment, Research Paper.

JOHNSON, M., COX, B. and CROSS, M. (1989), 'Paying for change? Section 11 and local authority social services', *New Community*, 15, 3: pp. 371–90.

JOHNSON, R. (1989), 'Thatcherism and English education: breaking the mould or confirming the pattern?', *History of Education*, 18, 2: pp. 91–121.

JOHNSON, T. (1972), *Professions and Power*, London: Macmillan.

JONES, T. (1985), 'A crisis in policing', *New Life*, 28 June.

— (1988), 'Crime Prevention and Local Authorities: Islington Council – A Case Study', Paper to the TVS/British Telecom Conference on 'Combatting Vandalism to Public Services', London, 28 June.

JONES, T., McLean, B. and YOUNG, J. (1986), *The Islington Crime Survey: crime, victimisation and policing in inner-city London*, Aldershot: Gower.

KATZ, J. (1978), *White Awareness*, Norman: University of Oklahoma Press.

KATZNELSON, I. (1976), *Black Men, White Cities*, Chicago: University of Chicago Press.

KEITH, M. (1987), 'Something Happened: The problems of explaining the 1980 and 1981 riots in British cities', in Jackson, P. ed. *Race and Racism*, London: Allen and Unwin
(forthcoming) *Lore and disorder : Policing a multi-racist society in the 1980s*

KINSEY, R., LEA, J and YOUNG, J. (1986), *Losing the Fight Against Crime*, Oxford: Blackwell.

KIRP, D. (1979), *Doing Good by Doing Little*, Berkeley: University of California Press.

KNIGHT, B. (1987), 'Managing the honeypots' in Thomas, H. and Simkins, T. (eds) *Economics and the Management of Education: Emerging Themes*, Lewes: Falmer Press.

LARKIN, G. (1983), *Occupational Monopoly and Modern Medicine*, London: Tavistock.

LANSLEY, S., GOSS, S. and WOLMAR, C. (1989), *Councils in Conflict: The Rise and Fall of the Municipal Left*, Basingstoke: Macmillan.

LAWRENCE, D. (1974), *Black Migrants, White Natives*, Cambridge: Cambridge University Press.

LEA, J. (1986), 'Police racism : some theories and their policy implications', in Matthews, R. and Young, J. (eds) *Confronting Crime*, London: Sage.

— (1987), 'Left realism: a defence', *Contemporary Crises*, 11: pp. 357–370.

LEA, J. and YOUNG, J. (1982a), 'Riots in Britain' in Cowell D., Jones, T., and Young, J. (eds) *Policing the Riots*, London: Junction Books.

— (1982b), 'A missed opportunity', *New Socialist*, Jan/Feb, p. 42.

— (1984), *What is to be Done About Law & Order*, Harmondsworth: Penguin.

LEA, J., JONES, T., and YOUNG, J. (1986), *Saving the Inner City. Broadwater Farm: A Strategy for Survival*, London: Middlesex Polytechnic,

LEA, J., MATTHEWS, R., and YOUNG, J. (1987), *Law and Order: Five Years On*, Middlesex Polytechnic: Centre for Criminology.

LEWIS, R. (1988), *Anti-Racism: A Mania Exposed*, London: Quartet.

LEWISHAM, LONDON BOROUGH OF (1980), 'Black People and Housing in Lewisham', Report to Housing Committee.

MACDONALD, I., BHAVNANI, R., KHAN, L. and JOHN G. (1989), *Murder in the playground: the report of the Macdonald Inquiry into racism and racial violence in Manchester schools*, London: Longsight Press.

MACFARLANE, A. (1978), *The Origins of English Individualism*, Oxford: Blackwell.

MACKINTOSH, M. and WAINWRIGHT, H. (1987), *A taste of power*, London: Verso.

MARKS, J. (1986), '"Anti-racism" – revolution not evolution', in Palmer, F. (ed) (1986), *Anti-Racism: an assault on education and value*, London: Sherwood Press.

MATTHEWS, R. (1987), 'Taking realist criminology seriously' *Contemporary Crises*, 11: pp. 371–398.

MATTHEWS, R. and YOUNG, J. (1986), *Confronting Crime*, London: Sage.

McCRUDDEN, C. (1988), 'The Northern Ireland Fair Employment White Paper: a critical assessment', *Industrial Law Journal*, 17, 3: pp. 162–81.

MEDIA RESEARCH GROUP (1987), *Media Coverage of London Councils*, London: Goldsmiths' College, University of London.

MESSINA, A. (1989), *Race and Party Competition in Britain*, London: Oxford University Press.

MILES, R. (1989), *Racism*, London: Routledge.

MODOOD, T. (1988), '"Black", racial equality and Asian identity', *New Community*, XIV, 3: pp. 397–404.

MULLINS, D. (1986), 'Ethnic Monitoring in Local Authority Housing Policy', M.Sc. Thesis, School of Advanced Urban Studies, Bristol.

— (1989) 'Housing and urban policy', *New Community*, 16, 1: pp. 145–52.

MURRAY, N. (1986), 'Anti-racists and other demons: the press and ideology in Thatcher's Britain', *Race and Class*, XXVII, 3: pp. 1-19.

NETTLETON, P. (1989), 'Ridley in documents row', *Guardian*, July 9.

OUSELEY, H. (1981) *The System*, London: Runnymede Trust and South London Equal Rights Consultancy.

— (1984) 'Local Authority Race Initiatives' in Boddy, M. and Fudge, C. (eds) *Local Socialism*, Basingstoke: Macmillan.

PALMER, F. (ed) (1986), *Anti-Racism: an assault on education and value*, London: Sherwood Press.

PAREKH, B. (1989), 'Between holy text and moral void', *New Statesman and Society*, 28 March, pp. 29–32.

PARKER, J. and DUGMORE, K. (1976), *Colour and Allocation of GLC Housing: the report of the GLC Letting Survey, 1974–75*, London: GLC.

PARKINS, G. (1984), *Reversing Racism: Lessons from America* London: Social Affairs Unit.

PARTINGTON, G. (1982a), 'Who taught the rioters?', *Police*, July, pp. 32–6.

— (1982b), 'Discipline's the answer', *Police*, August: pp. 28–30.

— (1986), 'History: rewritten to ideological fashion', in O'Keeffe, D. (ed) *The Wayward Curriculum: a cause for parents' concern?*, London: Social Affairs Unit.

PEARSON, M. (1988), *Social Services in a Multi-Racial Society*, Department of Health: Social Services Inspectorate.

PEARSON, R. (1988), 'Room at the top?', *Insight*, 28 February: pp. 12–14.

PHILLIPS, D. (1986), *What Price Equality? A report on the Allocation of GLC Housing in Tower Hamlets*, London: Greater London Council.

— (1987), 'Searching for a decent home: ethnic minority progress in the post-war housing market', *New Community*, XIV, 1/2: pp. 105–17.

RANSON, S. (1988), 'From 1944 to 1988: education, citizenship and democracy', *Local Government Studies*, 14, 1: pp. 1–19.

RATCLIFFE, P. (1986), *Race and Housing in Britain: A Bibliography*, Bibliographies in Ethnic Relations No 3, Centre for Research in Ethnic Relations, University of Warwick.

REX, J. and MOORE, R. (1967), *Race, Community and Conflict*, London: Oxford University Press.

REX, J. and TOMLINSON, S. (1979), *Colonial Immigrants in a British City: A Class Analysis*, London: Routledge and Kegan Paul.

RICHMOND, A. (1973), *Migration and Race Relations in an English City*, London: Oxford University Press.

RIDLEY, N. (1988), *The Local Right: Enabling not Providing*, London: Centre for Policy Studies.

ROBINSON, C. (1980), 'The origins of corporate structures for race relations policy in inner London borough councils', unpublished MSc. Thesis, London School of Economics.

ROBSON, B. (1988), *Those Inner Cities*, Oxford: Clarendon Press.

RUNNYMEDE TRUST (1975), *Race and Council Housing in London*, London: Runnymede Trust.

RYAN, M. and WARD, T. (1986), 'Law and order: left realism against the rest', *The Abolitionist*, 2: pp. 29–34.

— (1987), 'Left realism and the politics of law and order in Britain', Paper presented to the XIVth Conference of the EGSDSC on 'Justice and Ideology', 10–13 September 1987.

SCARMAN, Lord (1981), *The Brixton Disorders 10–12 April 1981 Report of Inquiry by the Rt. Hon. The Lord Scarman OBE*, London: HMSO.

SCRUTON, R., ELLIS-JONES, A., and O'KEEFE, D. (1985), *Education and Indoctrination: an attempt at definition and a review of social and political implications*, London: Educational Research Centre.

SIKORA, J. (1988), *An Assessment of One LEA's Attempts to Promote Multicultural Education in its Secondary Schools*, Unpublished Dissertation Submitted in Partial Fulfilment of M. Ed. Degree, University of Manchester.

SIM, J., SCRATON, P. and GORDON, P. (1987), 'Crime, the state and critical analysis', in Scraton, P., (ed) *Law, Order and the Authoritarian State*, Milton Keynes: Open University Press.

SIMON, B. (1989), *Bending the Rules: The Baker Reform of Education*, London: Lawrence and Wishart.

SIMPSON, A. (1981), *Stacking the Decks: A Study of Race, Inequality and Council Housing in Nottingham*, Nottingham: Nottingham Community Relations Council.

SIVANANDAN, A. (1985), 'RAT and the degradation of black struggle', *Race and Class*, XXVI, 4: pp. 1–33.

SKELLINGTON, R. S. (1980), *The Housing of Ethnic Minorities in Bedford*, Open University: Faculty of Social Sciences.

SMITH, D. (1977), *Racial Disadvantage in Britain*, Harmondsworth: Penguin.

SMITH, D. and WHALLEY, A. (1975), *Racial Minorities and Public Housing*, London: Political and Economic Planning.

SMITH, S. (1989), *The Politics of 'Race' and Residence*, Cambridge: Polity.

SOLOMOS, J. (1983), 'Black youth, unemployment and equal opportunities policies', in Troyna, B. and Smith, D. (eds) *Racism, School and the Labour Market*, Leicester: National Youth Bureau.
— (1988), *Black Youth, Racism and the State: The Politics of Ideology and Policy*, Cambridge: Cambridge University Press.
— (1989), *Race and Racism in Contemporary Britain*, Basingstoke: Macmillan.
SPENCER, K. M. (1989), 'Local Government and the Housing Reforms', in Stewart, J. and Stoker, G. (eds) *The Future of Local Government*, Basingstoke: Macmillan.
STEWART, J. and STOKER, G. (eds) (1989) *The Future of Local Government*, London: Macmillan.
STOKER, G. (1988), *The Politics of Local Government*, Basingstoke: Macmillan.
STUBBS, P. (1987), 'Crime, community and the multi-agency approach: a critical reading of the Broadwater Farm Inquiry Report', *Critical Social Policy*, 20: pp. 30–45.
TAYLOR, I. (1981), *Law and Order: Arguments for Socialism*, London: Macmillan.
THOMAS, D. N. (1986), *White Bolts, Black Locks: Participation in the Inner City*, London: Allen and Unwin.
TROYNA, B. (1984), '"Policy Entrepreneurs" and the development of multi-ethnic education policies: a reconstruction', *Educational Management and Administration*, 12, 3: pp. 203–212.
— (1990) 'Reform or Deform? The 1988 Education Reform Act and Racial Equality in Britain', *New Community*, 16, 2: forthcoming.
TROYNA, B. and BALL, W. (1983), 'Multicultural education policies: are they worth the paper they're written on?' *Times Educational Supplement*, 9 December: p. 20.
— (1985), *Views from the Chalk Face: School Responses to an LEA's Multicultural Education Policy*, Policy Papers in Ethnic Relations No 1, Centre for Research in Ethnic Relations, University of Warwick.
— (1986), 'Partnerships, consultation and influence: state rhetoric in the struggle for racial equality', in Hartnett, A. and Naish, M. (eds) *Education and Society Today*, Lewes: Falmer Press.
TROYNA, B. and WILLIAMS, J. (1986), *Racism, Education and the State: The Racialisation of Education Policy*, Beckenham: Croom Helm.

TUCK, D. (1988), 'Local financial management', *Educational Management and Administration*, 16, 2: pp. 140–148.

WANDSWORTH, LONDON BOROUGH OF (1979), 'Report by the Director of Housing on Ethnic Monitoring', Department of Housing, Report to Housing Committee.

WARD, R. (1984), *Race and Residence in Britain: Approaches to Differential Treatment in Housing*, Monograph on Ethnic Relations No 2, Centre for Research in Ethnic Relations, University of Warwick.

WELDON, F. (1989), *Sacred Cows*, London: Chatto.

WHITTY, G. (1985), *Sociology and School Knowledge, Curriculum Theory, Research and Politics*, London: Methuen.

WHITTY, G. and MENTER, I. (1989), 'Lessons of Thatcherism - Education Policy in England and Wales 1979–1988', *Journal of Law and Society*, 16, 1: pp. 42–64.

WRAGG, T. (1988), *Education in the Market Place. The Ideology Behind the 1988 Education Bill*, London: NUT.

WRENCH, J. (1989), 'Employment and the labour market', *New Community*, 15, 2: pp. 261–267.

YOUNG, J. (1987), 'The tasks facing a realist criminology', *Contemporary Crises*, 11: pp. 337–356.

YOUNG, K. (1979), '"Values' in the Policy Process', in Pollitt, C., Negro, J., Lewis, L., and Patten, J. (eds) *Public Policy in Theory and Practice*, London: Hutchinson.

— (1982), 'An Agenda for Sir George: Local Authorities and the Promotion of Racial Equality', *Policy Studies*, 3, 1: pp. 54–70.

— (1983), 'Ethnic Pluralism and the Policy Agenda in Britain', in Glazer, N. and Young, K. (eds) *Ethnic Pluralism and Public Policy*, London: Heinemann.

— (1985), 'Racial Disadvantage', in Ranson, S., Jones, G. W. and Walsh, K. (eds) *Between Centre and Locality*, London: Allen and Unwin

— (1987), 'The space between words: local authorities and the concept of equal opportunities', in Jenkins, R. and Solomos, J. (eds) *Racism and Equal Opportunities in the 1980s*, Cambridge: Cambridge University Press.

— (1988), 'Patterns of Service Provision and Recruitment: Ethnocentrism, Professional Cultures and Affirmative Action', in Allen, S. and Macey, M. (eds) *Race and Social Policy*, London: ESRC.

YOUNG, K. and CONNELLY, N. (1981), *Policy and Practice in the Multi-racial City*, London: Policy Studies Institute.
— (1984), 'After the Act: Local Authorities' Policy Reviews under the Race Relations Act, 1976', *Local Government Studies*, 10, 1: pp. 13–25.

Index